TEACHER'S ANNOTATED EDITION

Vocabulary Workshop

Lev

Jerome Shostak

Senior Series Consultant

Alex Cameron, Ph.D.
Department of English
University of Dayton
Dayton, Ohio

Series Consultants

Sylvia A. Rendón, Ph.D.
Coord., Secondary Language Arts
 and Reading
Cypress-Fairbanks I.S.D.
Houston, Texas

Mel H. Farberman
Supervisor of Instruction
Brooklyn High Schools
New York City Board of Education
Brooklyn, New York

John Heath, Ph.D.
Department of Classics
Santa Clara University
Santa Clara, California

Sadlier-Oxford
A Division of William H. Sadlier, Inc.

Reviewers

The publisher wishes to thank for their comments and suggestions the following teachers and administrators, who read portions of the series prior to publication.

Anne S. Crane
Clinician English Education
Georgia State University
Atlanta, GA

Arlene A. Oraby
Dept. Chair (Ret.), English 6–12
Briarcliff Public Schools
Briarcliff Manor, NY

Patricia M. Stack
English Teacher
South Park School District
South Park, PA

Susan W. Keogh
Curriculum Coordinator
Lake Highland Preparatory
Orlando, FL

Susan Cotter McDonough
English Department Chair
Wakefield High School
Wakefield, MA

Joy Vander Vliet
English Teacher
Council Rock High School
Newtown, PA

Mary Louise Ellena-Wygonik
English Teacher
Hampton High School
Allison Park, PA

Sr. M. Francis Regis Trojano
Sisters of St. Joseph (CSJ)
Educational Consultant
Boston, MA

Karen Christine Solheim
English Teacher
Jefferson High School
Jefferson, GA

Lisa Anne Pomi
Language Arts Chairperson
Woodside High School
Woodside, CA

Keith Yost
Director of Humanities
Tomball Ind. School District
Tomball, TX

Printed in the United States of America.
ISBN: 0-8215-7623-2
23456789/06 05 04 03

CONTENTS

INTRODUCTION

VOCABULARY WORKSHOP has for more than five decades been the leading program for systematic vocabulary development for grades 6–12. It has been proven a highly successful tool in helping students expand their vocabularies, improve their vocabulary skills, and prepare for the vocabulary strands of standardized tests.

This new edition of VOCABULARY WORKSHOP preserves and improves upon those key elements of the program that have made it so effective *and* introduces important new features that make the series more comprehensive in scope and current in approach to vocabulary instruction.

Key Elements

- At each Level, a **word list** of 300 main entries, plus hundreds of synonyms, antonyms, and other related words

- Proven and effective **five-step approach to instruction**, leading students to mastery of word meanings and usage

- Excellent **preparation for SAT I** and other standardized tests with strong correlations between word lists and words that frequently appear on the SAT, as well as practice in types and formats of exercises found on the SAT I

- Frequent **review and assessment** both in Student Text and in supplementary programs

New Features

- In each Unit and Review, **Vocabulary in Context**, a reading passage formatted to the SAT I reading comprehension sections that provides examples of how Unit words are used in context

- **Building with Classical Roots**, a Review exercise that acquaints students with Latin and Greek roots and provides a strategy for finding the meaning of words derived from these roots

- In each Review, **Writer's Challenge**, an exercise that helps students improve their writing skills by applying what they have learned about the meaning and proper usage of selected Unit words

- **Enriching Your Vocabulary**, a Cumulative Review feature designed to broaden and enhance the students' knowledge and understanding of the relationships, history, and origins of the words that make up our rich and dynamic language

- Instruction in and examples of key vocabulary **strategies**—using context and using word structure—for decoding word meaning

- In the Units, expanded **Definitions** sections, which now include synonyms, antonyms, and complete, illustrative sentences for each part of speech of every taught word

- **Synonyms** and **Antonyms** sections that offer more examples of range of contexts and distinctions of usage

- Stress marks in **Pronunciations** that now reflect the system used in most leading dictionaries

- **Photographs** and color to engage student interest and illustrate reading and enrichment features

---

New Components

- For each Level, an **Annotated Teacher's Edition** that includes answers to all exercise items in the Student Text as well as valuable background information to help in lesson planning, instruction in vocabulary strategies, and assessment

- For each of Levels A–F, a **Test Generator CD-ROM** that adds a new, secure assessment option to the program, eliminating the risk of "secondhand" tests that may distort assessment results

- For each of Levels A–F, an **Interactive Audio Pronunciation Program** now available in CD format as well as cassette—ideal for English Language Learners of all cultures and backgrounds and for use in ESL classrooms

In the following pages of this Teacher's Edition, you will learn more about the VOCABULARY WORKSHOP program, including these new features and components, as well as how to get the most out of the program in your classroom.

OVERVIEW

"Pure Vocabulary" Approach: Systematic Vocabulary Instruction

The VOCABULARY WORKSHOP program focuses on words themselves, their meanings (both literal and figurative), their ranges of application (or usage), and their relationships to other words.

The approach is systematic in the sense that it begins with and builds upon a word list compiled to provide students with vocabulary they will encounter in their reading both in and out of the classroom. It is designed to provide students with the vocabulary skills they will need in order to achieve higher-level reading proficiency and to succeed at standardized tests.

The VOCABULARY WORKSHOP systematic approach differs from a literature-based approach in that each Unit begins with a thorough consideration of the words themselves rather than with a reading selection featuring words to be studied. (This is not to say that VOCABULARY WORKSHOP cannot be profitably used as a complement to a literature-based approach. See pages T30–T31 for suggestions on how this might be done.)

Rather than in the circumstantial context of literature, VOCABULARY WORKSHOP introduces and exemplifies vocabulary usage in varied and controlled contexts. These range from short phrases to full sentences to the Vocabulary in Context reading passages that are new to this edition of the program.

For effective study, the "pure vocabulary" approach also offers these advantages:

- It provides unlimited flexibility in the choice and placement of grade-appropriate material.

- It avoids the problem of trying to deal with a literary passage both as literature and as a vehicle for vocabulary instruction.

- It focuses more directly and completely on the words themselves, their meanings, their usage, and their relationships to other words.

- By economizing space, it allows a greater range of practice, reinforcement, and enhancement.

- It allows maximum coverage to a maximum number of key words.

One of the cornerstones of the VOCABULARY WORKSHOP approach is intensive practice through varied and abundant "hands-on" exercises. This method ensures that students are provided with:

- maximum exposure to different meanings of the key words studied;

- maximum coverage of the range of each key word through its appearance in many different contexts;

• fullest understanding of the key words' relationships to other words.

The aim of the pattern of intensive practice is to include the words in the students' active, daily-use vocabulary. This implies the ability to use a given word not only in its literal, or narrow, sense but also in a figurative way. Furthermore, it means that students will be able to use the word with confidence both as speakers and as writers.

Grade-Level Placements

The chart below shows the suggested grade placement for each Level of VOCABULARY WORKSHOP, depending on the overall ability of the student population involved.

In determining "proper" placement of a particular Level of VOCABULARY WORKSHOP in a given situation, the following considerations should be taken into account:

• Grade placements are based on actual teacher experience and recommendations throughout the long course of VOCABULARY WORKSHOP's history.

• Differences in grade are reflected not only in the "difficulty" of the words presented but also in the "maturity" of the sentences and other contexts in which those words are used.

• Grade levels indicated in the chart should not be taken in too literal or rigorous a sense. A certain amount of experimentation, as well as the use of the diagnostic materials provided in the program, will establish the "correct" placement of a particular Level in a given situation.

• The use of Level H with "above-average" students is designed to enhance preparation for the SAT I and other college-entrance examinations.

Grade Placements			
"Average" Students		"Above-Average" Students	
Level	Grade	Level	Grade
A	6	A	5
B	7	B	6
C	8	C	7
D	9	D	8
E	10	E	9
F	11	F	10
G	12	G	11
		H	12

Word Lists

Each Student Text in the VOCABULARY WORKSHOP program for Levels A–H contains 300 words organized in 15 Units.

Criteria for Selection

The selection of words for the VOCABULARY WORKSHOP program is based on four major criteria:

- currency in and usefulness for present-day American oral or written communication;
- frequency on recognized vocabulary lists;
- applicability to standardized tests, especially the SAT I;
- current grade-placement research.

General Sources

The lists of key words were developed from many sources:

- traditional, classic, and contemporary literature, including novels, short stories, essays, newspaper and magazine articles, plays, films, videos, TV programs;
- spelling and vocabulary lists recognized as valid bases for teaching language skills at the middle and secondary levels;
- current subject-area textbooks, glossaries, and ancillary materials (especially for general, nontechnical terms).

Dictionary and Reference Sources

The following were the primary dictionary resources used for word (and definition) selection:

- *Webster's Third International Dictionary of the English Language* (unabridged)
- *Merriam-Webster's Collegiate Dictionary* (ninth and tenth editions)

Other supplementary dictionaries consulted included:

- *The American Heritage Dictionary of the English Language* (all four editions)
- *The Random House Dictionary of the English Language* (unabridged; both editions)
- *The Compact Edition of the Oxford English Dictionary*

Standard Word-Frequency Sources

Standard word-frequency studies were employed to evaluate and revise the words on the tentative lists. These included:

- *Primary*
  Dale-O'Rourke: *The Living Word Vocabulary*
  Carroll-Davies-Richman: *Word Frequency Book*

- *Supplementary*
  Harris-Jacobsen: *Basic Reading Vocabularies*
  Thorndike-Lorge: *The Teacher's Word Book of 30,000 Words*
  Zeno-Ivens-Millard-Duvvuri: *The Educator's Word Frequency Guide*

"Sliding-Scale" Placement

Each word list works on a sliding scale based on these principles:

- No word that Dale-O'Rourke indicates as known in a given grade is presented in that grade. Instead, where possible, it is presented 2 or 3 grades earlier.

- Each grade level contains a preponderance of words not known (according to Dale-O'Rourke) 2 or 3 grades later, with an admixture (in decreasing numbers) of words not known 4 or more grades later.

- The higher the grade, the larger the percentage of more difficult words contained on the word list. This was done to accommodate as many "SAT-type" words as possible in the key word lists for Grades 10–12.

PROGRAM COMPONENTS

This new edition of VOCABULARY WORKSHOP, Levels A–H, consists of the following components:

Components of the VOCABULARY WORKSHOP Program*

- **Student Texts,** 8 Levels (A–H)

- **Teacher's Annotated Editions,** 8 Levels (A–H)

- **Test Booklets**
  - Form A, 8 Levels (A–H)
  - Form B, 8 Levels (A–H)
  - Combined Answer Keys, 8 Levels (A–H)

- **Test Generator CD-ROM,** 6 Levels (A–F only)

- SAT-Type **TEST PREP Blackline Masters** (answers included), 8 Levels (A–H)

- **Interactive Audio Pronunciation Program,** 6 Levels (A–F only)

The components have been designed for use in an integrated year-long vocabulary program, as suggested in the chart on pages T23–T25.

*Note that, in its entirety, the VOCABULARY WORKSHOP program now includes Student Texts, Teacher's Editions, and Supplementary Testing Programs for Grades 3–5 (Levels Green, Orange, and Blue).

The Student Texts

All eight Student Texts (Levels A–H) present 300 key words and are organized in the same way: 15 Units of 20 words each; 5 Reviews (following Units 3, 6, 9, 12, and 15); and 4 Cumulative Reviews. Preceding the first Unit is a section titled The Vocabulary of Vocabulary and a Diagnostic Test. Concluding each Student Text is a Final Mastery Test.

Vocabulary of Vocabulary (Student Text pages 7–17)

The purpose of this section is to familiarize students with some of the terms, concepts, and strategies that will be introduced and applied in the program. The practice exercises that accompany the discussions are meant to clarify and consolidate the concepts involved.

Some of these terms (for example, *synonyms* and *antonyms*) will already be familiar to most students. However, teachers should not hesitate to review these terms if doing so seems advisable, even at the upper levels of the program. Other, more complex concepts (such as analogies and context), however, may require more instruction and practice, both as preparation for related exercises and as review or reteaching for any students who have difficulty in successfully completing those exercises.

This is particularly true of analogies, which many students find especially challenging. Four pages of Vocabulary of Vocabulary are devoted to this important critical-thinking exercise so often found on standardized tests.

Diagnostic Test (Student Text pages 18–20)

A Diagnostic Test has been provided at the beginning of each Level as a means of assessing the students' overall vocabulary and test-taking skills. The Test covers a selection of key words introduced in the Level in question and is presented in the form of 50 synonym and antonym items.

Although the Diagnostic Test may be presented as a timed speed test, with the specific aim of determining how many items students can answer in 10 or 15 minutes, it is better used as an informal assessment and/or motivational device. Speed will come when confidence and vocabulary fluency have developed.

The Units

At the heart of the Student Texts—and of the VOCABULARY WORKSHOP program—are the 15 Units in which the 300 key words are introduced.

The work of each Unit is divided into a unique 5-part structure designed to give maximum coverage to each of the key words within the space available.

Structure of the Unit
(20 words)
1. Definitions
2. Completing the Sentence
3. Synonyms and Antonyms
4. Choosing the Right Word
5. Vocabulary in Context

The following descriptions of the individual exercises in a typical Unit of Levels A–H are designed to aid the teacher in using the text to maximum effect in the classroom.

1. Definitions

The first section of each Unit provides definitions, parts of speech, pronunciation, synonyms, antonyms, and illustrative sentences.

Definitions

The definitions provided are not of the dictionary type. They are, for the most part, relatively brief and simple. The intent is to give students a reasonably good "core" idea of what each word means, without extensive detail or secondary connotations.

Generally, only a single meaning of maximum usefulness is given the student. However, several meanings may be indicated if they are distinct, if they appear to be more or less equally useful, or if they will enable students to prepare for the vocabulary-in-context strand of the Critical Reading section of the new SAT I.

Part of Speech

The part of speech of each word is indicated at the beginning of the definition, using a simple set of abbreviations. When a word functions as several parts of speech, the appropriate abbreviation appears before the corresponding definition. (An explanation of the abbreviations used can be found on page 6 of each Student Text.)

Pronunciation

With each word listing, the pronunciation is indicated by means of a simple set of diacritical marks presented at the beginning of every Student Text (page 6).

The practice has been to indicate only one pronunciation, even where alternate pronunciations are sanctioned by the dictionary. There are only a few exceptions to this—for example, when a word changes its pronunciation in accordance with its use as different parts of speech (ob´ ject and ob ject´).

Note that once they have completed the first section of each Unit, students may utilize the **Interactive Audio Pronunciation Program** (Levels A–F only) for that Unit. This program provides about four hours of spoken material per Student Text, including pronunciations, parts of speech, definitions, and illustrative usages. For further details about the use of the Audio Program in this and other ways, see page T21.

Synonyms and Antonyms

A list of synonyms and/or antonyms is given for each key word for which there is one or more of either. Some of these synonyms and antonyms will reappear in the Synonyms and Antonyms section (see page T13). By studying the given synonyms and antonyms, students will better understand the denotational family of words of which each key word is part; and by comparing specific usages of key words and their synonyms, students can better appreciate appropriate contexts for, and nuances in meaning and connotation represented by, these words.

Note that the lists of synonyms and antonyms are not meant to be exhaustive. Grade-level parameters have been taken into account; and obscure, archaic, and slang synonyms and antonyms have generally been avoided.

ILLUSTRATIVE SENTENCE

Concluding each key entry is an illustrative sentence including a blank space in which students must write the taught word. These sentences, although necessarily brief, provide a context that clarifies the meaning of each word and points up its idiomatic usage. By writing the word in such contextual settings, students begin to see how it can be used effectively in their own writing. Furthermore, the act of writing is in itself a form of reinforcement; and by writing the word, the student must focus attention on its spelling as well.

2. COMPLETING THE SENTENCE

The next activity, Completing the Sentence, is a simple completion exercise in which students are asked to choose and write the word that logically and meaningfully fits into a blank in a given sentence.

When using this activity in the classroom, the teacher should bear in mind the following considerations:

- The sentences in this activity call for the literal or direct (as opposed to the metaphorical or extended) meaning of the words involved. This is an easier usage for students to grasp and provides a good foundation for the more sophisticated contexts that appear in Choosing the Right Word.

- The sentences are designed so that one and only one of the words fits in the given blank. Selection of the proper word has been facilitated by the introduction of context clues into each sentence.

- The words are to be used as the part of speech given in Definitions. The only exceptions are: Nouns given in the singular in Definitions may be plural in the sentences; verbs given in the base form in Definitions may be used in any tense or form (including participial) required by the sentence.

3. SYNONYMS AND ANTONYMS

In this section students are given phrases that include synonyms or antonyms as presented in the Definitions section and must choose the appropriate key word for each phrase. Each of the 20 key Unit words is covered once in either the Synonyms or the Antonyms part of the section. Besides reinforcing meanings, this exercise provides students with further examples of usage and context.

4. Choosing the Right Word

The fourth activity in each Unit is called Choosing the Right Word. In it students are asked to choose the member of a pair of words that more satisfactorily completes the sentence. At first appearance this exercise may seem an easier activity than Completing the Sentence. In fact, however:

- sentences in this activity are more mature linguistically and in subject matter;

- in many cases the words covered are used in a more figurative, extended, or abstract meaning;

- the part of speech or form of the key word has been changed (for example, from an adjective to an adverb) whenever convenient.

Accordingly, this activity is in reality more difficult than Completing the Sentence and requires real effort and a thorough understanding of the range of a word to complete successfully.

5. Vocabulary in Context

The fifth, and last, section of each Unit is an activity titled Vocabulary in Context. The activity is presented in the form of a reading passage, approximating a standardized-test format, into which five or six of the key Unit words have been woven. Its purpose is threefold:

- to give further examples of usage for the selected words;

- to offer an opportunity to derive meaning from context;

- to provide practice in the sort of vocabulary exercises found on standardized tests.

With this activity, it may prove helpful to refer students, if necessary, to the section of Vocabulary of Vocabulary (see Student Text pages 7–17) that serves as an introduction to the strategies involved in studying vocabulary in context.

Follow-Up Activities

Once the work of the Unit is completed, you may find it useful to give a writing exercise in which students may apply and illustrate what they have learned about the words introduced in the Unit.

Writing Essays or Stories

Students might be invited to create their own brief essays or short stories and encouraged to use as many of the Unit's key words as is practical. (Students should, however, be discouraged from trying to "force" key words into their essays or stories indiscriminately, just for the sake of number alone. It is essential that students get in the habit of using these words correctly.) If they are to write essays, students might refer to the Vocabulary in Context passages as models.

WRITING SENTENCES

Depending on the ability level of individual students or of classes, you may prefer instead to administer a short writing exercise (5–10 items) such as the one shown below. This exercise is not so challenging as writing a story or essay but will give students an opportunity to "try out" some of the words they have learned and will provide the teacher with a means of assessing how well students have mastered the meaning and usage of these words.

Sample Writing Exercise (Level H)

Framing Sentences   *On the lines provided, write an **original** sentence that illustrates the meaning and use of each of the following words. Do **not** merely copy one of the sentences given in the Student Text.*

1. mirage

_____

_____

_____

2. fait accompli

_____

_____

_____

3. oblivious

_____

_____

_____

4. morass

_____

_____

_____

5. adjunct

_____

_____

_____

The Reviews

A Review follows every three Units. Every effort has been made to include all of the 60 key words at least once in the Review for the three corresponding Units.

Structure of the Review
1. Analogies
2. Word Associations
3. Vocabulary in Context
4. Choosing the Right Meaning
5. Antonyms
6. Word Families
7. Two-Word Completions
8. Building with Classical Roots
9. Writer's Challenge

SAT I SECTIONS

Four parts of each Review have been specially designed to meet the needs of students seriously preparing for the verbal part of the SAT I and similar standardized tests.

ANALOGIES (PART 1)

The first of these special SAT sections involves analogies.

- Analogies are valuable and revealing, not merely as a kind of mental gymnastics, but also as a means of pinning down the exact meanings of words and of remedying misconceptions or uncertainties about how those words are used.

- Analogies provide an excellent means for testing and refining the critical-thinking skills used on the college level.

- Words that receive the attention necessary to complete an analogy successfully are much more likely to become part of the student's active daily-use vocabulary.

It is impossible, of course, to catalog all the relationships that may be embodied in analogy questions. They are as open-ended as the mental capacity to manipulate ideas and terms. However, the analogies illustrated and discussed on Student Text pages 13–16 will be helpful in reviewing with the students a few of the general "types" that occur in the Reviews and Cumulative Reviews.

Note: In the supplemental answer key on pages T38–T46, you will find explanations for the correct answers to all analogy exercises in the Student Text.

VOCABULARY IN CONTEXT (PART 3)

Like the Unit exercises that bear the same name, this activity is meant primarily as preparation for the vocabulary questions that appear in the SAT I and other standardized tests. Its format is changed in the Reviews, however, to more closely reflect the columnar format of standardized tests.

CHOOSING THE RIGHT MEANING (PART 4)

Focusing on usage-discrimination skills, this part of the Review challenges students to choose, from among two or more taught meanings of a word, the only one that the specific context will reasonably allow. This activity gives students useful practice in determining a word's meaning by careful attention to the context in which it appears, a skill assessed in the critical reading section of the SAT I.

Note: Explanations for the correct answers to the Choosing the Right Meaning exercises can be found in the supplemental answer key on pages T38–T46.

TWO-WORD COMPLETIONS (PART 7)

This part of the Review has been designed to familiarize students with the type of word-omission (cloze) exercise that appears on typical standardized tests, including the SAT I. Again the aim here is to refine students' critical-thinking skills. Context clues are embedded within the passages to guide students to the correct choice.

Note: Explanations for the correct answers to the Two-Word Completions exercises can be found in the supplemental answer key on pages T38–T46.

OTHER SECTIONS OF THE REVIEW

WORD ASSOCIATIONS (PART 2)

The purpose of this activity is to reinforce and extend understanding of the meanings of key words with brief definitions or examples, situations, or allusions that in some way suggest key words.

ANTONYMS (PART 5)

As it requires of students that they recall the meaning of a key word in order to determine its opposite, this activity helps students "situate" a word within the cluster of words of related meanings.

WORD FAMILIES (PART 6)

This part extends the work of the Units by showing students that by learning one English word they often are acquiring a whole family of related words. It also provides practice in classifying words by part of speech.

BUILDING WITH CLASSICAL ROOTS (PART 8)

Building on the foundation laid down in the Vocabulary of Vocabulary section titled Vocabulary Strategy: Word Structure (Student Text pages 11–12), this part of the Review introduces students to English words derived from common Latin and Greek stems and gives practice in the strategy of finding meaning by analyzing the parts of a word.

WRITER'S CHALLENGE (PART 9)

The concluding part of each Review provides an opportunity for students to apply to the writing and revising process what they have learned about word meanings and usage. Note that it is important that students understand that, apart from the conventions of Standard English (when applicable), there are no "rights" or "wrongs" in writing and that this activity is meant to make them more aware of ways in which the choice of words affects the tone, clarity, and coherence of their written work.

The Cumulative Reviews

Once students have completed the Reviews (and any follow-up activities), they may turn to the Cumulative Reviews.

Of the four parts of the Cumulative Reviews, three mirror activities presented in the Reviews: Analogies, Choosing the Right Meaning, and Two-Word Completions. These are presented in the same format and serve the same purpose as their counterparts in the Reviews, primarily to give students practice in types of questions they will encounter on the SAT I and other standardized tests.

The fourth part of the Cumulative Review, Enriching Your Vocabulary, is designed to broaden and enhance student knowledge of the interesting origins, history, and relationships of the words that make up the English language.

The Final Mastery Test

The Final Mastery Test in the Student Text of Levels A–H is designed as a practice test of 100 items that gives students and teachers reasonably good insight into how much progress has been made during the year and what kind of additional work is in order.

The purpose of the Final Mastery Test is fourfold.

- It can serve as a dry run in preparation for the more formal (and "secure") tests available as optional components of this program.

- It can serve as an informal evaluation of achievement to date.

- It can serve as a reinforcement activity.

- It can serve as a before-and-after comparison when used in conjunction with the Diagnostic Test.

For whichever purpose the test is used, it is both a testing and a teaching device, the culminating step in a process involving many class periods and, therefore, should be given careful attention.

Supplemental Assessment Components (Optional)

Test Generator CD-ROM (Levels A–F)

New to this edition, the VOCABULARY WORKSHOP Test Generator CD-ROM provides an array of secure student tests that support the Student Texts for Levels A–F. With the Test Generator, teachers may create countless unique vocabulary tests with a variety of question formats, all within seconds. With a database of more than 3,000 questions per Level, teachers never have to administer the same test twice.

The Test Generator CD-ROM provides:

- new and secure Unit Tests, Mastery Tests, Cumulative Tests, Diagnostic Tests, Mid-Year Tests, and Final Mastery Tests

- a wide assortment of question types to choose from: pronunciation, part of speech, spelling, definitions, synonyms and antonyms, sentence completions, sentence framing

- the ability to customize tests to include any number of questions and to assess any Unit in the Student Text

- a method of flagging questions so that they will not appear on other tests

- the option to save a test for future use

- an on-screen Help program

- a printed Teacher's Manual

- technical support

The Test Generator provides a convenient and secure source of assessment and/or extra practice. With the Test Generator CD-ROM, teachers may tailor tests to suit the specific needs of either individual students or an entire class.

The flexibility of the Test Generator makes it easy to use either as needed or more systematically, as an integral part of the VOCABULARY WORKSHOP series. See pages T22–29 for recommendations on how it may be used in conjunction with the Student Text and other components of the program.

Test Booklets (Levels A–H)

Two Test Booklets (Form A and Form B) are available for each of Levels A–H. These Test Booklets have been designed to be used in alternating years, thereby reducing the risk of answers being passed on. Each Test Booklet contains a full set of testing materials and is designed to cover the work of one entire Level of the Student Text. Though the formats of the Test Booklets are the same, the items tested in any given section are completely different. The contents of the Test Booklets have been organized to reflect that of the Student Text and include the following:

- preparatory test-taking tips for students

- a Warm-Up Test (corresponding to the Diagnostic Test in the Student Text)

- 15 Unit Tests, each consisting of 25 items focusing on pronunciation, part of speech, spelling, definitions, synonyms, antonyms, and sentence completions

- 5 Cumulative Tests of 50 items each (plus 2 optional items)

The Warm-Up Test may serve either as an introduction to the Test Booklet as a whole or as an effective follow-up to the Diagnostic Test in the Student Text.

Each Unit Test has been designed for use as soon as the students have completed work on the Unit to which it corresponds or at any point thereafter.

Each Cumulative Test, including the Final Cumulative Test, covers all the work of the Student Text to the point at which it occurs and is designed to be used after the corresponding Review in the Student Text.

Note that these tests may also serve as effective "lead-ins" to the SAT-oriented Cumulative Reviews in the Student Texts and to the SAT-oriented PREP Worksheets in the corresponding TEST PREP Blackline Masters.

For recommendations on how to employ the Test Booklets as part of the complete VOCABULARY WORKSHOP program, see pages T22–T29.

TEST PREP Blackline Masters (Levels A–H)

For further assessment options, a booklet of reproducible TEST PREP Blackline Masters is available for each Level A–H. The TEST PREP component is designed to provide both practice in working with SAT I type test questions and formats *and* review tests covering the entire content of the corresponding Student Text.

- Prep Tests approximate as closely as possible, given the vocabulary that is to be covered, the analogy and word-omission sections of the SAT I and provide practice in the vocabulary-in-context strand with brief reading passages as well.

- Answer sheets provide an SAT I type test format to develop student ease and familiarity with standardized testing materials.

- Mastery Tests are meant to be used when students have completed the corresponding group of three Units in the Student Text. Each test covers basic meanings, synonyms, antonyms, sentence completions, and analogies.

- Answer keys, including selected answer rationales, are provided for all tests.

For recommendations on the implementation of the TEST PREP Blackline Masters as part of the complete VOCABULARY WORKSHOP program, see pages T22–T29.

Interactive Audio Pronunciation Program (Levels A–F)

Now available in CD format as well as cassette, the Interactive Audio Pronunciation Program provides teachers and students with a convenient and effective means of teaching and learning the recommended pronunciations of all key words introduced in the Student Texts for Levels A–F. It is designed to be used either by the teacher in a classroom setting or by the student (either individually or in small groups) in a language laboratory or at home.

- The audio program is ideal for English Language Learners of all cultures and backgrounds and for use in ESL classrooms.

- Students hear the recommended pronunciation of each word at least 6 times, both alone and in context.

- Full coverage is given to words with more than one recommended pronunciation.

- Students are provided with two opportunities to pronounce each word themselves.

- Pronunciations are followed by brief definitions based on those given in the Student Text.

- Usage examples in complete-sentence form extend student knowledge of how to use a word correctly in their speech and writing.

- Teacher's notes for the program are provided in Spanish as well as English.

For recommendations on when to use the program, see pages T22–T27.

IMPLEMENTING THE PROGRAM

The format of the VOCABULARY WORKSHOP program allows for great flexibility. The teacher can easily adjust the activity assignments to conform to the special needs of an entire class, of groups within the class, or of individual students.

Schedule for the Year (28 Weeks)

The chart on pages T23–T25 shows how the various components of the VOCABULARY WORKSHOP program for Levels A–H can be scheduled effectively over an academic year lasting 28 weeks.

The following notes should prove helpful when adapting the chart to individual needs:

- Though the chart shows a disposition of material over 28 weeks, the time period can be extended to as many as 34 weeks simply by increasing to two weeks the time allotment for the items under weeks 6, 11, 16, 21, 26, and 28.

- It is not to be supposed that every item listed under Follow-Up Activities is meant to be covered during the week specified. The listings here are designed to offer teacher options from which to choose in order to tailor the VOCABULARY WORKSHOP program to the specific needs of a particular class. This is also true of the sections or subsections into which some of the Follow-Up components are divided.

KEY

IAPP = Interactive Audio Pronunciation Program, Levels A–F only

BLM = TEST PREP Blackline Masters

TB A/B = Test Booklet Form A/Form B

TG = Test Generator CD-ROM

Using the Program Over the Year (28 Weeks)

Note: "Framing Sentences" and "Story/Essay Writing" are to be supplied by the teacher.

Week	Student Text	Follow-Up Activities
1	Vocabulary of Vocabulary	
2	Diagnostic Test	Warm-Up Test (TB A/B) Warm-Up Prep Test (BLM)
3	Unit 1 IAPP	Framing Sentences Story/Essay Writing Unit Test 1 (TB A/B) Unit Test 1 (TG)
4	Unit 2 IAPP	Framing Sentences Story/Essay Writing Unit Test 2 (TB A/B) Unit Test 2 (TG)
5	Unit 3 IAPP	Framing Sentences Story/Essay Writing Unit Test 3 (TB A/B) Unit Test 3 (TG)
6	Review 1-3	Mastery Test 1–3 (BLM) Mastery Test (TG)
7	—	Cumulative Test 1–3 (TB A/B) Prep Worksheet 1–3 (BLM)
8	Unit 4 IAPP	Framing Sentences Story/Essay Writing Unit Test 4 (TB A/B) Unit Test 4 (TG)
9	Unit 5 IAPP	Framing Sentences Story/Essay Writing Unit Test 5 (TB A/B) Unit Test 5 (TG)

(Continued on pg. T24)

(Continued from pg. T23)

Week	Student Text	Follow-Up Activities
10	Unit 6 IAPP	Framing Sentences Story/Essay Writing Unit Test 6 (TB A/B) Unit Test 6 (TG)
11	Review 4–6	Mastery Test 4–6 (BLM) Mastery Test (TG)
12	Cumulative Review 1–6	Cumulative Test 1–6 (TB A/B) Prep Worksheet 4–6 (BLM)
13	Unit 7 IAPP	Framing Sentences Story/Essay Writing Unit Test 7 (TB A/B) Unit Test 7 (TG)
14	Unit 8 IAPP	Framing Sentences Story/Essay Writing Unit Test 8 (TB A/B) Unit Test 8 (TG)
15	Unit 9 IAPP	Framing Sentences Story/Essay Writing Unit Test 9 (TB A/B) Unit Test 9 (TG)
16	Review 7–9	Mastery Test 7–9 (BLM) Mastery Test (TG) Mid-Year Test (TG)
17	Cumulative Review 1–9	Cumulative Test 1–9 (TB A/B) Prep Worksheet 7–9 (BLM) Cumulative Test (TG)
18	Unit 10 IAPP	Framing Sentences Story/Essay Writing Unit Test 10 (TB A/B) Unit Test 10 (TG)
19	Unit 11 IAPP	Framing Sentences Story/Essay Writing Unit Test 11 (TB A/B) Unit Test 11 (TG)

Week	Student Text	Follow-Up Activities
20	Unit 12 IAPP	Framing Sentences Story/Essay Writing Unit Test 12 (TB A/B) Unit Test 12 (TG)
21	Review 10–12	Mastery Test 10–12 (BLM) Mastery Test (TG)
22	Cumulative Review 1–12	Cumulative Test 1–12 (TB A/B) Prep Worksheet 10–12 (BLM) Cumulative Test (TG)
23	Unit 13 IAPP	Framing Sentences Story/Essay Writing Unit Test 13 (TB A/B) Unit Test 13 (TG)
24	Unit Test 14 IAPP	Framing Sentences Story/Essay Writing Unit Test 14 (TB A/B) Unit Test 14 (TG)
25	Unit 15 IAPP	Framing Sentences Story/Essay Writing Unit Test 15 (TB A/B) Unit Test 15 (TG)
26	Review 13–15	Mastery Test 13–15 (BLM) Mastery Test (TG)
27	Cumulative Review 1–15	Cumulative Test 1–15 (TB A/B) Prep Worksheet 13–15 (BLM) Cumulative Test (TG)
28	Final Mastery Test	Cumulative Mastery Test (BLM) Cumulative Prep Test (BLM) Final Test (TG)

Using the Units

On the top of these 2 pages the teacher will find 2 models for using the Units effectively on a weekly basis. Though there is no single formula or plan that will be sure to yield optimum results all the time, the models presented here and on the next 2 pages are designed to get the teacher thinking about how best to adapt the program to the needs of individual classes.

KEY: IAPP = Interactive Audio Pronunciation Program

TB = Test Booklet Form A or Form B

TG = Test Generator CD-ROM

** Item to be supplied by teacher/student

Assignment
Classwork
Homework

MODEL B: 5 Sessions/Periods (20 Minutes)		
Assignment	**Day 1**	**Day 2**
Classwork	**1.** Collect Framing Sentences** **2.** Review Unit Test **3.** Present Definitions	Review Completing the Sentences
Homework	**1.** Completing the Sentence **2.** IAPP	Synonyms and Antonyms

Using the Reviews

On the bottom of these 2 pages the teacher will find 2 models for using the Reviews effectively on a weekly basis.

Assignment
Classwork
Homework

MODEL B: 5 Sessions/Periods (20 Minutes)		
Assignment	**Day 1**	**Day 2**
Classwork	Present Analogies	**1.** Review homework **2.** Present Choosing the Right Meaning
Homework	**1.** Word Associations **2.** Antonyms	Vocabulary in Context

Weekly Lesson Plans

MODEL A: 3 Sessions/Periods (35–40 Minutes)

Day 1	Day 2	Day 3
1. Collect Framing Sentences** **2.** Present Definitions	**1.** Review Completing the Sentence, Synonyms and Antonyms **2.** Present Choosing the Right Word and Vocabulary in Context	**1.** Unit Test (TB or TG) **2.** Review last week's Framing Sentences**
1. Completing the Sentence, Synonyms and Antonyms **2.** IAPP	Test Study	Framing Sentences**

Day 3	Day 4	Day 5
Review Synonyms and Antonyms	**1.** Review Choosing the Right Word **2.** Present Vocabulary in Context	**1.** Unit Test (TB or TG) **2.** Review last week's Framing Sentences**
Choosing the Right Word	Test Study	Framing Sentences**

MODEL A: 3 Sessions/Periods (35–40 Minutes)

Day 1	Day 2	Day 3
Present: Word Associations Vocabulary in Context Word Families	Review homework Present: Antonyms Choosing the Right Meaning Building with Classical Roots	**1.** Mastery Test (TB or TG) **2.** Review homework
1. Analogies **2.** Two-Word Completions	**1.** Test Study **2.** Writer's Challenge	Remedial work as required

Day 3	Day 4	Day 5
1. Review homework **2.** Present Two-Word Completions	Mastery Test (TB or TG)	**1.** Review Mastery Test **2.** Review homework
1. Test Study **2.** Word Families	**1.** Building with Classical Roots **2.** Writer's Challenge	Remedial work as required

Using the Cumulative Reviews

On the top of these 2 pages the teacher will find 2 models for using the Cumulative Reviews effectively on a weekly basis.

Assignment
Classwork
Homework

MODEL B: 5 Sessions/Periods (20 Minutes)		
Assignment	Day 1	Day 2
Classwork	Present Cumulative Review	Cumulative Test Parts 1–4 (TB)
Homework	Test Study	Test Study

Implementing the Weekly Schedules

The following may prove helpful when adapting the foregoing schedules to specific situations.

• The models shown are, as their designation suggests, purely models—that is, starting points. Accordingly, the teacher is expected to adapt them to the particular situation at hand.

• The models make only minimal use of the Follow-Up Activities suggested earlier and no use whatsoever of the Alternative Approaches to Using the Program suggested on the following pages. The teacher should in all cases feel free to introduce such alternative approaches as are convenient.

• Place assignments and timings are to some extent hypothetical. Teachers should switch items around and adjust timings as needed. Similarly, items may be modified or deleted and new items inserted as the teacher sees fit.

• Multiple listings in a Day's entry for either Classwork or Homework are to be seen as options from which the teacher should select appropriate material. It is unlikely that the teacher could cover all the suggested material in the indicated time allotment.

• With some adjustment, the allotments for each Day can accommodate a 2- or 4-day arrangement. There is usually too much material to cover in 1 day, and a 1-day approach is, therefore, not suggested.

MODEL A: 3 Sessions/Periods (35–40 Minutes)		
Day 1	**Day 2**	**Day 3**
Present Cumulative Review	Cumulative Test (TB or TG)	**1.** Review Cumulative Test **2.** Review Prep Worksheet
Test Study	Prep Worksheet	Remedial work as required

Day 3	**Day 4**	**Day 5**
Cumulative Test Parts 5–6 (TB)	Review Cumulative Test	Review Prep Worksheet
—	Prep Worksheet	Remedial work as required

Alternative Approaches to Using the Program

Writing Approach

Research has shown that vocabulary acquisition is maximized when learning is authentically contextualized—when learners have a "real-life" purpose for acquiring and using a new word. Activities such as the following can provide these authentic contexts.

- Students can create journals or logs in which they use the key words to express experiences, thoughts, or feelings that are personally meaningful. They are free to keep these entries for their eyes only or to share them with others.

- Students can use the key words in personal letters to friends and relatives or in letters to the editor of the school or local newspaper. Students should write about subjects of real interest and concern to them.

- Students can use the key words to write descriptions of people they know or characters they are interested in. These character sketches or personality profiles may be written for a class yearbook, for a book report, or as a reference for a friend.

Literature-Based Approach

The VOCABULARY WORKSHOP program can be combined with some of the items listed below to form a *literature-based* approach to vocabulary study. Each of the items listed has been surveyed for use of some of the key words presented in the specified level of VOCABULARY WORKSHOP. Seeing the words they are studying in classic world literature will reinforce student appreciation of the value of possessing a good active-use vocabulary.

Classic Literature To Use With The Program

Levels D and E

Louisa May Alcott *Little Women*

Maya Angelou *I Know Why the Caged Bird Sings*

Ray Bradbury *Fahrenheit 451*

Charlotte Brontë *Jane Eyre*

Emily Brontë *Wuthering Heights*

Pearl S. Buck *The Good Earth*

Lewis Carroll *Alice's Adventures in Wonderland*

Willa Cather *My Antonia*

Sandra Cisneros *The House on Mango Street*

Daniel Defoe *Robinson Crusoe*

Charles Dickens *A Tale of Two Cities*

Arthur Conan Doyle *The Hound of the Baskervilles*

George Eliot *Silas Marner*

William Golding *Lord of the Flies*

Frank Herbert *Dune*

Harper Lee *To Kill a Mockingbird*

Carson McCullers *Member of the Wedding*

Nicholasa Mohr *El Bronx Remembered*

Walter Dean Myers *Fallen Angels*

George Orwell *Animal Farm*

Alan Paton *Cry, the Beloved Country*

John Steinbeck *The Pearl*

Level F

Sherwood Anderson *Winesburg, Ohio*

James Baldwin *Go Tell It on the Mountain*

Stephen Crane *The Red Badge of Courage*

Kate Chopin *The Awakening*

Ralph Ellison *Invisible Man*

Louise Erdrich *Love Medicine*

Jack Finney *Time and Again*

F. Scott Fitzgerald *The Great Gatsby*

Joseph Heller *Catch-22*

Ernest Hemingway *A Farewell to Arms*

Zora Neale Hurston *Their Eyes Were Watching God*

Nathaniel Hawthorne *The Scarlet Letter*

Henry James *Washington Square*

Maxine Hong Kingston *Woman Warrior*

N. Scott Momaday *The Way to Rainy Mountain*

Toni Morrison *Beloved*

John Steinbeck *The Grapes of Wrath*

Amy Tan *The Joy Luck Club*

Mark Twain *The Adventures of Huckleberry Finn*

Kurt Vonnegut, Jr. *Slaughterhouse Five*

Alice Walker *The Color Purple*

Edith Wharton *The House of Mirth* and *The Age of Innocence*

Richard Wright *Black Boy*

Levels G and H

Margaret Atwood *The Handmaid's Tale*

Chinua Achebe *Things Fall Apart*

Jane Austen *Pride and Prejudice*

Joseph Conrad *Lord Jim* and *Heart of Darkness*

Charles Dickens *David Copperfield*

Isak Dinesen *Out of Africa*

George Eliot *The Mill on the Floss*

Thomas Hardy *The Return of the Native*

Aldous Huxley *Brave New World*

James Joyce *A Portrait of the Artist as a Young Man*

Gabriel Garcia Marquez *One Hundred Years of Solitude*

Mark Mathabane *Kaffir Boy*

V.S. Naipaul *A House for Mr. Biswas*

Mary Shelley *Frankenstein*

Muriel Spark *The Prime of Miss Jean Brodie*

Jonathan Swift *Gulliver's Travels*

Virginia Woolf *A Room of One's Own* and *To the Lighthouse*

To coordinate reading and vocabulary study, the following may prove helpful:

- Instruct students to devote a special notebook to vocabulary. As they come across key words in their reading, they should head a page of the notebook with the word; copy the title of the work; and then indicate (a) the definition of the word used in that sentence, (b) its part of speech, and (c) whether it is used in a literal or figurative sense.

- Students may then be instructed to check *Bartlett's Familiar Quotations* for other famous examples of the use of the key word in question. These may be copied into the notebook and shared with others in the class.

Content-Area Approach

Vocabulary Workshop can be used to enhance student understanding and use of vocabulary in subjects such as social studies and history, science and health, and other curriculum areas.

In the following list of nonfiction print and video titles you will find works that relate in content to Vocabulary in Context exercises appearing in specific Units and Reviews of the Vocabulary Workshop Student Texts for Levels D–H. Students may wish to read or view some of these works and report on the topics and issues that they treat. In their reports, whether oral or written, students should be encouraged to use words they have come to know through their Student Texts.

Author & Title	Level & Unit
Lisa Aldred, *Thurgood Marshall*	Level G, U6; H, U6
Catherine Allgor, *Parlor Politics*	Level G, Unit 7
Isaac Asimov, "The Eureka Phenomenon" from *Left Hand of the Election*	Level E, Review 13–15
Russell Baker, *Growing Up*	Level E, U15; H, U4
Rachel Carson, *Silent Spring*	Level G, Unit 2
Agnes DeMille, "The Kosloff School" from *Dance to the Piper*	Level E, Unit 10
Benjamin Franklin, *The Autobiography*	Level E, Unit 3
James Herriot, *All Creatures Great and Small*	Level D, Unit 12
J.S. Holliday, *The World Rushed In*	Level E, Review 7–9
Washington Irving, *Dietrich Knickerbocker's A History of New York*	Level H, Review 10–12
Charles Kuralt, "Noah Webster's Dictionary" from *Dateline America*	Level H, Unit 2
Brian Lanker, "Daisy Bates," in *I Dream a World: Portraits of Black Women Who Changed America*	Level H, Unit 6
Patricia Lauber, *Volcano: The Eruption and Healing of Mt. St. Helens*	Level D, Unit 15
Bill Littlefield, *Champions*	F, Rev 4–6; H, U5, 12
John McPhee, "The Loch Ness Monster" from *Pieces of the Frame*	Level F, Unit 8
Tsuneo Nakamura, *Gentle Giant*	Level D, Unit 13
Ann Petry, *Harriet Tubman: Conductor on the Underground Railroad*	Level E, Unit 6
Franklin D. Roosevelt, *War Message to Congress, December 8, 1941*	Level F, Units 10, 11
Amy Tan, *The Joy Luck Club*	Level D, Unit 2
Ellen Harkins Wheat, *Jacob Lawrence, American Painter*	Level H, Unit 8

Title & Distributor Videos	Level & Unit
American Cinema (Discovery Channel Video)	Level F, Unit 1
American Photography (PBS Home Video)	Level F, Unit 7
American Visions (PBS Home Video)	E, U9; F, U3; G, U5; H, Rev. 1–3
Baseball: A Film by Ken Burns (PBS Home Video)	Level F, U5; Level H, U5
Bridges, Skyscrapers and Tunnels (Discovery Channel Video)	Level G, Unit 8
Cold War (PBS Home Video)	Level D, Unit 5
Flyers (PBS Home Video)	Level F, Review 1–3
Frank Lloyd Wright (PBS Home Video)	Level F, Unit 3
Gold Fever (PBS Home Video)	Level E, Review 7–9
The Great Depression (History Channel Video)	Level E, Unit 15
The Great Ships: Sailing Collection (History Channel Video)	Level E, Unit 7
John Ringling: Master of the Big Top (PBS Home Video)	Level E, Unit 1
Ken Burns' America: Statue of Liberty (PBS Home Video)	Level D, Unit 7
Liberty! The American Revolution (PBS Home Video)	D, U1, E, U3; F, U13; G, U4; H, U9
Not for Ourselves Alone (PBS Home Video)	Level H, Unit 7
Reflections on Elephants (National Geographic Video)	Level F, Review 7–9
Surviving the Dust Bowl (PBS Home Video)	Level H, Unit 14
Trains Unlimited (History Channel Video)	Level F, Unit 14
The Ultimate Guide: Birds of Prey (Discovery Channel Video)	Level E, Unit 12

Other content-related activities to which students might apply vocabulary study are:

- Working in pairs or small groups, they can choose sentences from Completing the Sentence or Choosing the Right Word and discuss a larger context in which these sentences could have appeared, such as a history or mathematics textbook, a daily newspaper, a book review, a personal letter, or a scientific article.

- Students can work together to link individual vocabulary words to a particular content area. Then working in pairs, they can find "real-world" examples of the words used in context in that content area.

- Students can work cooperatively to create sentence and paragraph contexts that illustrate the meaning of the content-area words that they have identified.

Useful Classroom Techniques

Classroom experience and research have shown that some students learn more readily when they can exercise a great deal of personal choice and can interact with others. VOCABULARY WORKSHOP can be adapted in the following ways to accommodate such students.

Cooperative Activities

Working cooperatively does not just mean working in proximity to other students or dividing an assignment or project into discrete tasks. Rather it means that students take individual and collective responsibility for the learning of all members of the group and for the successful completion of the group goal. Students who cooperate to develop their vocabulary should maintain an ongoing dialogue to monitor the comprehension of all group members.

Oral and Kinesthetic

- One student can write the key words in a given unit on the chalkboard while the rest of the class is divided into pairs or small groups. A member of each group will read a numbered item from the Unit aloud. The rest of the group will confer and then supply the required vocabulary word. The student reader will evaluate each answer and give reasons why it is correct or incorrect based on the word's definition and any context clues.

- Students in groups can discuss the shades of meaning or connotations among selected synonyms and antonyms for a given Unit and among the alternative answers in Choosing the Right Meaning.

- Students can work together to create puns, riddles, Tom Swifties, and limericks to illustrate the multiple meanings of appropriate vocabulary words. They may want to collect and publish their creations in illustrated books or an audio-anthology.

- Members of a group can work together to improvise stories, skits, or pantomimes that illustrate the meaning of a key word in a given Unit, while other group members guess the word being illustrated.

Written

- Students can work cooperatively to brainstorm their own vocabulary word lists based on their current reading and writing in all areas of the curriculum and on their personal reading and writing experiences.

- The class can collaborate to create their own Unit, covering vocabulary words they have chosen. Different groups can be assigned to develop each of the unit activities.

- Students may want to create their own minidictionaries, based on the word lists in VOCABULARY WORKSHOP or on categories of words that are especially meaningful or useful to them, such as sports, fashion, music, and career terms.

- Students can make use of semantic mapping and other graphic devices, such as flowcharts, to generate new vocabulary or to demonstrate understanding of word relationships. Semantic mapping, or webbing, can be used to illustrate word families, synonyms, and antonyms. Flowcharts can illustrate etymological and grammatical relationships.

Alternative Types of Assessment

The following types of assessment may be used in addition to or in lieu of the objective-scoring materials provided in the VOCABULARY WORKSHOP, Levels A–H. The emphasis here is on monitoring understanding rather than on ranking students.

Self-Evaluation

Students can use their journals to reflect on their own process of learning and use of new words. They may consider, for example, which words from VOCABULARY WORKSHOP they understood quickly and used frequently and why. They may want to use these insights to design their own vocabulary-acquisition strategies.

Teacher-Student Conferencing

Meetings take place at every stage of the vocabulary-acquisition process. Meeting over time allows teachers to assess students' developing understanding of words as used in specific contexts.

Observation

Using a checklist of 2 or 3 important criteria, the teacher can observe and evaluate students while they are interacting in groups or engaging in other oral activities. Teachers can also probe for deeper levels of comprehension by asking students to clarify or give reasons for their choice of word or context.

Peer Evaluation

Students meet in pairs or small groups to develop standards or criteria to evaluate their vocabulary acquisition. They then apply their standards to their peers' oral or written expression, giving positive feedback and concrete suggestions for improvement.

Portfolio Assessment

By having students collect and save self-selected samples of their writing over a period of time, teachers have an ongoing record of students' vocabulary development and of their facility in using words in context.

Multimodal Assessment

Students with strong nonverbal competencies can be given the opportunity to demonstrate in nonverbal media their understanding of new vocabulary. For example, they can draw, paint, model, dance, compose music, or construct objects to communicate their comprehension of a word and its definition.

TEACHER RESOURCES

The following lists have been compiled to assist the teacher in the effective presentation of the VOCABULARY WORKSHOP program, Levels A–H.

I. DICTIONARIES

Recommended

Merriam-Webster *Collegiate Dictionary* [Tenth Edition] (Springfield, MA: Merriam-Webster, 2000)

Webster's Third New International Dictionary (Springfield, MA: G. & C. Merriam, 1993)

American Heritage Dictionary (Boston: Houghton Mifflin, 2000)

Oxford English Dictionary [Compact Edition] (Oxford: Oxford University Press, 1971)

Skeat, W.W. *A Concise Etymological Dictionary of the English Language* (NY: G.P. Putnam, 1980)

Supplemental

12,000 Words [A Supplement to Webster's *Third International Dictionary*] (Springfield, MA: Merriam-Webster, 1993)

The Random House Dictionary of the English Language [Unabridged Edition] (NY: Random House, 1987)

II. THESAURI

Recommended

Roget's II The New Thesaurus (Boston: Houghton Mifflin, 1995)

Random House Roget's Thesaurus (NY: Random House, 2001)

Rodale, J. [Revised by Urdang, L. and La Roche, N.] *The Synonym Finder* (Emmaus, PA: Rodale Press, 1979)

Supplemental

Chapman, R.L. (Ed.). *Roget A to Z* (NY: Harper Perennial, 1994)

Laird, C. *Webster's New World Thesaurus* (NY: Warner Books, 1990)

Roget's International Thesaurus [Fifth Edition] (NY: HarperCollins, 1992)

Abate, F. *The Oxford Dictionary and Thesaurus: The Ultimate Language Reference for American Readers* (NY: Oxford University Press, 1996)

III. OTHER REFERENCE WORKS

Recommended

Carroll, J., Davies, P., and Richman, B. *Word Frequency Book* (Boston: Houghton Mifflin, 1971)

Dale, E. and O'Rourke, J. *The Living Word Vocabulary* (Chicago: Scott & Fetzer, 1981)

Supplemental

Harris, A. and Jackson, M. *Basic Reading Vocabularies* (NY: Macmillan, 1982)

Thorndike, E. and Lorge, I. *The Teacher's Book of 30,000 Words* (NY: Teachers College Press, Columbia University, 1968)

IV. HISTORY

General

Baugh, A.C. and Cable, T. *A History of the English Language* [Third Edition] (Englewood Cliffs, NJ: Prentice-Hall, 1992)

Carver, C. *A History of English in Its Own Words* (NY: HarperCollins, 1991)

Jespersen, O. *Growth and Structure of the English Language* (Chicago: University of Chicago Press, 1982)

McCrum, R., Cran, W., and MacNeil, R. *The Story of English* (NY: Penguin, 1993)

Myers, L.M. *The Roots of Modern English* (Boston: Little, Brown, 1961)

Pyles, T. *The Origins and Development of the English Language* [Fourth Edition] (NY: Harcourt, Brace, Jovanovich, 1993)

Robinson, O. *Old English and Its Closest Relatives* (Stanford, CA: Stanford University Press, 1993)

American English

Dillard, J.L. *All-American English* (NY: Random House, 1975)

Dillard, J.L. *American Talk* (NY: Random House, 1976)

Flexner, S.B. *I Hear America Talking* (NY: Simon & Schuster, 1976)

Mencken, H.L. *The American Language* (NY: Alfred A. Knopf, 1979)

V. OTHER USEFUL RESOURCES

A Dictionary of American Idioms (Woodbury, NY: Barron's Educational Series, Inc., 1995)

Bryson, B. *A Dictionary of Troublesome Words* (NY: Viking Penguin, 1988)

Carroll, D. *Dictionary of Foreign Terms in the English Language* (NY: Hawthorn Books, 1973)

Dixson, R. *Essential Idioms in English* (Englewood Cliffs, NJ: Pearson ESL, 1993)

Evans, I.H. (Ed.) *Brewer's Dictionary of Phrase & Fable* (NY: Harper & Row, 2000)

Harrison, G. *Vocabulary Dynamics* (NY: Warner Books, 1992)

Hendrickson, R. *The Dictionary of Eponyms* (NY: Stein and Day, 1985)

Morris, W. and M. *Morris Dictionary of Word & Phrase Origins* (NY: Harper & Row, 1988)

Orgel, J.R. *Building an Enriched Vocabulary* (NY: William H. Sadlier, Inc., 1999)

Paxson, W. *New American Dictionary of Confusing Words* (NY: NAL-Dutton, 1990)

Room, A. *Dictionary of Contrasting Pairs* (NY: Routledge Educational Series Inc., 1988)

Room, A. *The Penguin Dictionary of Confusibles* (NY: Penguin Books, 1989)

Shipley, J. *Dictionary of Word Origins* (Glenville, IL: Greenwood Press, 1988)

Smith, R. *Dictionary of English Word-Roots* (Totowa, NJ: Littlefield, Adams & Co., 1980)

Spears, R. *Slang and Euphemisms* (NY: NAL-Dutton, 1991)

Webster's Word Histories (Springfield, MA: Merriam-Webster, 1989)

ANSWERS TO EXERCISES IN REVIEWS AND CUMULATIVE REVIEWS

Analogies (page 42)

1. (c) When you A something, you take material B; when you C something, you put it D.
2. (b) An A is something that would by definition B a community or population.
3. (a) An A is by definition B.
4. (d) An A is a person who would by definition try to B you.
5. (a) Someone who is A lacks B.
6. (b) Someone who is A consumes more B than is advisable.
7. (d) When you A something, you lessen its B.
8. (b) An A functions as a B.
9. (d) An A provides B.
10. (c) An A is by definition B.

Choosing the Right Meaning (page 43)

1. (d) (Clue: What sort of person would seek antiques and objets d'art?) (a), (b): wrong sense of word for context (ws); (c): irrelevant to meaning of word (ir).

2. (a) (Clue: What sort of claim for a paper towel might be made in a commercial?) (b), (c): ws; (d): ir.

3. (b) (Clue: What is the color of a rose?) (a), (c), (d): ws.

4. (c) (Clue: How might a tyrannical ideologue be characterized?) (a), (b): ws; (d): ir.

Two-Word Completions (page 46)

1. (c) melee (Inference clue: What would be likely to happen when two enemy forces unexpectedly collide?) . . . vassals (Inference clue: What would be the Duke of Orleans' relationship to the King of France?)

2. (d) solecisms (Inference clue: What would you use a grammar book to correct?) . . . lexicon (Inference clue: To what reference book would you go to correct a malapropism?)

3. (b) hierarchical (Inference clue: How would you describe a social structure that had rigid levels?) . . . Hidebound (Inference clue: What sort of notions would discourage social mobility?)

4. (a) polarized (Inference clue: What would a controversy about a point of doctrine be likely to do to ecclesiastical opinion?) . . . schism (Inference clue: What would divided opinion be likely to produce?)

Analogies (page 72)

1. (a) A are ceremonies that are performed when you B.
2. (b) Something that is A is impossible to B.
3. (c) An A remark would be typical of a B, or an A remark would likely come from a B.
4. (c) Something that is A has too much B in it.
5. (b) Something that is A would by definition be likely to B you.
6. (c) An A is a person who is B about some subject or form of endeavor.
7. (d) Someone who is A would by definition lack B.
8. (a) An A is a device used to B something.
9. (b) An A is by definition B.
10. (d) You would use an A to B someone.

Choosing the Right Meaning (page 73)

1. (a) (Clue: What might be the local standing of someone who enjoys "great fame"?) (b), (c): ws; (d): ir.

2. (b) (Clue: For what reason might believers "forbear to utter" a name?) (a), (c): ws; (d): ir.

3. (d) (Clue: Meaning restated in "hidden.") (a), (b), (c): ws.

4. (d) (Clue: What sort of treatment might be offered for a malady for which there is no cure?) (a), (b): ws; (c): ir.

Two-Word Completions (page 76)

1. (c) aficionado (Inference clue: What name would you apply to someone who relished a particular literary form?) . . . genre (Restatement clue: "literary form.")

2. (a) dicta (Inference clue: What is Dorothy Parker's comment an example of? *NB:* Remember that Parker was famous for her caustic wit.) . . . gamut (Inference clue: What in respect to emotions is a role likely to run?)

3. (d) forays (Inference clue: On what type of mission would a cavalry commander be likely to lead his men?) . . . panache (Inference clues: With what would a daring and colorful cavalry commander be likely to lead his men? With what did Charlemagne's legendary paladins perform their feats of derring-do?)

4. (b) browbeat (Inference clue: If flattery doesn't work, how might you next try to get someone to do what you wanted?) . . . abortive (Inference clue: How might you best describe an attempt or effort that was getting you nowhere?)

Analogies (page 81)

1. (c) An A is a literary form that is by definition B.
2. (a) A means the opposite of B.
3. (d) Something that is A is conducive to one's B.
4. (c) A remark that is A is designed to produce B.
5. (b) An A is a kind of speech that is by definition B.
6. (d) You would be likely to hear an A in a B.
7. (b) Clothing that is A is reminiscent of B.
8. (a) An A is a type of person who is B.
9. (b) An A is designed to help one's B.
10. (a) Someone who is A lacks B about something; someone who is C lacks D of it.

Choosing the Right Meaning (pages 81–82)

1. (a) Clue: (Correct meaning is indicated by contrast of "parents' hidebound views" to "more liberal attitudes.") (b), (c), (d): ir.

2. (c) (Clue: What were eclipses once believed to do? Correct meaning also suggested in "sequent effects.") (a): ws (derived from adjectival form); (b), (d): ir.

3. (d) (Clue: What would etymological entries and quoted passages comprise?) (a), (b), (c): ws.

4. (c) (Clue: Correct sense is indicated as in contrast to "change with the times.") (a), (b), (d): ws.

5. (b) (Clue: Correct sense is restated in "everyday scenes.") (d): ws; (a), (c): ir.

Two-Word Completions (page 82)

1. (b) Elixir (Restatement clue: "love potion"; Inference clue: What is the name of Donizetti's most famous comic opera?) . . . cozens (Inference clue: What would a charlatan be likely to do to an overly gullible country bumpkin?)

2. (c) ribald (Restatement clue: "salacious") . . . bowdlerized (Inference clue: In what sort of version would the prudish Victorians have been likely to read Shakespeare if his works contained ribald jokes and salacious language?)

3. (b) verisimilitude (Inference clue: What would sketches possess if the reader was left with the impression that he or she actually knew the people being described?) . . . vignettes (Restatement clue: "sketches")

4. (d) liturgies (Inference clue: What do many Christian denominations use in their services?) . . . obfuscate (Inference clue: What would an obsolete word or phrase tend to do to the meaning of a sentence?)

Analogies (page 105)

1. (b) Something that is A is easy to B.
2. (c) An A is a person who is overly concerned with B.
3. (b) An A is a person who would by definition B someone.
4. (c) An A is a person who is by definition B.
5. (b) A means the same as B.
6. (a) Something that is A is easy to B.
7. (d) A is an essential part of a nation's B.
8. (c) You would try to A someone by using B.
9. (d) An A is by definition an agent of B.
10. (a) An A is something that would by definition B you.

Choosing the Right Meaning (page 106)

1. (d) (Clue: Context indicates sense having to do with legal jurisdiction.) (a), (b), (c): (ws).

2. (c) (Clue: What sort of person might be warned off a movie that contains scenes of "mayhem and carnage"?) (a), (b), (d): ws.

3. (a) (Clue: What about an ailment might prompt drastic measures by doctors?) (b), (c), (d): ws.

4. (b) (Clue: What, if drunk, might cause death?) (a), (d): ws; (c): ir.

Two-Word Completions (page 109)

1. (d) philistine (Inference clue: What word would Wagner probably have used of people with benighted musical tastes?) . . . pander (Inference clue: What, given his opinion of the average operagoer, would Wagner probably not have done in regard to these people's musical tastes?)

2. (b) sycophants (Restatement clue: "toadies and") . . . truckling (Inference clue: What would a toady or sycophant be by definition likely to do?)

3. (c) prototype (Inference clue: What did the adventures of Gil Blas provide?) . . . picaresque (Restatement clue: "roguish")

4. (a) beleaguered (Inference clue: What would a band of marauders be likely to do to a provincial governor in his own capital?) . . . depredations (Inference clue: What do marauders commit?)

Analogies (page 114)

1. (c) Something that is A would by definition make a person feel B.
2. (d) An A is by definition B.
3. (d) An A is something that is by definition B.
4. (a) An A is a person whose tastes could aptly be described as B.
5. (d) A is something that is by definition B.
6. (b) Something that is A is by definition lacking in B.
7. (b) You would try to A someone by using B.
8. (a) An A is an animal that is proverbially B.
9. (a) An A is a person who would by definition perform with B.
10. (c) An A is a person who is by definition B.

Choosing the Right Meaning (pages 114–115)

1. (b) (Clue: Context indicates scientific meaning.) (a), (c), (d): ws.

2. (a) (Clue: What would be the consequence if the Mississippi breached levees?) (b), (c), (d): ws (too general).

3. (c) (Clue: What condition might lead to "newspaper death," or the cessation of public notice?) (a), (b), (d): ws (all derived from adjectival form).

4. (d) (Clue: Correct meaning restated in "encircled.") (b): ws; (a), (c): ir.

5. (d) (Clue: What sort of audience might fail to laugh at jokes?) (a), (b), (c): ws.

Two-Word Completions (page 115)

1. (d) iconoclast (Inference clue: What might you call an artist who flouted the canons of classical ballet?) . . . sacrosanct (Inference clue: To an iconoclast, what would received or traditional ideas *not* be?)

2. (a) hedonist (Inference clue: As what sort of person is King Edward VII often pictured?) . . . gargantuan (Inference clue: What adjective would aptly describe King Edward VII's appetites if they were comparable to his physical size?)

3. (c) pander (Inference clue: What does a book with no redeeming social or artistic value usually do?) . . . prurient (Inference clue: To what sort of tastes does such a book cater?)

4. (a) rapacious (Inference clue: What adjective would aptly characterize a hungry shark?) . . . depredations (Inference clue: What did Boss Tweed and his cronies commit on the treasury if they left New York City in severe financial straits?)

5. (d) maladroit (Restatement clue: "awkward and") . . . savoir-faire (Inference clue: With what does a born diplomat handle a ticklish problem?)

Analogies (page 138)

1. (a) If something is A, a person cannot B it.
2. (c) If you are A, it would be easy to B you.
3. (d) If you wanted to A something, you would use B.
4. (c) An A is a person who by definition dislikes B.
5. (b) Someone who is A possesses a great deal of B.
6. (b) An A is a person whose actions could aptly be described as B.
7. (a) Someone who is A is proverbially said to have a B.
8. (b) A position that is A is full of B.
9. (d) An A is a person who would by definition B a matter.
10. (a) An A is by definition B.

Choosing the Right Meaning (page 139)

1. (d) (Clue: What would hailstones do to produce a "staccato drumming"?) (a), (b), (c): (ws).

2. (d) (Clue: Context indicates meaning having to do with duration.) (a), (b), (c): ws.

3. (c). (Clue: Context indicates meaning having to do with cooking. (a), (b), (d):ws.

4. (a) (Clue: Context indicates meaning related to "geneology.") (b), (c): ws; (d): ir.

Two-Word Completions (page 142)

1. (d) impasse(Restatement clue: "deadlock"). . . adjudicate (Inference clue: What is an outside mediator supposed to do in a labor-management dispute?)

2. (c) apostate (Inference clue: How would you describe a lover who fled from his or her loved one?). . . immolated (Inference clue: What would Dido have used a large pyre for?)

3. (c) patrician (Inference clue: Socially speaking, to what sort of family would a duke or earl belong?) . . . lackeys (Inference clue: "servants and")

4. (b) apocryphal (Inference clue: How would you characterize an anecdote that had been devised long after the death of the person it concerned?). . . anachronisms (Inference clue: What do apocryphal stories or anecdotes often contain?)

Analogies (page 147)

1. (b) You would be likely to find an A in a B novel.
2. (c) An A is a person who divines the future through the inspection of B.
3. (d) A indicates that there is B of something; C indicates that there is only D.
4. (c) An A is a mistake in B.
5. (d) An A is a person who would by definition be likely to tell/deliver B.
6. (a) A means the same as B.
7. (a) If you are in a state of A, you feel extremely B.
8. (c) A means the same as B.
9. (d) An A is a person who is by definition B.
10. (b) An A is by definition a member of the B.

Choosing the Right Meaning (pages 147–148)

1. (b) (Clue: Of what nature must fighting have been so that the site was nicknamed "Bloody Lane"?) (a), (c), (d): ws.

2. (a) (Clue: From what sort person might issue "baseless slanders"?) (b), (c), (d): ws.

3. (d) (Clue: Context indicates contrast with "grand design.") (a), (b), (c): ws.

4. (d) (Clue: Context indicates meaning related to architecture.) (a), (b), (c): ws.

5. (c) (Clue: With what might a shaman be endowed so that he/she can heal the sick and converse with ghosts?) (a), (b), (d): ws.

Two-Word Completions (page 148)

1. (b) parameters (Restatement clue: "broad outlines"). . . . carte blanche (Restatement clue: "discretion")

2. (d) propitiated (Inference clue: For what purpose did ancient peoples make human sacrifices?). . . immolating (Inference clue: For what purpose would they have erected huge pyres in sacred groves and other such places?)

3. (a) raconteur (Inference clue: What would you call someone who told tales?) . . . ribald (Restatement clue: "broad, earthy, and")

4. (c) bibulous (Inference clue: What sort of person would be in his or her cups in the local pub?) . . . maudlin (Restatement clue: "teary-eyed and")

Analogies (page 171)

1. (b) Something that is A is without B.
2. (a) Something that is A is designed to B.
3. (d) Someone who is A moves like B.
4. (a) Of something that is A there is only a B.
5. (c) If something is A, a person cannot justly B it.
6. (b) An A would by definition be guilty of B.
7. (d) If you A a person, you make him/her a B.
8. (b) A would by definition aptly be described as B.
9. (b) An A would by definition aptly be described as B.
10. (c) An A would by definition B a person.

Choosing the Right Meaning (page 172)

1. (c) (Clue: Context indicates a physical property.) (a): ws; (b), (d): ir.

2. (b) (Clue: Correct sense restated in "embrace" and "kiss.") (a), (c), (d): ws.

3. (d) (Clue: Correct sense restated in "memoranda.") (a), (b), (c): ws.

4. (c) (Clue: What about an illness might be termed "remarkable"?) (a), (b), (d): ws.

Two-Word Completions (page 175)

1. (c) complementary (Inference clue: If both of two purposes are needed to complete something, how would you describe their relationship?)... didactic (Inference clue: What adjective would describe a purpose that aims "to point a moral"?)

2. (d) polemicist (Inference clue: What name would you give a person who wasn't a disinterested observer but a sort of soapbox orator?)... fulminate (Inference clue: What does a polemicist usually do?)

3. (a) factional (Restatement clue: "regional") . . . bickering (Restatement clue: "strife")

4. (b) inhibited (Inference clue: What would the South's lack of manpower have done to General Lee's freedom of choice in military matters?). . . attrition (Inference clue: What is one way in which an army sustains losses?)

Analogies (page 180)

1. (a) Something that is A would by definition literally B.
2. (c) An A would be likely to exhibit B.
3. (a) An A expresses B.
4. (b) An A is by definition B.
5. (b) An A is designed to be B.
6. (d) One would accord an A to a B.
7. (d) A means the same as B.
8. (d) A are things that people would B.
9. (b) Something that is A would lead to (bring about) B.
10. (c) A means the same as B.

Choosing the Right Meaning (pages 180-181)

1. (c) (Clue: In what might an analgesic be suspended to make it more palatable to children?) (a), (b), (d): (ws).

2. (a) (Clue: What might a brook be said to do?) (b), (c), (d): ws.

3. (d) (Clue: What might "serving men" appear in?) (a), (b), (c): ws.

4. (b) (Clue: What might be said of a people who are to be "forcibly relocated"?) (a), (c): ws; (d): ir.

5. (d) (Clue: Context indicates a meaning related to clothing and accessories.) (a), (b), (c): ws.

Two-Word Completions (page 181)

1. (d) élan (Restatement clue: "verve and"). . . lackluster (Restatement clue: "and indifferent")

2. (b) traumatized (Inference clue: What effect would the sudden assassination of your spouse have on you?). . . obsequies (Inference clue: After the assassination of John F. Kennedy, in what did Jacqueline Kennedy play a part?)

3. (a) opportunist (Inference clue: What name might you apply to someone who was self-seeking?) . . . probity (Inference clue: About what might you be concerned in the dealings of someone who was prepared to use any means at hand to achieve his or her ends?)

4. (a) homily (Inference clue: What might you call something that had an underlying didactic purpose?). . . imbue (Inference clue: In order to achieve an underlying didactic purpose, what might a composer have done to his or her music?)

5. (c) metamorphosis (Inference clue: what process does a larva go through to become a butterfly?). . . flamboyantly (Inference clue: How might you aptly describe the coloration of a monarch or swallowtail butterfly?)

NOTES

Vocabulary Workshop

Level H

Jerome Shostak

Senior Series Consultant

Alex Cameron, Ph.D.
Department of English
University of Dayton
Dayton, Ohio

Series Consultants

Sylvia A. Rendón, Ph.D.
Coord., Secondary Language Arts
and Reading
Cypress-Fairbanks I.S.D.
Houston, Texas

Mel Farberman
Supervisor of Instruction
Brooklyn High Schools
New York City Board of Education
Brooklyn, New York

John Heath, Ph.D.
Department of Classics
Santa Clara University
Santa Clara, California

Sadlier-Oxford
A Division of William H. Sadlier, Inc.

Reviewers

The publisher wishes to thank for their comments and suggestions the following teachers and administrators, who read portions of the series prior to publication.

Anne S. Crane
Clinician English Education
Georgia State University
Atlanta, GA

Susan W. Keogh
Curriculum Coordinator
Lake Highland Preparatory
Orlando, FL

Mary Louise Ellena-Wygonik
English Teacher
Hampton High School
Allison Park, PA

Lisa Anne Pomi
Language Arts Chairperson
Woodside High School
Woodside, CA

Arlene A. Oraby
Dept. Chair (Ret.), English 6–12
Briarcliff Public Schools
Briarcliff Manor, NY

Susan Cotter McDonough
English Department Chair
Wakefield High School
Wakefield, MA

Sr. M. Francis Regis Trojano
Sisters of St. Joseph (CSJ)
Educational Consultant
Boston, MA

Keith Yost
Director of Humanities
Tomball Ind. School District
Tomball, TX

Patricia M. Stack
English Teacher
South Park School District
South Park, PA

Joy Vander Vliet
English Teacher
Council Rock High School
Newtown, PA

Karen Christine Solheim
English Teacher
Jefferson High School
Jefferson, GA

Photo Credits

Corbis: 34,182; Paul Almasy: 149; Bettmann: 27, 41, 71, 104; Mark E. Gibson: 57; Gordon Whitten: 156; used with the permission of the Estate of Zora Neale Hurston: 170. *Getty*/The Image Bank: 83, 116. *Jacob and Gwendolyn Lawrence Foundation*, © 2002 Gwendolyn Knight Lawrence: 97. *Library of Congress, Prints & Photographs Division*/Dorothea Lange, LC-USF34-9095: 163. *Museum of Modern Art*, New York; Gift of Mrs. David M. Levy: 97. *PhotoEdit*/Richard Hutchings: 90; Dennis MacDonald: 137. *The Granger Collection*: 64. *The Viesti Collection*/Joe Viesti: 130.

PREFACE

For over five decades, VOCABULARY WORKSHOP has proven a highly successful tool for guiding systematic vocabulary growth. It has also been a valuable help to students preparing for the vocabulary-related parts of standardized tests. In this, the latest edition of the series, many new features have been added to make VOCABULARY WORKSHOP even more effective in increasing vocabulary and improving vocabulary skills.

The **Definitions** sections in the fifteen Units, for example, have been expanded to include synonyms and antonyms and for each taught word an illustrative sentence for each part of speech.

In the **Synonyms** and **Antonyms** sections, exercise items are now presented in the form of phrases, the better to familiarize you with the range of contexts and distinctions of usage for the Unit words.

New to this edition is **Vocabulary in Context**, an exercise that appears at the end of each Unit and in the Reviews. In this exercise, you will read an expository passage containing a selection of Unit words. In addition to furnishing you with further examples of how and in what contexts Unit words are used, this exercise will also provide you with practice with vocabulary questions in standardized-test formats.

In the five Reviews, you will find two important new features, in addition to Analogies, Two-Word Completions, and other exercises designed to help you prepare for standardized tests. One of these new features, **Building with Classical Roots**, will acquaint you with Latin and Greek roots from which many English words stem and will provide you with a strategy that may help you find the meaning of an unknown or unfamiliar word.

Another new feature, **Writer's Challenge**, is designed to do just that—challenge you to improve your writing skills by applying what you have learned about meanings and proper usage of selected Unit words.

Finally, another new feature has been introduced in the four Cumulative Reviews. **Enriching Your Vocabulary** is meant to broaden and enhance your knowledge and understanding of the relationships, history, and origins of the words that make up our rich and dynamic language.

In this Level of VOCABULARY WORKSHOP, you will study three hundred key words, and you will be introduced to hundreds of other words in the form of synonyms, antonyms, and other relatives. Mastery of these words will make you a better reader, a better writer and speaker, and better prepared for the vocabulary parts of standardized tests.

CONTENTS

PRONUNCIATION KEY

The pronunciation is indicated for every basic word introduced in this book. The symbols used for this purpose, as listed below, are similar to those appearing in most standard dictionaries of recent vintage. The author has consulted a large number of dictionaries for this purpose but has relied primarily on *Webster's Third New International Dictionary* and *The Random House Dictionary of the English Language (Unabridged)*.

There are, of course, many English words for which two (or more) pronunciations are commonly accepted. In virtually all cases where such words occur in this book, the author has sought to make things easier for the student by giving just one pronunciation. The only significant exception occurs when the pronunciation changes in accordance with a shift in the part of speech. Thus we would indicate that *project* in the verb form is pronounced prə jekt', and in the noun form, präj' ekt.

It is believed that these relatively simple pronunciation guides will be readily usable by the student. It should be emphasized, however, that the *best* way to learn the pronunciation of a word is to listen to and imitate an educated speaker.

Vowels						
	ā	lake	e	stress	ü	loot, new
	a	mat	ī	knife	ů	foot, pull
	â	care	i	sit	ə	rug, broken
	ä	bark, bottle	ō	flow	ər	bird, better
	aů	doubt	ô	all, cord		
	ē	beat, wordy	oi	oil		

Consonants						
	ch	child, lecture	s	cellar	wh	what
	g	give	sh	shun	y	yearn
	j	gentle, bridge	th	thank	z	is
	ŋ	sing	th̶	those	zh	measure

All other consonants are sounded as in the alphabet.

Stress	The accent mark *follows* the syllable receiving the major stress: en rich'

Abbreviations						
	adj.	adjective	*n.*	noun	*prep.*	preposition
	adv.	adverb	*part.*	participle	*v.*	verb
	int.	interjection	*pl.*	plural		

THE VOCABULARY OF VOCABULARY

There are some interesting and useful words that are employed to describe and identify words. The exercises that follow will help you to check and strengthen your knowledge of this "vocabulary of vocabulary."

Denotation and Connotation

The **denotation** of a word is its specific dictionary meaning. Here are a few examples:

Word	Denotation
benevolent	kind or charitable
callous	emotionally hardened or unfeeling
reiterate	repeat

The **connotation** of a word is its **tone**—that is, the emotions or associations it normally arouses in people using, hearing, or reading it. Depending on what these feelings are, the connotation of a word may be *favorable* (*positive*) or *unfavorable* (*negative, pejorative*). A word that does not normally arouse strong feelings of any kind has a *neutral* connotation. Here are some examples of words with different connotations:

Word	Connotation
benevolent	favorable
callous	unfavorable
reiterate	neutral

Exercises *In the space provided, label the connotation of each of the following words F for "favorable," U for "unfavorable," or N for "neutral."*

__N__ **1.** precedent   __U__ **3.** contentious   __U__ **5.** deride

__F__ **2.** deft   __F__ **4.** alacrity   __N__ **6.** allocate

Literal and Figurative Usage

When a word is used in a **literal** sense, it is being employed in its strict (or primary) dictionary meaning in a situation (or context) that "makes sense" from a purely logical or realistic point of view. For example:

> The corn was not harvested while it was still *green*.

In this sentence, *green* is employed literally. Corn that is not yet ripe is green.

Sometimes words are used in a symbolic or nonliteral way in situations that do not "make sense" from a purely logical or realistic point of view. We call this nonliteral application of a word a **figurative** or **metaphorical** usage. For example:

> It takes a *green* young rookie years to become a seasoned, streetwise veteran.

In this sentence, *green* is not being used in a literal sense. That is, *green* is being used figuratively to indicate that the young rookie has not yet gained maturity and experience.

Exercises *In the space provided, write **L** for "literal" or **F** for "figurative" next to each of the following sentences to show how the italicized expression is being used.*

__L__ **1.** The *musty* odor in the dark, damp cellar was most unpleasant.

__F__ **2.** Teenagers sometimes dismiss their parents' ideas as *musty* and antiquated.

__F__ **3.** Only a singer with a *supple* voice can do full justice to the elaborate music of the baroque era.

Synonyms

A **synonym** is a word that has *the same* or *almost the same* meaning as another word. Here are some examples:

guile—trickery
brash—brazen
skulk—lurk

delete—remove
somber—gloomy
askew—lopsided

Exercises *In each of the following groups, circle the word that is most nearly the **synonym** of the word in **boldface** type.*

1. pinnacle	**2. placate**	**3. dearth**	**4. tentative**
a. article	(a. mollify)	a. surplus	(a. uncertain)
b. viewpoint	b. cure	b. failure	b. thoughtful
(c. summit)	c. ridicule	c. supply	c. conclusive
d. pause	d. provoke	(d. scarcity)	d. interested

Antonyms

An **antonym** is a word that means *the opposite* of or *almost the opposite* of another word. Here are some examples:

elated—depressed
chastise—commend
disperse—collect

dour—cheery
repose—exertion
harmony—rancor

Exercises *In each of the following groups, circle the word that is most nearly the **antonym** of the word in **boldface** type.*

1. stolid	**2. deride**	**3. limpid**	**4. urbane**
(a. emotional)	a. forestall	a. blatant	a. naive
b. relaxed	(b. extol)	b. colorful	b. suave
c. impassive	c. amuse	(c. murky)	(c. crude)
d. flighty	d. decide	d. subtle	d. diffident

VOCABULARY STRATEGY: USING CONTEXT

How do you go about finding the meaning of an unknown or unfamiliar word that you come across in your reading? You might look the word up in a dictionary, of course, provided one is at hand. But there are two other useful strategies that you might employ to find the meaning of a word that you do not know at all or that is used in a way that you do not recognize. One strategy is to analyze the **structure** or parts of the word. (See pages 11 and 12 for more on this strategy.) The other strategy is to try to figure out the meaning of the word by reference to context.

When we speak of the **context** of a word, we mean the printed text of which that word is part. By studying the context, we may find **clues** that lead us to its meaning. We might find a clue in the immediate sentence or phrase in which the word appears (and sometimes in adjoining sentences or phrases, too); or we might find a clue in the topic or subject matter of the passage in which the word appears; or we might even find a clue in the physical features of a page itself. (Photographs, illustrations, charts, graphs, captions, and headings are some examples of such features.)

One way to use context as a strategy is to ask yourself what you know already about the topic or subject matter in question. By applying what you have learned before about deserts, for example, you would probably be able to figure out that the word *arid* in the phrase "the arid climate of the desert" means "dry."

The **Vocabulary in Context** exercises that appear in the Units and Reviews and the **Choosing the Right Meaning** exercises that appear in the Reviews and Cumulative Reviews both provide practice in using subject matter or topic to determine the meaning of given words.

When you do the various word-omission exercises in this book, look for **context clues** built into the sentence or passage to guide you to the correct answer. Three types of context clues appear in the exercises in this book.

A **restatement clue** consists of a *synonym* for, or a *definition* of, the missing word. For example:

A _____ person may be too timid to speak to strangers at a party.
a. disheveled   b. diffident   c. brash   d. droll

In this sentence, *timid* is a synonym of the missing word, *diffident*, and acts as a restatement clue for it.

A **contrast clue** consists of an *antonym* for, or a phrase that means the *opposite* of, the missing word. For example:

Although the actor's laughter seemed (**spontaneous,** raucous), I knew that it had been carefully rehearsed.

In this sentence, *rehearsed* is an antonym of the missing word, *spontaneous*. This is confirmed by the presence of the words *although* and *seemed*, which indicate that the answer must be the opposite of *rehearsed*.

An **inference clue** implies but does not directly state the meaning of the missing word or words. For example:

Only _____ amounts of rain this spring will _____ the severe drought in the northeastern states.

a. mandatory . . . fathom

c. copious . . . alleviate

b. palatable . . . waive

d. opulent . . . stipulate

This sentence contains inference clues: (a) the words *severe drought* suggest that the amount of rain needed must be *copious*; (b) the phrase *only copious amounts of rain* suggests the word *alleviate* because that is what so much rain will do to a drought.

Exercises *Use context clues to choose the word or words that complete each of the following sentences or sets of sentences.*

1. Some people are so _____ that they are always ready to argue about anything whatsoever.

a. secretive

c. contentious

b. predictable

d. sneaky

2. I don't understand how someone who is normally so (**meticulous, tepid**) could do such a careless job.

3. Utter _____ erupted when the noisy, _____ crowd saw their adored rock star alight from the limousine.

a. compassion . . . grotesque

c. pandemonium . . . raucous

b. conflagration . . . obnoxious

d. animosity . . . belligerent

VOCABULARY STRATEGY: WORD STRUCTURE

One important way to build your vocabulary is to learn the meaning of word parts that make up many English words. These word parts consist of prefixes, suffixes, and **roots**, or **bases**. A useful strategy for determining the meaning of an unknown word is to "take apart" the word and think about the parts. For example, when you look at the word parts in the word *invisible,* you find the prefix *in-* ("not") + the root *-vis-* ("see") + the suffix *-ible* ("capable of"). From knowing the meanings of the parts of this word, you can figure out that *invisible* means "not capable of being seen."

Following is a list of common prefixes. Knowing the meaning of a prefix can help you determine the meaning of a word in which the prefix appears.

Prefix	Meaning	Sample Words
bi-	two	bicycle, biannual
com-, con-	together, with	compatriot, contact
de-, dis-	lower, opposite	devalue, disloyal
fore-, pre-	before, ahead of time	forewarn, preplan
il-, im-, in-, ir, non-, un-	not	illegal, impossible, inactive, irregular, nonsense, unable
in-, im-	in, into	inhale, import
mid-	middle	midway, midday, midterm
mis-	wrongly, badly	mistake, misbehave
re-	again, back	redo, repay
sub-	under, less than	submarine, subzero
super-	above, greater than	superimpose, superstar
tri-	three	triangle

Following is a list of common suffixes. Knowing the meaning and grammatical function of a suffix can help you determine the meaning of a word.

Noun Suffix	Meaning	Sample Nouns
-acy, -ance, -ence, -hood, -ity, -ment, -ness, -ship	state, quality, or condition of, act or process of	adequacy, attendance, persistence, neighborhood, activity, judgment, brightness, friendship
-ant, -eer, -ent, -er, -ian, -ier, -ist, -or	one who does or makes something	contestant, auctioneer, resident, banker, comedian, financier, dentist, doctor
-ation, -ition, -ion	act or result of	organization, imposition, election

Verb Suffix	Meaning	Sample Verbs
-ate	to become, produce, or treat	validate, salivate, chlorinate
-en	to make, cause to be	weaken, shorten, lengthen
-fy, -ify, -ize	to cause, make	liquefy, glorify, legalize

Adjective Suffix	Meaning	Sample Adjectives
-able, -ible	able, capable of	believable, incredible
-al, -ic,	relating to, characteristic of	natural, romantic
-ful, -ive, -ous	full of, given to, marked by	beautiful, protective, poisonous
-ish, -like	like, resembling	foolish, childlike
-less	lacking, without	careless

A **base** or **root** is the main part of a word to which prefixes and suffixes may be added. Many roots come to English from Latin, such as *-socio-,* meaning "society," or from Greek, such as *-logy-,* meaning "the study of." Knowing Greek and Latin roots can help you determine the meaning of a word such as *sociology,* which means "the study of society."

In the **Building with Classical Roots** sections of this book you will learn more about some of these Latin and Greek roots and about English words that derive from them. The lists that follow may help you figure out the meaning of new or unfamiliar words that you encounter in your reading.

Greek Root	Meaning	Sample Word
-astr-, -aster-, -astro-	star	astral, asteroid, astronaut
-auto-	self	autograph
-bio-	life	biography
-chron-, chrono-	time	chronic, chronological
-cosm-, -cosmo-	universe, order	microcosm, cosmopolitan
-cryph-, -crypt-	hidden, secret	apocryphal, cryptographer
-dem-, -demo-	people	epidemic, democracy
-dia-	through, across, between	diameter
-dog-, -dox-	opinion, teaching	dogmatic, orthodox
-gen-	race, kind, origin, birth	generation
-gnos-	know	diagnostic
-graph-, -graphy-, -gram-	write	graphite, autobiography, telegram
-log-, -logue-	speech, word, reasoning	logic, dialogue
-lys-	break down	analysis
-metr-, -meter-	measure	metric, kilometer
-micro-	small	microchip
-morph-	form, shape	amorphous
-naut-	sailor	cosmonaut
-phon-, -phone-, -phono-	sound, voice	phonics, telephone, phonograph
-pol-, -polis-	city, state	police, metropolis
-scop-, -scope-	watch, look at	microscopic, telescope
-tele-	far off, distant	television
-the-	put or place	parentheses

Latin Root	Meaning	Sample Word
-cap-, -capt-, -cept-, -cip-	take	capitulate, captive, concept, recipient
-cede-, -ceed-, -ceas-, -cess-	happen, yield, go	precede, proceed, decease, cessation
-cred-	believe	incredible
-dic-, -dict-	speak, say, tell	indicate, diction
-duc-, -duct-, -duit-	lead, conduct, draw	educate, conduct, conduit
-fac-, -fact-, -fect-, -fic-, -fy-	make	faculty, artifact, defect, beneficial, clarify
-ject-	throw	eject
-mis-, -miss-, -mit-, -mitt-	send	promise, missile, transmit, intermittent
-note-, -not-	know, recognize	denote, notion
-pel-, -puls-	drive	expel, compulsive
-pend-, -pens-	hang, weight, set aside	pendulum, pension
-pon-, -pos-	put, place	component, position
-port-	carry	portable
-rupt-	break	bankrupt
-scrib-, -scribe-, -script-	write	scribble, describe, inscription
-spec-, -spic-	look, see	spectator, conspicuous
-tac-, -tag-, -tang-, -teg-	touch	contact, contagious, tangible, integral
-tain-, -ten-, -tin-	hold, keep	contain, tenure, retinue
-temp-	time	tempo, temporary
-ven-, -vent-	come	intervene, convention
-vers-, -vert-	turn	reverse, invert
-voc-, -vok-	call	vocal, invoke

WORKING WITH ANALOGIES

Today practically every standardized examination involving vocabulary, especially the SAT-I, employs the **analogy** as a testing device. For that reason, it is an excellent idea to learn how to read, understand, and solve such verbal puzzles.

What Is an Analogy?

An analogy is a kind of equation using words rather than numbers or mathematical symbols and quantities. Normally, an analogy contains two pairs of words linked by a word or symbol that stands for an equal sign (=). A complete analogy compares the two pairs of words and makes a statement about them. It asserts that the logical relationship between the members of the first pair of words is *the same as* the logical relationship between the members of the second pair of words. This is the only statement a valid analogy ever makes.

Here is an example of a complete analogy. It is presented in two different formats.

Format 1
maple is to tree as rose is to flower

Format 2
maple : tree :: rose : flower

Reading and Interpreting Analogies

As our sample indicates, analogies are customarily presented in formats that need some deciphering in order to be read and understood correctly. There are a number of these formats, but you need concern yourself with only the two shown.

Format 1:   Let's begin with the format that uses all words:

maple is to tree as rose is to flower

Because this is the simplest format to read and understand, it is the one used in the student texts of VOCABULARY WORKSHOP. It is to be read exactly as printed. Allowing for the fact that the word pairs change from analogy to analogy, this is how to read every analogy, no matter what the format is.

Now you know how to read an analogy. Still, it is not clear exactly what the somewhat cryptic statement "maple is to tree as rose is to flower" means. To discover this, you must understand what the two linking expressions *as* and *is to* signify.

- The word *as* links the two word pairs in the complete analogy. It stands for an equal sign (=) and means "is the same as."

- The expression *is to* links the two members of each word pair, so it appears twice in a complete analogy. In our sample, *is to* links *maple* and *tree* (the two words in the first pair) and also *rose* and *flower* (the two words in the second word pair). Accordingly, the expression *is to* means "the logical relationship between" the two words it links.

Putting all this information together, we can say that our sample analogy means:

> The logical relationship between a *maple* and a *tree* is *the same as* (=) the logical relationship between a *rose* and a *flower*.

Now you know what our sample analogy means. This is what every analogy means, allowing for the fact that the word pairs will vary from one analogy to another.

Format 2: Our second format uses symbols, rather than words, to link its four members.

> maple : tree :: rose : flower

This is the format used on the SAT-I and in the *TEST PREP Blackline Masters* that accompany each Level of Vocabulary Workshop. In this format, a single colon (:) replaces the expression *is to*, and a double colon (::) replaces the word *as*. Otherwise, format 2 is the same as format 1; that is, it is read in exactly the same way ("maple is to tree as rose is to flower"), and it means exactly the same thing ("the logical relationship between a *maple* and a *tree* is the same as the logical relationship between a *rose* and a *flower*").

Completing Analogies

So far we've looked at complete analogies. However, standardized examinations do not provide the test taker with a complete analogy. Instead, the test taker is given the first, or key, pair of words and then asked to *complete* the analogy by selecting the second pair from a given group of four or five choices, usually lettered *a* through *d* or *e*.

Here's how our sample analogy would look on such a test:

1. maple is to tree as
a. acorn is to oak
b. hen is to rooster
c. rose is to flower
d. shrub is to lilac

or

1. maple : tree ::
a. acorn : oak
b. hen : rooster
c. rose : flower
d. shrub : lilac

It is up to the test taker to complete the analogy correctly.

Here's how to do that in just four easy steps!

Step 1: *Look at the two words in the key (given) pair, and determine the logical relationship between them.*

In our sample analogy, *maple* and *tree* form the key (given) pair of words. They indicate the key (given) relationship. Think about these two words for a moment. What is the relationship of a maple to a tree? Well, a maple is a particular kind, or type, of tree.

Step 2: *Make up a short sentence stating the relationship that you have discovered for the first pair of words.*

For our model analogy, we can use this sentence: "A maple is a particular kind (type) of tree."

Step 3: *Extend the sentence you have written to cover the rest of the analogy, even though you haven't completed it yet.*

The easiest way to do this is to repeat the key relationship after the words *just as*, leaving blanks for the two words you don't yet have. The sentence will now read something like this:

A maple is a kind (type) of tree, just as a ? is a kind of ? .

Step 4: *Look at each of the lettered pairs of words from which you are to choose your answer. Determine which lettered pair illustrates the same relationship as the key pair.*

The easiest and most effective way to carry out step 4 is to substitute each pair of words into the blanks in the sentence you made up to see which sentence makes sense. Only one will.

Doing this for our sample analogy, we get:

a. A maple is a kind of tree, just as an acorn is a kind of oak.
b. A maple is a kind of tree, just as a hen is a kind of rooster.
c. A maple is a kind of tree, just as a rose is a kind of flower.
d. A maple is a kind of tree, just as a shrub is a kind of lilac.

Look at these sentences. Only *one* of them makes any sense. Choice *a* is clearly wrong because an acorn is *not* a kind of oak. Choice *b* is also wrong because a hen is *not* a kind of rooster. Similarly, choice *d* is incorrect because a shrub is *not* a kind of lilac, though a *lilac* is a kind of shrub. In other words, the two words are in the wrong order. That leaves us with choice *c*, which says that a rose is a kind of flower. Well, that makes sense; a rose is indeed a kind of flower. So, choice *c* must be the pair of words that completes the analogy correctly.

Determining the Key Relationship

Clearly, determining the nature of the key relationship is the most important and the most difficult part of completing an analogy. Since there are literally thousands of key relationships possible, you cannot simply memorize a list of them. The table on page 16, however, outlines some of the most common key relationships. Study the table carefully.

Table of Key Relationships

Complete Analogy	Key Relationship
big is to **large** as **little** is to **small**	**Big** means the same thing as **large**, just as **little** means the same thing as **small**.
tall is to **short** as **thin** is to **fat**	**Tall** means the opposite of **short**, just as **thin** means the opposite of **fat**.
brave is to **favorable** as **cowardly** is to **unfavorable**	The tone of **brave** is **favorable**, just as the tone of **cowardly** is **unfavorable**.
busybody is to **nosy** as **klutz** is to **clumsy**	A **busybody** is by definition someone who is **nosy**, just as a **klutz** is by definition someone who is **clumsy**.
cowardly is to **courage** as **awkward** is to **grace**	Someone who is **cowardly** lacks **courage**, just as someone who is **awkward** lacks **grace**.
visible is to **see** as **audible** is to **hear**	If something is **visible**, you can by definition **see** it, just as if something is **audible**, you can by definition **hear** it.
invisible is to **see** as **inaudible** is to **hear**	If something is **invisible**, you cannot **see** it, just as if something is **inaudible**, you cannot **hear** it.
frigid is to **cold** as **blistering** is to **hot**	**Frigid** is the extreme of **cold**, just as **blistering** is the extreme of **hot**.
chef is to **cooking** as **tailor** is to **clothing**	A **chef** is concerned with **cooking**, just as a **tailor** is concerned with **clothing**.
liar is to **truthful** as **bigot** is to **fair-minded**	A **liar** is by definition not likely to be **truthful**, just as a **bigot** is by definition not likely to be **fair-minded**.
starvation is to **emaciation** as **overindulgence** is to **corpulence**	**Starvation** will cause **emaciation**, just as **overindulgence** will cause **corpulence**.
practice is to **proficient** as **study** is to **knowledgeable**	**Practice** will make a person **proficient**, just as **study** will make a person **knowledgeable**.
eyes are to **see** as **ears** are to **hear**	You use your **eyes** to **see** with, just as you use your **ears** to **hear** with.
sloppy is to **appearance** as **rude** is to **manner**	The word **sloppy** can refer to one's **appearance**, just as the word **rude** can refer to one's **manner**.
learned is to **knowledge** as **wealthy** is to **money**	Someone who is **learned** has a great deal of **knowledge**, just as someone who is **wealthy** has a great deal of **money**.

Exercises   *In each of the following, circle the item that best completes the analogy. Then explain the key relationship involved.*

1. adroit is to **favorable** as
a. craven is to unfavorable
b. obnoxious is to favorable
c. scrupulous is to unfavorable
d. officious is to favorable

2. stipulate is to **specify** as
a. disperse is to collect
b. extirpate is to nourish
c. rescind is to ratify
d. elucidate is to explain

3. insuperable is to **overcome** as
a. inopportune is to understood
b. insidious is to studied
c. indomitable is to conquered
d. inclement is to predicted

4. premeditated is to **spontaneous** as
a. innocuous is to harmless
b. mandatory is to optional
c. rampant is to widespread
d. august is to stately

VOCABULARY AND WRITING

When you study vocabulary, you make yourself not only a better reader but also a better writer. The greater the number of words at your disposal, the better you will be able to express your thoughts. Good writers are always adding new words to their personal vocabularies, the pool of words that they understand *and* know how to use properly. They use these words both when they write and when they revise.

There are several factors to consider when choosing words and setting the tone of your writing. First, your choice of words should suit your purpose and your audience. If you are writing an essay for your history teacher, you will probably want to choose words that are formal in tone and precise in meaning. If you are writing a letter to a friend, however, you will probably choose words that are more informal in tone and freer in meaning. Your **audience** is the person or people who will be reading what you write, and your **purpose** is the reason why you are writing. Your purpose, for example, might be to explain; or it might be to describe, inform, or entertain.

Almost any kind of writing—whether a school essay, a story, or a letter to a friend—can be improved by careful attention to vocabulary. Sometimes you will find, for example, that one word can be used to replace a phrase of five or six words. This is not to say that a shorter sentence is always better. However, readers usually prefer and appreciate **economy** of expression. They grow impatient with sentences that plod along with vague, unnecessary words rather than race along with fewer, carefully chosen ones. Writing can also be improved by attention to **diction** (word choice). Many writers use words that might make sense in terms of *general* meaning but that are not precise enough to convey *nuances* of meaning. In the **Writer's Challenge** sections of this book, you will have an opportunity to make word choices that will more clearly and precisely convey the meaning you intend.

Exercises   *Read the following sentences, paying special attention to the words and phrases underlined. From the words in the box, find better choices for the underlined words and phrases.*

1. The unexpectedly warm day gave us a brief period of relief or rest from winter's chill.

solace	assent	respite	redress

2. A co-worker who is excessively forward in assuming authority can be very disruptive.

officious	garrulous	zealous	vivacious

3. If you are able to use both hands equally well, you may have the ability to become a juggler.

dour	ambidextrous	sinuous	ironic

4. We stared with open mouths as we looked out over the vast expanse of the Grand Canyon.

waived	gaped	lolled	concurred

5. It is time to put aside ancient strong dislikes and strive to make the world a safer, more peaceful place.

pretexts	misnomers	antipathies	panaceas

This test contains a sampling of the words that are to be found in the exercises in this Level of VOCABULARY WORKSHOP. It will give you an idea of the types of words to be studied and their level of difficulty. When you have completed all the units, the Final Mastery Test at the end of this book will assess what you have learned. By comparing your results on the Final Mastery Test with your results on the Diagnostic Test below, you will be able to judge your progress.

Synonyms

*In each of the following groups, circle the word or phrase that **most nearly** expresses the meaning of the word in **boldface** type in the given phrase.*

1. an **ecumenical** conference
   a. financial (b. worldwide) c. moral d. uninteresting

2. a **niggardly** allowance
   a. generous b. lavish c. adequate (d. stingy)

3. **opt** to leave
   a. prepare b. refuse (c. choose) d. fail

4. the **bane** of my life
   a. mainstay b. joy c. hobby (d. ruin)

5. contributed **sub rosa** to the campaign
   (a. covertly) b. legally c. exceptionally d. routinely

6. a **quizzical** look
   a. solemn b. caustic c. querulous (d. puzzled)

7. find the **mot juste**
   a. perfect gift (b. right word) c. lost child d. trouble spot

8. my **bête noire**
   (a. nemesis) b. success c. favorite d. aspiration

9. an **insouciant** attitude
   a. serious b. ambivalent (c. carefree) d. phlegmatic

10. a **noisome** atmosphere
    a. charming (b. noxious) c. loud d. explosive

11. a **risible** development
    a. unexpected b. fortunate (c. laughable) d. recent

12. **adjudicate** the dispute
    a. define (b. mediate) c. overhear d. start

13. receive something as a **lagniappe**
    (a. bonus) b. warning c. visitor d. honor

14. **gambol** on the green
    (a. romp) b. lie c. sleep d. loiter

15. begin **in medias res**
    a. again b. at the beginning (c. in the middle) d. at the conclusion

16. chimerical hopes
a. buoyant   (b. unrealistic)   c. modest   d. achievable

17. a **touchstone** of valor
a. medal   (b. yardstick)   c. champion   d. amulet

18. a **maudlin** story
a. hilarious   b. terrifying   c. long   (d. sentimental)

19. condescend to see us
a. refuse   (b. stoop)   c. attempt   d. plan

20. a terrible **faux pas**
a. job   b. pain   c. loss   (d. blunder)

21. under the **aegis** of the university
(a. auspices)   b. roof   c. solicitude   d. morass

22. an inadvertent **solecism**
a. donnybrook   (b. mistake)   c. persiflage   d. fait accompli

23. an **affinity** for math
a. jurisdiction   b. yearning   c. ignominy   (d. penchant)

24. strutted with **panache**
(a. flamboyance)   b. lucubration   c. lagniappe   d. obloquy

25. always a fascinating **raconteur**
a. aristocrat   b. mountebank   c. virtuoso   (d. storyteller)

26. steelworkers on their **precarious** perch
(a. perilous)   b. sturdy   c. fervid   d. dank

27. no **vestige** of their culture
a. liason   (b. artifact)   c. pastiche   d. harbinger

28. horrified by their **execrable** behavior
a. insipid   b. pragmatic   (c. reprehensible)   d. picaresque

29. the ambassador's **unimpeachable** credentials
a. pertinent   b. sullied   c. dubious   (d. irrefutable)

30. their **disparate** backgrounds
a. questionable   (b. dissimilar)   c. irrelevant   d. similar

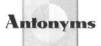 **Antonyms**   *In each of the following groups, circle the word that is **most nearly opposite** in meaning to the word in **boldface** type in the given phrase.*

31. quixotic schemes
a. fanciful   b. extravagant   (c. realistic)   d. visionary

32. a **lackluster** performance
a. early   (b. dazzling)   c. exhausting   d. mediocre

33. an **apocryphal** story
(a. authentic)   b. fictitious   c. romantic   d. sordid

34. a **mellifluous** voice
a. sweet   b. unusual   c. low   (d. shrill)

35. an inexplicable sense of **euphoria**
a. happiness   b. drowsiness   c. contentment   (d. melancholy)

36. a **diaphanous** curtain
(a. opaque)   b. flimsy   c. colorful   d. full

37. **minuscule** amounts
a. small   (b. huge)   c. unknown   d. profitable

38. a **viable** arrangement
a. attractive   (b. impracticable)   c. reasonable   d. dangerous

39. a **gargantuan** appetite
a. depraved   (b. tiny)   c. stimulated   d. immense

40. deliver a lengthy **philippic**
(a. panegyric)   b. diatribe   c. harangue   d. invective

41. an **ineluctable** conclusion
a. tragic   b. decisive   (c. avoidable)   d. peaceful

42. **constrict** the flow
a. control   b. end   c. inspect   (d. enlarge)

43. a **waggish** fellow
a. mature   b. childish   c. unbalanced   (d. dour)

44. a **malleable** mind
a. costly   b. indestructible   (c. intractable)   d. brilliant

45. **apropos of** our discussion
(a. irrelevant to)   b. needed for   c. germane to   d. stemming from

46. a **hidebound** view
(a. liberal)   b. epic   c. ribald   d. narrow-minded

47. an **ancillary** role
a. auxiliary   b. indigenous   (c. principal)   d. pessimistic

48. the critic's **bilious** review
a. ludicrous   b. benevolent   c. cowardly   (d. delightful)

49. a member of the **hoi polloi**
a. mumbo jumbo   b. faux pas   (c. upper class)   d. derring-do

50. speak to the **contumacious** students
(a. cooperative)   b. unruly   c. bored   d. ineluctable

Definitions

Note carefully the spelling, pronunciation, part(s) of speech, and definition(s) of each of the following words. Then write the word in the blank space(s) in the illustrative sentence(s) following. Finally, study the lists of synonyms and antonyms given at the end of each entry.

1. adjunct
(aj′ ənkt)

(*n.*) something added to something else as helpful or useful but not essential; an assistant or helper; a valuable quality or characteristic; (*adj.*) added or connected in a subordinate capacity; attached to a faculty or staff in an auxiliary capacity

The test manual was an _____**adjunct**_____ provided free with purchases of the new textbook series.

An _____**adjunct**_____ art professor will be hired.

SYNONYMS: (*n.*) associate, addition, accessory

2. bellwether
(bel′ weth ər)

(*n.*) the male sheep that leads the flock to the slaughterhouse; a leader, as in a desperate or violent undertaking; an indicator of trends

When their _____**bellwether**_____ was captured, the mob disbanded.

SYNONYMS: ringleader, initiator, barometer
ANTONYMS: follower, imitator, emulator

3. caterwaul
(kat′ ər wôl)

(*v.*) to howl or screech like a cat; to quarrel; (*n.*) a harsh or noisy cry; a racket

The desperate survivors _____**caterwauled**_____ about their suffering.

The _____**caterwaul**_____ in the alley kept us awake.

SYNONYMS: (*v.*) whine; (*n.*) wail, screech

4. chimerical
(ki mer′ i kəl)

(*adj.*) absurd; wildly fantastic; impossible

They proposed yet another _____**chimerical**_____ get-rich-quick scheme.

SYNONYMS: fanciful, visionary, quixotic, pie-in-the-sky
ANTONYMS: realistic, down-to-earth, practicable

5. effete
(i fēt′)

(adj.) lacking in wholesome vigor or energy; worn-out or exhausted; sterile or unable to produce; out-of-date

The _____**effete**_____ society was once a thriving and vigorous one.

SYNONYMS: decadent, enfeebled, outmoded
ANTONYMS: thriving, burgeoning, vigorous, dynamic

6. fait accompli
(fe ta kôm plē′)

(*n.*) an accomplished and presumably irreversible deed, fact, or action

The proud generals confidently declared the fall of the rebel stronghold a _____**fait accompli**_____.

SYNONYM: accomplished fact

7. hidebound
(hīd′ baůnd)

(*adj.*) narrow-minded and rigid, especially in opinions or prejudices;stubbornly and unthinkingly conservative

The _____**hidebound**_____ administrator stood by the outdated ways of previous administrations.

SYNONYMS: intolerant, inflexible
ANTONYMS: open-minded, tolerant, liberal, progressive

8. hierarchy
(hi′ ə rär kē)

(*n.*) any system of things or people arranged or graded one above another in order of rank, wealth, class, etc.

Within the governmental _____**hierarchy**_____, the voice of the junior senator was not a powerful one.

SYNONYMS: chain of command, pecking order

9. liturgy
(lit′ ər jē)

(*n.*) a religious service or rite; the form of a ritual or other act of public worship

The _____**liturgy**_____ has been modernized.

SYNONYMS: ceremony, observance

10. mirage
(mi räzh′)

(*n.*) something illusory, without substance, or without a basis in reality; an illusion

Deceived by a _____**mirage**_____, the desert travelers perked up at the thought of water and shade.

SYNONYM: optical illusion

11. morass
(mə ras′)

(*n.*) a patch of low, soft, wet ground; a swamp; a confusing situation in which one is entrapped, as in quicksand

After several bad performances, the aging athlete wallowed in a _____**morass**_____ of self doubt.

SYNONYMS: bog, quagmire
ANTONYMS: solid ground, bedrock, terra firma

12. noisome
(noi′ səm)

(*adj.*) offensive or disgusting; foul-smelling; harmful or injurious

The _____**noisome**_____ atmosphere of the slaughterhouse overwhelmed the visitors.

SYNONYMS: fetid, noxious, vile, loathsome
ANTONYMS: wholesome, pleasant, sweet-smelling

13. oblivious
(ə bliv′ ē əs)

(*adj.*) forgetful; unaware

The climbers were totally _____**oblivious**_____ of the dangers ahead.

SYNONYM: insensible
ANTONYMS: aware, mindful, cognizant, alert

14. poltroon
(pol trün′)

(*n.*) a base coward

The _____ **poltroon** _____ was caught in the act of deserting.

SYNONYMS: craven, dastard, "chicken"
ANTONYMS: hero, stalwart, gallant

15. proselyte
(pros′ ə līt)

(*n.*) a convert; a disciple

A group of zealous _____ **proselytes** _____ demonstrated in the square.

SYNONYMS: novice, neophyte
ANTONYMS: master, teacher, guide, guru

16. quasi
(kwā′ zī) *or*
(kwä′ zē)

(*adj.*) resembling but not actually being; seemingly but not actually or completely

They formed a _____ **quasi** _____ partnership.

SYNONYMS: kind of, semi-, as if
ANTONYMS: totally, completely, actually, in fact

17. raillery
(rā′ lər ē)

(*n.*) good-humored ridicule; teasing

The good-natured _____ **raillery** _____ in the locker room pleased the coach.

SYNONYMS: banter, persiflage

18. ribald
(rib′ əld)

(*adj.*) irreverently mocking; coarse, vulgar, or indecent in language

The actor tells _____ **ribald** _____ stories about life in the theater world.

SYNONYMS: bawdy, risqué
ANTONYMS: seemly, proper, decorous

19. supine
(sù pīn′)

(*adj.*) lying flat on one's back; listless or lethargic; apathetic or passive

The hiker relaxed in a _____ **supine** _____ position.

SYNONYMS: prone, prostrate; inert
ANTONYMS: upright, erect, perpendicular, vertical

20. vignette
(vin yet′)

(*n.*) a short description or sketch; a picture or illustration with edges that gradually shade off; a decorative design on the title page of a book or at the beginning or end of a chapter

All enjoyed the writer's _____ **vignette** _____ of country life.

SYNONYMS: thumbnail sketch, anecdote
ANTONYMS: epic, full-length treatment

Completing the Sentence

From the words for this unit, choose the one that best completes each of the following sentences. Write the word in the space provided.

1. If you think that the literature of earlier ages was always staid and proper, take a look at some of the _____ribald_____ stories in the *Decameron*, written more than 600 years ago.

2. Failure in itself is no disgrace, but the _____supine_____ acceptance of failure certainly is.

3. Taking advantage of the young man's naïve idealism, they sought to make him a(n) _____proselyte_____ to serve in their wild revolutionary plots.

4. Their youthful enthusiasm for literature had degenerated over the years into a(n) _____effete_____ preoccupation with quibbling criticism and minor details.

5. I detected an undertone of hostility and ridicule in the remarks, which were ostensibly no more than good-natured _____raillery_____.

6. The local Parents' Association has on many occasions served as a willing _____adjunct_____ to the administration and staff of our school.

7. Since the Smithsonian Institution is only partly under the control of the United States government, it is considered a(n) _____quasi-_____ governmental institution.

8. The newspaper published a series of charming _____vignettes_____ by my Aunt Alice—brief sketches of the town she grew up in.

9. I regret Fred's resignation as much as anyone, but I think that we must regard it as a(n) _____fait accompli_____ and find someone to take his place.

10. I think that the critic was a little harsh when he observed that the band's lead vocalist did not sing so much as _____caterwaul_____.

11. A handful of self-appointed "leaders" served as the _____bellwethers_____ who induced the mob to surge through the barriers.

12. Cynics may say that the goal of universal and lasting peace is no more than a(n) _____mirage_____, but we must continue to hope and strive for it.

13. As late as the seventeenth century, researchers called "alchemists" devoted their lives to the pursuit of _____chimerical_____ schemes for turning iron into gold.

14. She used talent, charm, energy, and determination to fight her way up the corporate _____hierarchy_____ until she attained the highest position in the company.

15. Don Quixote dismissed as a mere _____poltroon_____ anyone who refused to join in his crusade against the forces of evil.

16. Polluted by the spill from a nearby chemical plant, the once beautiful lake had become a foul pool, _____noisome_____ and hideous.

17. Advocates of equal rights maintain that we must reject the _____hidebound_____ prejudices that bar the physically impaired from many occupations.

18. The use of English rather than traditional languages in religious ceremonies is evidence of efforts to modernize and revitalize the _____liturgies_____ of various denominations.

19. Ever since she learned of the failure of her project, she has been mired in a(n) _____morass_____ of disappointment and self-recrimination.

20. As a rule, I am not a particularly proud or combative person, but I cannot be _____oblivious_____ to the fact that you have deliberately insulted me.

Synonyms

*Choose the word from this unit that is **the same** or **most nearly the same** in meaning as the **boldface** word or expression in the given phrase. Write the word on the line provided.*

1. brought another **neophyte** into the fold _____proselyte_____

2. a **thumbnail sketch** of urban life _____vignette_____

3. has a **fanciful** notion of what the future holds _____chimerical_____

4. found themselves in a **quagmire** _____morass_____

5. a steady stream of **banter** _____raillery_____

6. entranced by the **optical illusion** _____mirage_____

7. angered by the **outmoded** views of the leader _____effete_____

8. startled by the sudden **wail** _____caterwaul_____

9. embarrassed by the **bawdy** prose _____ribald_____

10. tempted by the idea of **semi**-retirement _____quasi_____

11. recognized the **irreversible situation** _____fait accompli_____

12. unfamiliar with the **ceremony** _____liturgy_____

13. at the pinnacle of the **pecking order** _____hierarchy_____

14. an **associate** hired for the summer _____adjunct_____

15. hasty instructions from the **ringleader** _____bellwether_____

Antonyms

*Choose the word from this unit that is **most nearly opposite** in meaning to the **boldface** word or expression in the given phrase. Write the word on the line provided.*

16. known as a **progressive** thinker _____hidebound_____

17. nauseated by the **pleasant** odor _____noisome_____

18. seemed **mindful** of the chaos all around _____oblivious_____

19. placed in a **perpendicular** position _____supine_____

20. enjoyed a deserved reputation as a **hero** _____poltroon_____

Choosing the Right Word

*Circle the **boldface** word that more satisfactorily completes each of the following sentences.*

1. Overly sensitive to any suggestion of ridicule, young Rogers seemed to be hurt even by a friend's good-natured (**raillery,** **proselytes**).

2. The lyrics of the song, presented as though they were devastating wit, were in my opinion no more than a course and (**supine,** **ribald**) jest.

3. They have confronted us not with a theoretical possibility but with a(n) (**adjunct,** **fait accompli**); now we must decide what we can do about it.

4. With penetrating insight and a marvelous ear for dialogue, the author gave us in a few words an unforgettable (**adjunct,** **vignette**) of a confused but hopeful adolescent.

5. After a brief period of popularity, their cheap and vulgar novels lost their appeal and sank into well-deserved (**proselyte,** **oblivion**).

6. Failure to stand up for your rights is not being "prudent" or "moderate"; it is the behavior of a (**poltroon,** **bellwether**).

7. Although the old Senator no longer holds any public office, her fame and prestige are so great that she is still regarded as a (**quasi,** **hidebound**) public figure.

8. Martin Luther King, Jr. appealed to his countrymen to abandon the (**noisome,** **hidebound**) stereotypes of racism and rise to a new level of understanding.

9. Financial analysts carefully watch the performance of certain stocks, which they regard as (**bellwethers,** **mirages**) for indications of economic trends.

10. How can you expect a prompt response from an agency that is bogged down in a veritable (**morass,** **liturgy**) of unnecessary red tape?

11. By late imperial times, centuries of soft living had turned the once hardy Romans into an (**oblivious,** **effete**) and indolent people.

12. We have lived to see the acceptance and enactment of reform programs that, when first proposed, were dismissed as absolutely (**chimerical,** **oblivious**).

13. The great historian Edward Gibbon sought to explain how and why the (**proselytizing,** **liturgical**) efforts of the early Christian church met with such extraordinary success.

14. As I listened to the talk of those unlettered folk, suffused with love and reverence, I felt that their simple words were a (**raillery,** **liturgy**) worthy of respect.

15. A superintendent is at the head of the (**hierarchy,** **vignette**) of educators responsible for the schooling of our children and young people.

16. I am willing to listen to any reasonable grievances you may have, but this constant (**caterwauling,** **hierarchy**) about trivia has exhausted my patience.

17. He is so (**ribald,** **hidebound**) in his political views that he won't even listen to opinions that differ from his own.

18. Her unfailing courtesy to others is not a mere (**adjunct,** **morass**) of her personality; it reflects the essential values and standards by which she lives.

19. Almost incredibly, a formidable resistance movement had been organized by people whom we had always associated with (**supine,** **noisome**) submission to authority.

20. Your serene confidence that "everything will come out all right in the end" may be reassuring, but it is no more than a (**morass,** **mirage**).

Vocabulary in Context

*Read the following passage, in which some of the words you have studied in this unit appear in **boldface** type. Then complete each statement given below the passage by circling the letter of the item that is **the same** or **almost the same** in meaning as the highlighted word.*

Before There Were Movies

(Line)

From the 1880s to the 1930s, the most popular form of entertainment in the United States was vaudeville. The roots of vaudeville, a French term for an amusing play with music, lay in the **ribald** variety shows popular in mid-nineteenth-century saloons. The purpose of these shows was to attract men who would spend money in the saloon.

(5)   One of the first important vaudeville producers, B. F. Keith, sought to expand the audience to include women and children. To do so, he imposed upon his performers strict rules forbidding vulgarity and hired the best talent he could find in Europe as well as the United States.

(10)   The results were phenomenal. Gone were the **noisome** antics of the saloon performances. Within twenty-five years, nearly 1,000 vaudeville theaters across the country filled up with two million spectators each day.

(15)   Audiences saw jugglers, singers, and comedians, as well as **vignettes** both humorous and dramatic. A typical show included from eight to ten acts. Comedians Jack Benny, George Burns, and W. C.

(20)   Fields were among the stars.

The advent of motion pictures brought doom to vaudeville. To the enthusiasts of the new medium, vaudeville must have seemed an **effete** entertainment, one that had seen its

Vaudeville comics tickled audiences' funny bones with slapstick skits and zany jokes.

(25)   day. Vaudeville producers tried to hold onto their dwindling audiences by showing motion pictures between acts. It didn't work. People flocked to the movies instead.

The old vaudeville stars are gone, but their legacy remains. Today, a new generation of vaudevillians has recreated the **chimerical** world of juggling, acrobatics, mime, silly skits, and eye-popping sight gags. Knee-slapping corny jokes

(30)   are back and so are magic tricks, sword swallowing, and animal acts. Audiences have returned, and entertainment for the whole family is back on center stage.

---

1. The meaning of **ribald** (line 3) is
a. apathetic
c. bawdy
b. rich
d. intolerant

2. Noisome (line 11) most nearly means
a. auxiliary
c. fanciful
b. insensible
d. offensive

3. Vignettes (line 16) is best defined as
a. sketches
c. quagmires
b. performers
d. illusions

4. The meaning of **effete** (line 24) is
a. visionary
c. outmoded
b. inflexible
d. decorous

5. Chimerical (line 28) most nearly means
a. vigorous
c. cognizant
b. quixotic
d. proper

Definitions

Note carefully the spelling, pronunciation, part(s) of speech, and definition(s) of each of the following words. Then write the word in the blank space(s) in the illustrative sentence(s) following. Finally, study the lists of synonyms and antonyms given at the end of each entry.

1. aegis
(ē′ jis)

(*n.*) protection; patronage; sponsorship

The arts and education programs of the United Nations are under the _____**aegis**_____ of UNESCO.

SYNONYM: auspices

2. apprise
(ə prīz′)

(*v.*) to inform of; to make aware of by giving oral or written notice

The spokesperson will _____**apprise**_____ us of the latest developments.

SYNONYMS: acquaint, notify
ANTONYMS: keep secret, withhold information

3. bibulous
(bib′ yə ləs)

(*adj.*) fond of or inclined to drink; absorbent

The retired sailor was a _____**bibulous**_____ old codger.

SYNONYMS: inebrious, alcoholic
ANTONYMS: teetotaling, abstemious, temperate

4. claque
(klak)

(*n.*) a group of people hired to applaud a performer or performance; enthusiastic or fawning admirers; an opera hat

The soprano's _____**claque**_____ was in attendance, as usual.

SYNONYMS: fan club, flatterers, hangers-on

5. deracinate
(di ras′ ə nāt)

(*v.*) to pull up by the roots; to root out, uproot, or dislocate; to eliminate all traces of

One way to _____**deracinate**_____ prejudice from our society is to heighten public awareness.

SYNONYMS: extirpate, eradicate, expunge
ANTONYMS: implant, nurture, foster, instill

6. eleemosynary
(el i mos′ ə ner ē)

(*adj.*) charitable; dependent upon or supported by charity; derived from or provided by charity

Some _____**eleemosynary**_____ institutions use phone solicitations to obtain contributions.

SYNONYMS: philanthropic, beneficent
ANTONYMS: selfish, self-seeking, uncharitable

7. indigenous
(in dij' ə nəs)

(*adj.*) originating in the country or region where found, native; inborn; inherent

Grizzly bears and mountain lions are two examples of wildlife _____ indigenous _____ to the Rockies.

SYNONYMS: endemic, domestic, homegrown
ANTONYMS: foreign, alien, exoteric, imported

8. lachrymose
(lak' rə mōs)

(*adj.*) given to tears or weeping; causing to shed tears; mournful, lugubrious

It was a _____ lachrymose _____ tale of poverty and woe.

SYNONYMS: tearful, doleful, dolorous
ANTONYMS: dry-eyed, cheerful, merry, hilarious

9. lexicon
(lek' sə kən)

(*n.*) a dictionary of a language; the special vocabulary of a person, group, or subject; a compendium

The _____ lexicon _____ of computer technology is large and growing.

SYNONYMS: wordbook, glossary

10. melee
(mā' lā)

(*n.*) a confused struggle; a violent free-for-all; a tumultuous mingling

Many fans were hurt in the _____ melee _____ that followed the soccer match.

SYNONYMS: fracas, brawl, scuffle, donnybrook
ANTONYMS: friendly chat, peace and quiet

11. microcosm
(mī' krə kos əm)

(*n.*) a miniature world or universe; a group or system viewed as the model of a larger group or system

The ocean liner is a _____ microcosm _____ of society in the novel *Ship of Fools*.

SYNONYMS: epitome, world in little
ANTONYMS: universe, macrocosm, cosmos, totality

12. minuscule
(min' əs kyül)

(*adj.*) very small, tiny; (*n.*) a lowercase letter

I ate only a _____ minuscule _____ portion of the dessert.

In the typeface that the poet chose, every letter used in the poem is a _____ minuscule _____.

SYNONYMS: (*adj.*) infinitesimal, insignificant
ANTONYMS: (*adj.*) huge, massive, monumental

13. obfuscate
(ob' fə skāt)

(*v.*) to darken or obscure; to confuse or bewilder

The pedantic lecturer's long-winded explanation served only to _____ obfuscate _____ the meaning of the thesis.

SYNONYM: muddy the waters
ANTONYMS: clarify, elucidate, explicate

14. paternalism
(pə tûr′ nə liz əm)

(*n.*) the policy or practice of treating or governing people in the manner of a father dealing with his children

The President won over the worried populace with his attitude of kind _____ paternalism _____.

SYNONYMS: benevolence, solicitude, fatherliness

15. polarize
(pō′ lə rīz)

(*v.*) to cause to concentrate around two conflicting or contrasting positions; to cause light to vibrate in a pattern

The debate served to _____ polarize _____ public opinion on the issue.

SYNONYMS: split, divide, alienate, estrange
ANTONYMS: unite, unify, reconcile

16. purview
(pər′ vyü)

(*n.*) the range, extent, or scope of something; in law, the scope or limit of what is provided in a statute

The subject was outside the _____ purview _____ of the mayor's authority.

SYNONYMS: jurisdiction, orbit

17. sanguine
(saŋ′ gwin)

(*adj.*) having a ruddy complexion; of a naturally cheerful, confident, or optimistic outlook

Scientists remain _____ sanguine _____ about the chances of finding a cure for the deadly disease.

SYNONYMS: flushed, rosy
ANTONYMS: bloodless, ashen, pessimistic, gloomy

18. solecism
(sol′ ə siz əm)

(*n.*) a substandard or ungrammatical usage; a breach of etiquette; any impropriety or mistake

One common _____ solecism _____ is "irregardless."

SYNONYMS: misusage, blunder, faux pas
ANTONYM: correct usage

19. vassal
(vas′ el)

(*n.*) a person under the protection of a feudal lord to whom he or she owes allegiance; a subordinate or dependent; a servant; (*adj.*) subservient

The duke's _____ vassal _____ was forced to fight for the king, to whom the duke owed allegiance.

As a _____ vassal _____ nation, India provided troops for British armies.

SYNONYMS: (*n.*) menial, minion; (*adj.*) servile
ANTONYM: (*n.*) overlord

20. verisimilitude
(ver ə si mil′ ə tüd)

(*n.*) the quality of appearing to be true, real, likely, or probable

The play's _____ verisimilitude _____ won praise from critics.

SYNONYMS: realism, lifelikeness, authenticity

Completing the Sentence

From the words for this unit, choose the one that best completes each of the following sentences. Write the word in the space provided.

1. I am not given to undue optimism, but the preliminary results of the polls make me _____**sanguine**_____ about the outcome of the election.

2. A hard-line speech may gain her the applause of her followers, but overall it will _____**polarize**_____ sentiments throughout the country and impair national unity.

3. Is the expression "It is me" to be regarded as a(n) _____**solecism**_____ or as an acceptable idiomatic form?

4. He came to realize that the inner city in which he had been raised was a(n) _____**microcosm**_____ of the sufferings of poor people all over the world.

5. She defended her policy of hiring a(n) _____**claque**_____ by noting that even with a supportive audience, someone is needed to get the applause started.

6. The third period was marred by a bench-clearing _____**melee**_____ that left the hockey rink littered with discarded gloves and sticks.

7. A case of that type, which does not involve a Federal law or constitutional issue, does not come within the _____**purview**_____ of the Supreme Court.

8. "The rash and _____**bibulous**_____ behavior of that young hothead almost cost us the battle, to say nothing of the war," the general remarked sourly.

9. Without expressing opinions, simply _____**apprise**_____ us as promptly as possible of the results of the conference.

10. No matter how fantastic and far-fetched the themes of Ray Bradbury's stories may be, he seems able to achieve an extraordinary effect of _____**verisimilitude**_____.

11. Both sides let on that the negotiators were still miles apart, when in fact the distance that separated them was _____**minuscule**_____.

12. Only within recent years has a complete _____**lexicon**_____ of the Latin language been compiled.

13. The issue is basically a simple one, and your efforts to _____**obfuscate**_____ it by raising endless technical objections will have no effect on us.

14. It is easy to be cynical about the motives that lie behind their _____**eleemosynary**_____ activities, but I truly believe that they want to help people.

15. Surprisingly, the white potato, which I have always associated with Ireland, is _____**indigenous**_____ to the Americas.

16. _____**Deracinated**_____ from their Old World environments, European immigrants had difficult adjustments to make.

17. The people of this impoverished area need a program that will "help them to help themselves"—not a form of _____**paternalism**_____ that will make them completely dependent on outside aid.

18. If you are ever to get out of this tangled mess, now is the time for action, not indulgence in _____**lachrymose**_____ self-pity.

19. When South Korea was invaded, the United States organized a collective defense effort under the _____**aegis**_____ of the United Nations.

20. At the outset of World War II, Lithuania lost its sovereignty and became an unwilling _____**vassal**_____ of the Soviet Union.

Synonyms

*Choose the word from this unit that is **the same** or **most nearly the same** in meaning as the **boldface** word or expression in the given phrase. Write the word on the line provided.*

1. acknowledged for its **authenticity** — verisimilitude

2. under the **auspices** of the church — aegis

3. left early and missed the **donnybrook** — melee

4. within the **jurisdiction** of the sheriff — purview

5. neglected to **notify** the townspeople — apprise

6. a small, private, **philanthropic** organization — eleemosynary

7. the **hangers-on** waiting by the stage door — claque

8. using the programmers' **special vocabulary** — lexicon

9. a **menial** in the royal family's service — vassal

10. to **divide** voters' sympathies — polarize

11. **native** to the region — indigenous

12. hopes to **expunge** the bad blood — deracinate

13. commits a **faux pas** at every turn — solecism

14. the **benevolence** of the dictator — paternalism

15. a **model** of the entire park — microcosm

Antonyms

*Choose the word from this unit that is **most nearly opposite** in meaning to the **boldface** word or expression in the given phrase. Write the word on the line provided.*

16. sought to **clarify** my view of the event — obfuscate

17. **pessimistic** about the test results — sanguine

18. invited all their **teetotaling** relatives — bibulous

19. in the **cheerful** moment that followed — lachrymose

20. had a **monumental** effect on the crowd — minuscule

Choosing the Right Word

*Circle the **boldface** word that more satisfactorily completes each of the following sentences.*

1. Their standards are so rigid and so devoid of a sense of proportion that they elevate every minor (**lexicon, solecism**) to the level of a major crime.

2. Falstaff, as conceived by Shakespeare, is not just a (**lachrymose, bibulous**) old braggart but an archetype of human appetites and joy in living.

3. Is it any wonder that the young quarterback is getting a swelled head when he seems always to be surrounded by a(n) (**claque, aegis**) of fawning admirers?

4. It is not enough merely to push aside our prejudices and pretend they don't exist; we must (**deracinate, apprise**) these evils from our minds and personalities.

5. From the observatory atop the Empire State Building, the pedestrians on the streets below look as (**sanguine, minuscule**) as ants.

6. Even the public opinion polls, which showed a strong trend toward our candidate, did not make us overly (**indigenous, sanguine**) about our chances of winning.

7. Those later scenes, in the opinion of many critics, had so much self-conscious pathos that they lacked conviction and (**verisimilitude, microcosm**).

8. For many years, there was a tendency among Americans and Europeans to ignore the highly developed (**eleemosynary, indigenous**) cultures of the peoples of Africa.

9. Compared to today's free agents, the ballplayers of yesteryear were practically the (**lexicon, vassals**) of the team owners.

10. A basketball team will be sent to the Far East under the (**claque, aegis**) of the State Department to play native teams in various countries.

11. I think it was very inconsiderate of her to wait until this late date before she (**apprised, obfuscated**) us of her intention to quit the class show.

12. In spite of the development of social security and insurance plans by the government, there is still a need for private (**minuscule, eleemosynary**) institutions to provide special services for needy people.

13. If we disregard the emotions and desires of other groups in our area, we are simply going to increase partisanship and (**deracinate, polarize**) the whole community.

14. The movie started off well, but the later scenes, with the beautiful young heroine slowly dying of cancer, became overwrought and (**bibulous, lachrymose**).

15. In the tragedy that overtakes the pathetic Lennie in *Of Mice and Men*, we see in (**microcosm, purview**) the cruelty and injustice that pervade our society.

16. Please do not try to (**apprise, obfuscate**) your responsibility in this matter by irrelevant criticisms of other people's behavior.

17. I came to resent the company's (**solecism, paternalism**) because it assumed that employees lacked the self-reliance to take care of themselves.

18. Under the American system of personal liberty, there are many aspects of daily life that are not within the (**claque, purview**) of any governmental authority.

19. Morality is not a criterion that can be used to judge whether or not a word belongs in a (**microcosm, lexicon**) of the language in which it is used.

20. At rush hour, I always have a hard time fighting my way through the (**melee, claque**) of tired commuters scurrying through the station.

Read the following passage, in which some of the words you have studied in this unit appear in **boldface** *type. Then complete each statement given below the passage by circling the letter of the item that is* **the same** *or* **almost the same** *in meaning as the highlighted word.*

Noah's Mark

(Line)

In his lifetime, Noah Webster compiled and published two major works that irrevocably distinguished the English spoken in the United States from that spoken in Great Britain. These works eloquently expressed their author's **sanguine** conviction that the citizens of the burgeoning United States ought to express themselves in an idiom as unique and rich as their young nation's spirit. (5)

The first of the two, *A Grammatical Institute of the English Language,* was published in 1783, when Webster was twenty-five years old. The "Blue-Backed Speller," so nicknamed for its blue cover, quickly replaced the British textbooks then in use. Within the author's **purview** was no less than the creation of a uniform American-English language, with American (10) words and American spellings. Webster sought to simplify spellings in order to differentiate them from those in British dictionaries. *Musick* became *music. Colour* became *color.* Such changes in spelling became the American (15) standard.

During its one hundred years of use, Webster's book eradicated many distinctions between different provincial colonial dialects. It became one of the most popular books of its time, with (20) sales second only to those of the Bible.

In 1828, after laboring for nearly thirty years, Webster published his masterpiece, the first comprehensive **lexicon** of American English.

The word for this animal first appeared in Webster's 1828 dictionary.

An American Dictionary of the English Language contained 70,000 entries and (25) was published in two volumes. In addition to revising spellings and pronunciations to reflect national practice, Webster included a number of words **indigenous** to North America. So it was that the words *hickory, skunk, squash,* and others made their first appearance in a dictionary.

Sales of Webster's highly praised but expensively priced dictionary were (30) lackluster. When Charles and George Merriam acquired the rights to publish new editions, they lowered the price—a sound business decision. Sales of the first Merriam-Webster dictionary boomed.

---

1. The meaning of **sanguine** (line 3) is
  a. abandoned   c. confident
  b. recovered   d. closed

2. The meaning of **purview** (line 9) is
  a. sponsorship   c. fan club
  b. scope   d. struggle

3. Lexicon (line 24) most nearly means
  a. orbit   c. model
  b. clarification   d. wordbook

4. Indigenous (line 27) most nearly means
  a. native   c. doleful
  b. given   d. paternal

Definitions

Note carefully the spelling, pronunciation, part(s) of speech, and definition(s) of each of the following words. Then write the word in the blank space(s) in the illustrative sentence(s) following. Finally, study the lists of synonyms and antonyms given at the end of each entry.

1. ancillary
(an' sə ler ē)

(*adj.*) subordinate or supplementary

The aide serves in an _____ancillary_____ position.

SYNONYMS: auxiliary, subsidiary, accessory
ANTONYMS: central, key, primary, principal, main

2. bowdlerize
(bōd' lə rīz)

(*v.*) to remove material considered offensive (from a book, play, film, etc.)

The writers refused to _____bowdlerize_____ the book when they turned it into a screenplay.

SYNONYMS: censor, purge, expurgate

3. condescend
(kon di send')

(*v.*) to come down or stoop voluntarily to a lower level; to deal with people in a patronizing manner

The fashion designer _____condescended_____ to speak to reporters.

SYNONYM: deign

4. cozen
(kəz' ən)

(*v.*) to trick; to cheat or swindle

Some taxi drivers _____cozen_____ unsuspecting tourists.

SYNONYMS: dupe, deceive, beguile, inveigle

5. enclave
(en' klāv)

(*n.*) an enclosed district, region, or area inhabited by a particular group of people or having a special character

The mountains afforded the displaced townspeople and the local militia an _____enclave_____ of resistance.

SYNONYMS: island, subgroup

6. forte
(fôrt) *or* (fôr' tā)

(*n.*) a person's strong point; what a person does best

Although I love listening to piano music, playing the instrument is not my _____forte_____ .

SYNONYMS: gift, aptitude, specialty
ANTONYMS: weakness, shortcoming, foible

7. gratis
(gra' tis)

(*adj.*) free; (*adv.*) without charge

The food provided was _____ **gratis** _____ .

During the filming, a local restaurant provided meals to the crew _____ **gratis** _____ .

SYNONYMS: (*adj.*) on the house; (*adv.*) freely
ANTONYM: (*adv.*) for a price

8. icon
(ī' kän)

(*n.*) a representation or image of a sacred personage, often considered sacred itself; an image or picture; a symbol; a graphic symbol on a computer monitor display; an object of blind devotion

The museum's exhibit of _____ **icons** _____ included several from Czarist Russia.

SYNONYMS: emblem, idol

9. interstice
(in tər' stis)

(*n.*) a small, narrow space between things or parts of things

Once it slipped through the _____ **interstice** _____ in the fence, the rabbit headed straight for the vegetables.

SYNONYMS: gap, slot, crevice, interval, lacuna

10. macrocosm
(mak' rō koz əm)

(*n.*) the universe considered as a whole; the entire complex structure of something

During the course of their college education, many students study the economic _____ **macrocosm** _____ .

SYNONYMS: cosmos, entirety
ANTONYMS: model, miniature, microcosm

11. mountebank
(màun' tə baŋk)

(*n.*) a trickster or swindler; a charlatan

The _____ **mountebank** _____ who sold surefire remedies for every imaginable ailment was finally exposed.

SYNONYMS: impostor, quack
ANTONYMS: sucker, dupe, "mark," "pigeon"

12. paean
(pē' ən)

(*n.*) a song of praise, joy, or triumph

The audience responded with a _____ **paean** _____ of exultation when the ceremony ended.

SYNONYMS: hymn, ode, anthem
ANTONYMS: dirge, elegy, lament, threnody

13. persiflage
(pər' sə fläzh)

(*n.*) lighthearted joking, talk, or writing

The friends engaged in _____ **persiflage** _____ from the moment their reunion began until the last of them left.

SYNONYMS: banter, jesting, repartee, badinage

14. plethora
(pleth′ ə rə)

(*n.*) overfullness; superabundance; superfluity

The inquisitive journalists besieged the harried celebrity with a _____**plethora**_____ of personal questions.

SYNONYMS: surplus, surfeit, glut, excess
ANTONYMS: shortage, paucity, dearth, scarcity

15. pragmatic
(prag mat′ ik)

(*adj.*) concerned with practical considerations or values; dealing with actions and results rather than with abstract theory

The mayor takes a _____**pragmatic**_____ approach to the city's problems.

SYNONYMS: down-to-earth, businesslike
ANTONYMS: idealistic, impractical, visionary

16. quizzical
(kwiz′ i kəl)

(*adj.*) puzzled; mocking; odd; equivocal

The politician's unexpected comment left all who heard it with _____**quizzical**_____ expressions on their faces.

SYNONYMS: peculiar, perplexed, mystified, derisive
ANTONYMS: unequivocal, crystal-clear, unambiguous

17. rapacity
(rə pas′ ə tē)

(*n.*) inordinate greed; the disposition to obtain one's desires by force, extortion, or plunder

With the _____**rapacity**_____ of a shark, the ruthless new company went after its competitors' clients.

SYNONYMS: avarice, cupidity, voraciousness
ANTONYMS: liberality, generosity, altruism

18. schism
(siz′ əm) *or*
(skiz′ əm)

(*n.*) a formal split within a religious organization; any division or separation of a group or organization into hostile factions

What began as a disagreement over a minor issue led to a bitter _____**schism**_____ within the party.

SYNONYMS: rift, breach
ANTONYMS: united front, reconciliation

19. therapeutic
(ther ə pyü′ tik)

(*adj.*) having the power to heal or cure; beneficial

Many believe in the _____**therapeutic**_____ effects attributed to the waters of natural hot springs.

SYNONYMS: curative, salutary, salubrious
ANTONYMS: harmful, injurious, deleterious

20. virtuoso
(vər chü ō′ sō)

(*n.*) a brilliant performer; a person with masterly skill or technique; (*adj.*) masterly or brilliant

Franz Liszt was a piano _____**virtuoso**_____.

I was treated to a _____**virtuoso**_____ performance.

SYNONYMS: (*n.*) expert, master, prodigy, maestro
ANTONYMS: (*n.*) amateur, beginner, novice; (*adj.*) mediocre

 **Completing the Sentence**

From the words for this unit, choose the one that best completes each of the following sentences. Write the word in the space provided.

1. Playing on his vanity and his desire to be known as a "good guy," I tried to _____**cozen**_____ him into lending me his car.

2. To promote circulation, the publisher offered to throw in home delivery _____**gratis**_____ for new subscribers to the Sunday edition.

3. She thought of herself as a combination of Mark Twain and H. L. Mencken, but her attempts at "devastating _____**persiflage**_____" were not very funny.

4. In attempting to make the novel acceptable to the general public, the editor so _____**bowdlerized**_____ it that it lost its quality of stark realism.

5. His self-importance stems from his inability to appreciate the very minor part he plays in the _____**macrocosm**_____ of human affairs.

6. His exaggerated claims for an expensive painkiller that turned out to be no more than aspirin exposed him as a(n) _____**mountebank**_____.

7. He considers himself such a marvelous chess player that I'm surprised he would _____**condescend**_____ to sit down at the board with a beginner like me.

8. The "minor difference of opinion" developed into a(n) _____**schism**_____ that split the political party into two opposing factions.

9. The situation is growing worse because there is a(n) _____**plethora**_____ of good intentions but a dearth of common sense and willingness to work hard.

10. The stubborn old-timers who refused to sell their homes came to form a(n) _____**enclave**_____ of "natives" surrounded by "city people."

11. A good laugh invariably makes me feel better; I honestly believe that it has a(n) _____**therapeutic**_____ effect on my disposition.

12. When the soldiers realized that they had defeated the far more numerous enemy, their cheers rose in a great _____**paean**_____ of jubilation and victory.

13. At the height of Beatlemania in the mid-1960s the Fab Four assumed the stature of pop _____**icons**_____.

14. Although we pride ourselves on the advance of civilization, the sad fact is that the _____**rapacity**_____ of twentieth-century humanity has resulted in more destruction and suffering than ever before in history.

15. I would have welcomed any firm answer, no matter how unfavorable, but all that I got from her was a(n) _____**quizzical**_____ smile.

16. When she neatly faked out the guard, pivoted, and drove in for a layup, I realized that I was seeing a true _____**virtuoso**_____ on the basketball court.

17. My classmates selected me to address the community affairs committee because public speaking is a(n) _____**forte**_____ of mine.

38 ▪ Unit 3

18. Once the advance and royalties were settled, the publisher and agent negotiated _____ancillary_____ rights to be covered in the author's contract.

19. The coach used diagrams to show our receivers how to slip through the _____interstice(s)_____ in our opponent's zone pass coverage.

20. What point is there in dwelling on unproven theories when the problem we are facing demands that we be as _____pragmatic_____ as possible?

Synonyms

*Choose the word from this unit that is **the same** or **most nearly the same** in meaning as the **boldface** word or expression in the given phrase. Write the word on the line provided.*

1. **deign** to respond to the question — condescend
2. wormed its way through the **crevice** — interstice
3. worshipped the **idol** — icon
4. participated in the witty **repartee** — persiflage
5. urges writers to **censor** their screenplays — bowdlerize
6. offered a **hymn** of praise — paean
7. awed by the gifts of the young **master** — virtuoso
8. gave their assistance **freely** — gratis
9. the **curative** benefits of mineral water — therapeutic
10. caused a **breech** in their ranks — schism
11. received a **surfeit** of gifts — plethora
12. a charmer, ever ready to **deceive** — cozen
13. belonging to a **subsidiary** organization — ancillary
14. the **universe** of Western society — macrocosm
15. an **island** of safety — enclave

Antonyms

*Choose the word from this unit that is **most nearly opposite** in meaning to the **boldface** word or expression in the given phrase. Write the word on the line provided.*

16. gave a **crystal-clear** response — quizzical
17. known for their **idealistic** views — pragmatic
18. with a **generosity** heretofore unseen — rapacity
19. marked as a **sucker** by the others — mountebank
20. shown not to be a **shortcoming** — forte

Choosing the Right Word

*Circle the **boldface** word that more satisfactorily completes each of the following sentences.*

1. The sun left its mottled imprint on the wall as the rays filtered through the (**enclaves, interstices**) of the iron grating.

2. In this situation, when I desperately needed material help, I was deluged with a(n) (**plethora, enclave**) of glib and gratuitous advice.

3. A truly great leader must possess both the inspiration of a visionary and the (**quizzical, pragmatic**) skills of an experienced politician.

4. In the great crises of life, you must depend basically on yourself; the help you get from others can only be (**pragmatic, ancillary**).

5. A political candidate who promises to solve all our social problems without ever mentioning higher taxes would certainly be dismissed as a (**mountebank, schism**).

6. Our little group of would-be writers, painters, and musicians formed an (**enclave, ancillary**) of culture in what we considered a hostile world.

7. Because he sees life as a pattern of ambiguities and contradictions, he likes to express himself in the form of (**quizzical, ancillary**) witticisms.

8. The dictum "There's no such thing as a free lunch" means that nothing worthwhile in life comes to us (**forte, gratis**).

9. They can't force you to do anything, but it is quite possible that they will be able to (**condescend, cozen**) you into actions against your best interests.

10. A theory that seems valid in the confines of a small family group may be proved useless when applied in the (**macrocosm, interstice**) of society at large.

11. Simply because we have dropped a few objectionable words from the dialogue does not justify the critic's statement that we have (**cozened, bowdlerized**) the play.

12. In sandpainting, an art still practiced by the Navajos and Pueblos of the American Southwest, designs are created of (**icons, fortes**) representing animals, deities, and natural phenomena.

13. Your (**virtuosity, pragmatism**) as a public speaker and campaigner may earn you votes, but it cannot make up for your lack of experience and knowledge of public affairs.

14. If, as they say, they find those people so vulgar and unpleasant, why do they (**cozen, condescend**) to associate with them?

15. The clash of wits between those two brilliant columnists was no mere (**persiflage, paean**), but an exchange of deadly insults.

16. The first serious (**schism, enclave**) in the Communist world of the postwar era occurred in 1948, when Yugoslavia began in earnest to distance itself from the Soviet Union.

17. Her easygoing attitude and resilience, far from being a weakness, proved to be her (**mountebank, forte**) in surviving during that trying period.

18. Though acupuncture has been practiced in Eastern medicine for centuries, its (**therapeutic, quizzical**) value has only recently been acknowledged in the West.

19. It is a common mistake to assume that shrewdness in business affairs must be accompanied by extreme (**rapacity, mountebank**).

20. After the great victory, his quiet and modest statements were far more impressive than the most effusive (**paean, interstice**) could have been.

Vocabulary in Context

Read the following passage, in which some of the words you have studied in this unit appear in **boldface** type. Then complete each statement given below the passage by circling the letter of the item that is **the same** or **almost the same** in meaning as the highlighted word.

Patently Dangerous

(Line)

In the latter half of the nineteenth century, a **plethora** of diseases plagued Americans living in frontier settlements. Without the benefit of vaccines and antibiotics, an ailing settler was forced to choose from among a variety of grim options. Bleeding and blistering were among the treatments regular, licensed doctors commonly offered.

(5) To treat diphtheria, doctors would boil sulfur in lime water and then pour it into a patient's nose. Dreary procedures like these often compelled the pioneers to seek the aid of unlicensed, less-reputable practitioners, known as irregulars.

Some irregulars extolled the **therapeutic** powers of hot spring waters. Others swore to the efficacy
(10) of the latest patented tonic. Settlers often favored the services of the crafty irregulars, with their patent medicines and promises of good health.

By 1900, the patent-medicine industry offered a vast array of tonics, most full of alcohol and some
(15) containing narcotics or poisons. Lydia Pynkham's Vegetable Compound claimed to cure all kinds of ills; it also contained 18 percent alcohol. Peddlers of the patented tonics managed to **cozen** susceptible patients out of millions of dollars each year. To the
(20) medical community, the patent-medicine industry's increasing **rapacity** and success must have been very disheartening.

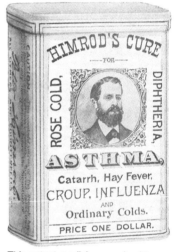

This patent medicine promised to cure eight diseases for one dollar!

Yet within the space of a few years, a group of tireless investigative reporters, nicknamed
(25) muckrakers, kicked off an era of significant reforms. In 1904, Edward Bok published a series of trenchant articles in *Ladies' Home Journal*, exposing the **mountebanks** who ran the patent-medicine industry. In 1906, the American government finally stepped in and passed the Pure Food and Drug Act. It was a small step, but one
(30) that set a precedent for further reforms and cleared the way for the rapid medical advances of the mid-1900s.

---

1. The meaning of **plethora** (line 1) is
  a. symbol
  b. shortage
  c. cosmos
  d. glut

2. Therapeutic (line 8) most nearly means
  a. harmful
  b. curative
  c. expert
  d. proven

3. Cozen (line 18) is best defined as
  a. dupe
  b. censor
  c. banter
  d. harm

4. The meaning of **rapacity** (line 21) is
  a. altruism
  b. weakness
  c. aptitude
  d. avarice

5. Mountebanks (line 27) most nearly means
  a. islanders
  b. climbers
  c. swindlers
  d. suckers

Analogies

In each of the following, circle the item that best completes the comparison.

See pages T38–T46 for explanations of answers.

1. bowdlerize is to **out** as
a. abbreviate is to in
b. annotate is to out
c. interpolate is to in
d. duplicate is to out

2. schism is to **polarize** as
a. controversy is to reconcile
b. merger is to unite
c. covenant is to antagonize
d. compromise is to estrange

3. mirage is to **illusory** as
a. will-o-the-wisp is to elusive
b. thunderclap is to noisome
c. rainbow is to chimerical
d. eclipse is to luminous

4. mountebank is to **cozen** as
a. turncoat is to cheat
b. panhandler is to kill
c. embezzler is to abduct
d. highwayman is to rob

5. oblivious is to **awareness** as
a. comatose is to consciousness
b. serene is to composure
c. erudite is to knowledge
d. adroit is to skill

6. bibulous is to **drink** as
a. rapacious is to clothing
b. gluttonous is to food
c. altruistic is to money
d. vegetarian is to meat

7. obfuscate is to **clarity** as
a. illuminate is to light
b. deracinate is to precision
c. invigorate is to energy
d. adulterate is to purity

8. bellwether is to **barometer** as
a. proselyte is to spark plug
b. cynosure is to magnet
c. morass is to catalyst
d. liturgy is to lightning rod

9. aegis is to **protection** as
a. hierarchy is to experience
b. maelstrom is to sanctuary
c. vignette is to encouragement
d. buttress is to support

10. poltroon is to **pusillanimous** as
a. jester is to lachrymose
b. dynamo is to supine
c. optimist is to sanguine
d. progressive is to hidebound

Word Associations

In each of the following groups, circle the word that is best defined or suggested by the given phrase.

1. "For you, our special customer, it's on the house."
a. gratis   b. polarized   c. quizzical   d. ancillary

2. I'm glad I done it!
a. purview   b. verisimilitude   c. aegis   d. solecism

3. He certainly fooled us!
a. proselyte   b. mountebank   c. schism   d. pragmatist

4. delighted to listen to their clever give-and-take
a. persiflage   b. paean   c. lexicon   d. paternalism

5. It's hardly worth bothering about.
a. macrocosm   b. minuscule   c. condescend   d. rapacity

6. The chairperson brought the committee up to date on the new developments.
a. apprise   b. caterwaul   c. defer   d. bowdlerize

7. Is it inside or outside of our jurisdiction?

    a. vassal   b. adjunct   (c. purview)   d. claque

8. The instincts of a "shark"

    (a. rapacity)   b. virtuoso   c. melee   d. raillery

9. like nails on a chalkboard

    (a. caterwaul)   b. polarize   c. obfuscate   d. deracinate

10. looking at the large picture

    a. verisimilitude   b. mountebank   (c. macrocosm)   d. persiflage

11. a person's "long suit"

    a. interstice   b. gratis   c. therapeutic   (d. forte)

12. "It's no use crying over spilled milk."

    a. hierarchy   (b. fait accompli)   c. poltroon   d. vignette

Choosing the Right Meaning

Read each sentence carefully. Then circle the item that best completes the statement below the sentence.

See pages T38–T46 for explanations of answers.

Adopting the role of virtuoso, newspaper magnate William Randolph Hearst scoured Europe in the 1920s for antiques and objets d'art with which to furnish San Simeon, his immense California estate.   (2)

1. In line 1 the word **virtuoso** is used to mean

    a. maestro   b. prodigy   c. tycoon   (d. connoisseur)

Despite the claims advanced in commercials, I find it hard to believe that one brand of paper towel is more bibulous than another.   (2)

2. The best definition for the word **bibulous** in line 2 is

    (a. absorbent)   b. inebrious   c. fond of the bottle   d. soft

"This fellow here, with envious carping tongue,
Upbraided me about the rose I wear;   (2)
Saying, the sanguine color of the leaves
Did represent my master's blushing cheeks . . ."   (4)
      (Shakespeare, *I Henry VI*, IV, i, 90–93)

3. In line 3 the word **sanguine** most nearly means

    a. cheerful   (b. red)   c. optimistic   d. confident

Attached to units of the Red Army were political commissars, Communist party ideologues whose pragmatic and tyrannical ways made them the objects of fear and contempt on the part of the common soldiers.   (2)

4. The word **pragmatic** in line 2 most nearly means

    a. practical   b. businesslike   (c. doctrinaire)   d. conspiratorial

Antonyms

*In each of the following groups, circle the word or expression that is most nearly the **opposite** of the word in **boldface** type.*

1. quizzical
a. amused
b. unequivocal *(circled)*
c. contorted
d. dissimilar

2. paean
a. lament *(circled)*
b. sonnet
c. soliloquy
d. appear

3. deracinate
a. implant *(circled)*
b. twist
c. conceal
d. flourish

4. quasi
a. tacitly
b. noisily
c. semi
d. completely *(circled)*

5. chimerical
a. impossible
b. fortunate
c. comprehensive
d. realistic *(circled)*

6. poltroon
a. follower
b. stalwart *(circled)*
c. milksop
d. employer

7. proselyte
a. gallant
b. novice
c. guide *(circled)*
d. proper

8. eleemosynary
a. unworthy
b. uncharitable *(circled)*
c. unenthusiastic
d. unemployable

9. noisome
a. wholesome *(circled)*
b. quiet
c. tasty
d. loathsome

10. oblivious
a. thankful
b. tolerant
c. smug
d. cognizant *(circled)*

11. ancillary
a. dependent
b. concomitant
c. relevant
d. primary *(circled)*

12. plethora
a. surfeit
b. dearth *(circled)*
c. contrast
d. supply

13. effete
a. vigorous *(circled)*
b. exhausted
c. lax
d. awkward

14. pragmatic
a. earthy
b. prominent
c. idealistic *(circled)*
d. inquisitive

15. bibulous
a. limited
b. sedate
c. abstemious *(circled)*
d. convivial

16. obfuscate
a. bedim
b. exemplify
c. clarify *(circled)*
d. slander

Completing the Sentence

From the following list of words, choose the one that best completes each of the following sentences. Write the word in the space provided.

condescend	hierarchy	macrocosm	rapacity
cozen	interstice	quasi	sanguine

1. Ben quickly learned his lowly place in the ___**hierarchy**___ of employees in the busy supermarket.

2. How could you have allowed them to ___**cozen**___ you into voting for their ticket?

3. Will Earth be able to survive the ___**rapacity**___ of humanity in the name of progress?

4. I was amazed that the august senior would ___**condescend**___ to allow me to drive him home.

5. Even a person of his ___**sanguine**___ temperament could not maintain his optimism in the face of such a series of misfortunes.

6. Helen soon learned to fill the ___**interstices**___ between the intense workouts with relaxation exercises.

Interesting Derivations

From the following list of words, choose the one that best completes each of the sentences below. Write the word in the space provided.

aegis	**chimerical**	**lexicon**	**plethora**
bowdlerize	**claque**	**paean**	**proselyte**

1. One of the many epithets of Apollo, the god of music, poetry, and the arts, is the basis for the English noun _____**paean**_____.

2. The fire-breathing mythological monster with the head and forepaws of a lion, the body and hind legs of a goat, and the tail of a dragon is the source of the English adjective _____**chimerical**_____.

3. The goatskin shield or breastplate bearing the head of Medusa and used by Zeus and Athena is the source of the English noun _____**aegis**_____.

4. The name of the early 19th-century English editor who rigorously excised "questionable" words, phrases, lines, and scenes from his "family edition" of Shakespeare's plays is remembered in the verb _____**bowdlerize**_____.

Word Families

A. *On the line provided, write the word you have learned in Units 1–3 that is related to each of the following nouns.*

EXAMPLE: obfuscation—**obfuscate**

1. condescension — condescend
2. deracination — deracinate
3. bowdlerization, bowdlerizer — bowdlerize
4. polarization, polarity — polarize
5. pragmatism, pragmatist — pragmatic
6. chimera, chimerism — chimerical
7. lachrymosity — lachrymose
8. indigenousness — indigenous
9. therapy, therapist, therapeutics — therapeutic
10. oblivion, obliviousness — oblivious
11. ribaldry — ribald
12. liturgist, liturgiology — liturgy
13. poltroonery — poltroon
14. vignettist — vignette
15. claqueur — claque
16. lexicology, lexicographer — lexicon

B. *On the line provided, write the word you have learned in Units 1–3 that is related to each of the following verbs.*

EXAMPLE: indigenize—**indigenous**

17. proselytize _____ proselyte

18. quiz _____ quizzical

19. schismatize _____ schism

20. supinate _____ supine

Two-Word Completions

Circle the pair of words that best complete the meaning of each of the following passages.

See pages T38–T46 for explanations of answers.

1. As the detachment of knights galloped over the crest of the hill, it collided with a column of enemy foot soldiers moving up the other side. In the brief but bloody _____ that ensued, two of the king's most prominent _____ lost their lives, and the Duke of Orleans was wounded.
a. schism . . . proselytes
b. purview . . . mountebanks
c. melee . . . vassals
d. vignette . . . bellwethers

2. Your composition is so full of _____, malapropisms, and general gobbledygook that I suggest you study a grammar book, a _____, and a style manual before you ever again put pen to paper.
a. interstices . . . liturgy
b. raillery . . . microcosm
c. persiflage . . . plethora
d. solecisms . . . lexicon

3. The social structure of the South in the days before the Civil War was rigidly _____, with the gentleman planter at the summit of the edifice and the chattel slave at its base. _____ notions of caste discouraged whites from moving freely within the system, and the "peculiar institution" denied blacks any mobility whatsoever.
a. pragmatic . . . Polarized
b. hierarchical . . . Hidebound
c. therapeutic . . . Cozened
d. chimerical . . . Obfuscated

4. On more than one occasion during the Middle Ages, controversy about some point of doctrine _____ ecclesiastical opinion and produced a temporary _____ in the Christian church.
a. polarized . . . schism
b. bowdlerized . . . fait accompli
c. obfuscated . . . enclave
d. deracinated . . . macrocosm

Read the following passage, in which some of the words you have studied in Units 1–3 appear in **boldface** type. Then complete each statement given below the passage by circling the item that is **the same** or **almost the same** in meaning as the highlighted word.

Drawn to the Sea

(Line)

Winslow Homer's dramatic seascapes continue to fascinate museum visitors and collectors. Born in Boston in 1836, he was just
(5) nineteen when his father's importing business soured. Lacking funds for college, he answered an ad and became a lithographer's apprentice. After two years of making bland
(10) drawings, he vowed never to be bound to an employer again.

Homer moved to New York to join the city's artistic community. After a mere five art lessons in night school,
(15) where he learned the basics of oil painting, he boldly embarked on a career as a freelance illustrator. In 1861, under the **aegis** of *Harper's Weekly*, he attached himself to
(20) General George McClellan's Army of the Potomac to draw scenes of Civil War army life in the encampments and at or near the front lines.

His drawings and sketches
(25) showed that he was not a mere realist. His **forte** was his ability to capture the emotional pain and desperation of his subjects, using shape and color to convey his
(30) sympathy for the combatants.

Harper's regularly published his unsentimental images of the fear and despair of Civil War soldiers. By the end of the war, Homer was famous.
(35) Not content to be just another **hidebound** artist painting whatever would sell, he traveled to France and, later, to England where he painted the people of the fishing village of
(40) Tynemouth, whose daily lives were affected by their constant struggles with the sea. Returning to America, in a seemingly **quizzical** move he settled in Prout's Neck, finding the solitude
(45) he needed on the remote and rugged Maine coast. His new paintings depicted the drama of man's heroic battles with the forces of nature.

Except for excursions to Florida and
(50) the Caribbean, Homer remained in Maine, far from the celebrity he spurned. Nonetheless, by the late 1880s, he was recognized as America's **virtuoso** seascape painter.
(55) Homer died in 1910. This self-taught, fiercely independent artist fully deserves his exalted place in the **hierarchy** of great American painters.

---

1. The meaning of **aegis** (line 18) is
a. auspices
b. roof
c. discipline
d. mistake

2. Forte (line 26) most nearly means
a. fortress
b. foible
c. strong suit
d. weakness

3. Hidebound (line 36) is best defined as
a. clothed
b. narrow-minded
c. flexible
d. enfeebled

4. The meaning of **quizzical** (line 43) is
a. test-taking
b. peculiar
c. typical
d. expected

5. Virtuoso (line 54) most nearly means
a. virtuous
b. amateur
c. masterly
d. mediocre

6. Hierarchy (line 58) is best defined as
a. court
b. swampland
c. anecdotes
d. pecking order

Building with Classical Roots

sem, simil, simul—like; together, at the same time

This root appears in **verisimilitude** (page 30), which means "the appearance of being true." Some other words based on the same root are listed below.

assemblage	**disassemble**	**simile**	**simulation**
assimilation	**resemblance**	**simulacrum**	**simulcast**

From the list of words above, choose the one that corresponds to each of the brief definitions below. Write the word in the blank space in the illustrative sentence below the definition.

1. an image or representation of something; an unreal or superficial semblance

The first 1950s television sitcoms presented a cheery ____**simulacrum**____ of family happiness.

2. to take apart

After the science fair, it took the exhibitors and maintenance crew several hours to fully ____**disassemble**____ the many displays and booths.

3. a similarity in form or appearance; a likeness

Grandma glows over the strong family ____**resemblance**____ she already sees in her newborn grandson.

4. a collection of people or things; a gathering

The most experienced journalists were sent to cover the annual ____**assemblage**____ of notables in the field of medical research.

5. a comparison, introduced by *like* or *as*; an analogy

A nonfiction piece on a dreary topic can be enlivened by poetic use of ____**simile**____.

6. the act or process of taking in or absorbing; the state of being absorbed

The healthy human brain is uniquely designed for constant ____**assimilation**____ of knowledge.

7. to broadcast over radio and television at the same time

She had some friends over to enjoy the ____**simulcast**____ of the rock concert with her.

8. the act or process of taking on the appearance or form of something; a feigning or pretending

Although the children were unable to keep the secret from their mother, she put on a convincing ____**simulation**____ of surprise at the presentation of their gift.

From the list of words above, choose the one that best completes each of the following sentences. Write the word in the space provided.

1. French purists have gone to great lengths to resist any further ____**assimilation**____ of English words and phrases into their language.

2. Displayed in Madame Tussaud's museum in London are _____ **simulacra** _____ fashioned in wax of historical personages and notorious criminals.

3. We watched the _____ **simulcast** _____ of Puccini's *La Boheme* on television while listening to it on our local public radio station.

4. The mechanic was forced to _____ **disassemble** _____ the entire transmission in order to replace the faulty part.

5. The instructor cautioned his creative-writing students against relying on such timeworn _____ **similes** _____ as "red as a rose" and "blue as the sky."

6. Members of the police emergency negotiating team rehearse their demanding roles in lifelike _____ **simulations** _____ of hostage situations.

7. It was a matchless _____ **assemblage** _____ of politicians and philosophers who gathered in Philadelphia in 1787 to frame our Constitution.

8. Though they were not related by blood, the _____ **resemblance** _____ between them was so strong that many took them for sisters.

---

*Circle the **boldface** word that more satisfactorily completes each of the following sentences.*

1. In American Studies class, we prepared a detailed (**simulation,** assemblage) of the landmark *Brown v. Board of Education* case that the U.S. Supreme Court heard in 1954.

2. Part of a soldier's basic training is to learn to (simulcast, **disassemble**) and then put back together a weapon, within a time limit, while blindfolded.

3. In many cases, sociologists have noted that the younger the immigrant, the more likely his or her (simulation, **assimilation**) into the local culture will progress smoothly and quickly.

4. Robert Burns's well-loved poem "A Red, Red Rose" begins with two very basic yet romantic (resemblances, **similes**) about the object of the poet's affection.

5. In the closing credits for most movies, you will see in small print a legal disclaimer that any (**resemblance,** simulacrum) to actual persons, living or dead, is purely coincidental.

6. The pageantry of the opening ceremonies of the Olympic Games is a thrilling experience for the (**assemblage,** assimilation) of world-class athletes who take part.

7. It takes advanced planning, flexible scheduling, and technological precision to effectively (disassemble, **simulcast**) a program on two media.

8. In recurring dreams, he was tormented by the astonishing (simile, **simulacrum**) of the horrific fire he had witnessed as a young child.

Writer's Challenge

Read the following sentences, paying special attention to the words and phrases underlined. From the words in the box below, find better choices for these underlined words and phrases. Then use these choices to rewrite the sentences.

WORD BANK

apprise	(hidebound)	melee	ribald	therapeutic
deracinate	icon	mirage	schism	verisimilitude
(enclave)	indigenous	mountebank	solecism	(vignette)
forte	(lachrymose)	(pragmatic)	supine	(virtuoso)

Django Reinhardt

1. A group of itinerant Gypsy musicians and acrobats formed the traveling <u>subgroup</u> into which Jean Baptiste "Django" Reinhardt was born on January 24, 1910.
enclave

---

2. Django's family wandered in caravans across Europe and North Africa. They camped in empty fields, away from the <u>narrow-minded and prejudiced</u> communities that neither welcomed nor accepted Gypsies.
hidebound

---

3. <u>Thumbnail sketches</u> of Django's youth attest to his gifts. He once won a bet by playing on a banjo—from memory and in order—seventeen tunes he'd heard played only once on an accordion.
vignettes

---

4. An accidental fire burned off two fingers of Reinhardt's left hand and left him partly paralyzed. <u>Weepy</u> and in great pain for well over a year, Django feared an end to his musical dreams.
lachrymose

---

5. To cheer him up, Django's brother got him a guitar. With it, Django began a <u>down-to-earth</u> yet bold rehabilitation plan. He spent painful hours inventing an original musical technique.
pragmatic

---

6. Django Reinhardt emerged as the undisputed <u>brilliant performer</u> of the jazz guitar. He played with the best musicians of his day until his untimely death at age 43.
virtuoso

Definitions

Note carefully the spelling, pronunciation, part(s) of speech, and definition(s) of each of the following words. Then write the word in the blank space(s) in the illustrative sentence(s) following. Finally, study the lists of synonyms and antonyms given at the end of each entry.

1. affinity
(ə fin′ ə te)

(*n.*) a natural attraction to a person, thing, or activity; a relationship, connection

The mysterious _____ **affinity** _____ between the two leaders could not be explained.

SYNONYMS: inclination, penchant
ANTONYMS: distaste, aversion

2. bilious
(bil′ yəs)

(*adj.*) peevish or irritable; sickeningly unpleasant

The room was painted a _____ **bilious** _____ shade of green.

SYNONYMS: choleric, irascible, peevish, splenetic
ANTONYMS: sweet-tempered, genial, pleasant, delightful

3. cognate
(kog′ nāt)

(*adj.*) closely related in origin, essential nature, or function; (*n.*) such a person or thing

_____ **Cognate** _____ languages, such as Spanish, Italian, and French, share a common root.

When I studied Latin, I learned that the words *pater* and *father* are _____ **cognates** _____.

SYNONYMS: (*adj.*) allied, affiliated; (*n.*) relative
ANTONYMS: (*adj.*) dissimilar, unrelated

4. corollary
(kôr′ ə ler ē)

(*n.*) a proposition that follows from one already proven; a natural consequence or result; (*adj.*) resultant or consequent

Learning the axiom and its _____ **corollary** _____ was no simple matter.

The _____ **corollary** _____ effects of today's findings remain to be seen.

SYNONYMS: (*n.*) deduction, conclusion
ANTONYMS: (*n.*) axiom, postulate, premise

5. cul-de-sac
(kəl′ də sak)

(*n.*) a blind alley or dead-end street; any situation in which further progress is impossible; an impasse

Much to their dismay, the once-optimistic negotiators found themselves in a hopeless _____ **cul-de-sac** _____.

6. derring-do
(der′ iŋ dü)

(*n.*) valor or heroism; daring deeds or exploits (often used to poke fun at false heroics)

Breathtaking feats of _____ **derring-do** _____ are all in a day's work for a Hollywood stuntperson.

SYNONYMS: audacity, bravado, pyrotechnics
ANTONYMS: cowardice, timidity, poltroonery

7. divination
(div ə nā′ shən)

(*n.*) the art or act of predicting the future or discovering hidden knowledge

Claiming skill in _____divination_____, the fortune teller took my money and then told me what my future held.

SYNONYMS: prophesy, augury

8. elixir
(i lik′ sər)

(*n.*) a potion once thought capable of curing all ills and maintaining life indefinitely; a panacea; a sweet liquid used as a vehicle in medicines

Allegedly, the explorer Ponce de León spent years searching for the _____elixir_____ of eternal life.

SYNONYMS: cure-all, nostrum, tonic

9. folderol
(fol′ də rol)

(*n.*) foolish talk, ideas, or procedures; nonsense; a trifle

Right from the outset, the sergeant informed her troops that she would not tolerate any _____folderol_____.

SYNONYMS: hoopla, gibberish
ANTONYMS: sense, significance

10. gamut
(gam′ ət)

(*n.*) an entire range or series

The reviews of the newest Broadway musical extravaganza ran the _____gamut_____ from praise to scorn.

SYNONYMS: scope, compass, sweep

11. hoi polloi
(hoi pə loi′)

(*n.*) the common people, the masses

By catering to the _____hoi polloi_____, the studio was able to make one very successful movie after another.

SYNONYM: rank and file
ANTONYMS: aristocracy, elite, upper class

12. ineffable
(in ef′ ə bəl)

(*adj.*) not expressible in words; too great or too sacred to be uttered

The _____ineffable_____ joy of parenthood is the subject of a psychologist's new bestseller.

SYNONYMS: inexpressible, indescribable

13. lucubration
(lü kyü brā′ shən)

(*n.*) laborious study or thought, especially at night; the result of such work

The scientist's _____lucubration_____ took place after midnight, secretly, in the quiet of the laboratory.

SYNONYMS: burning the midnight oil, deep thought

14. mnemonic
(ni mon′ ik)

(*adj.*) relating to or designed to assist the memory; (*n.*) a device to aid the memory

PPMDAS is a _____**mnemonic**_____ device used to remember the order of mathematical operations.

The _____**mnemonic**_____ HOMES can help people to recall the names of the Great Lakes.

SYNONYMS: (*n.*) reminder, cue

15. obloquy
(ob′ lə kwē)

(*n.*) public abuse indicating strong disapproval or censure; the disgrace resulting from such treatment

The press heaped _____**obloquy**_____ on the head of the offending official.

SYNONYMS: discredit, opprobrium, ignominy, dishonor
ANTONYMS: praise, acclaim, approbation

16. parameter
(pə ram′ ə tər)

(*n.*) a determining or characteristic element; a factor that shapes the total outcome; a limit, boundary

The committee analyzed the _____**parameter**_____ of the nation's military potential.

17. pundit
(pən′ dit)

(*n.*) a learned person; one who gives authoritative opinions

A renowned _____**pundit**_____ of the theater, the critic had the power to affect a show's success.

SYNONYMS: expert, authority, savant
ANTONYMS: layman, amateur, dilettante

18. risible
(riz′ ə bəl)

(*adj.*) pertaining to laughter; able or inclined to laugh; laughable

All in the crowd, not just the children, were delighted by the _____**risible**_____ antics of the clowns.

SYNONYMS: droll, ludicrous
ANTONYMS: depressing, poignant, heartrending

19. symptomatic
(simp tə mat′ ik)

(*adj.*) typical or characteristic; being or concerned with a symptom of a disease

According to certain sociologists, vulgarity and indulgence are _____**symptomatic**_____ of a nation's decline.

SYNONYM: indicative

20. volte-face
(volt fäs′)

(*n.*) an about-face; a complete reversal

The prosecution's witness's testimony amounted to a completely unexpected _____**volte-face**_____.

SYNONYM: turnabout

Completing the Sentence

From the words for this unit, choose the one that best completes each of the following sentences. Write the word in the space provided.

1. The role calls for an actor who can express a(n) _____**gamut**_____ of emotions, from speechless rage to utter bliss.

2. After having strongly supported the teaching of foreign languages, they made a complete _____**volte-face**_____ and advocated that this part of the curriculum be dropped or limited to a small minority.

3. In reading a passage in French, I can often guess the meanings of words I have never seen before because they are recognizable _____**cognates**_____ of familiar English words.

4. The _____**bilious**_____ tenor of the remarks that they offered to us as "constructive criticism" betrayed just how sorely they envied our success.

5. The suggestion was so _____**risible**_____ that I couldn't help laughing out loud as soon as I heard it.

6. The intensive merchandising and tremendous sale of patent medicines shows that mankind has never really ceased its search for an all-purpose _____**elixir**_____.

7. Foreign visitors sometimes dismiss our national political conventions as mere _____**folderol**_____ because of all the surface pageantry.

8. All kittens display a natural _____**affinity**_____ for mischief, but I have never known one so bent on monkey business as our Mickie.

9. The relief we felt when we realized they were safe was so profound and overwhelming as to be utterly _____**ineffable**_____.

10. Is our blind faith in computerized analysis any different in its essentials from the belief of so-called primitive peoples in _____**divination**_____?

11. Having been maneuvered into a(n) _____**cul-de-sac**_____, the retreating troops could do nothing but turn and fight a battle for survival against superior forces.

12. No sooner did the press conference end than the network correspondent turned to a group of political _____**pundits**_____ for an instant analysis.

13. Your ponderous _____**lucubration(s)**_____ seemed to me intended much more to emphasize your own brilliance and importance than to shed any real light on the subject.

14. It is true that capital punishment has not been proved to be a deterrent to murder, but it would be invalid to draw from this the _____**corollary**_____ that it has been proved *not* to be a deterrent.

15. In estimating the relative military strength of the two powers, we must concentrate on the _____**parameters**_____ by which ability to carry on modern warfare may be judged.

16. The lecturer said that the soaring crime statistics are _____**symptomatic**_____ of a society in which traditional values and standards are breaking down.

17. This short sentence will serve as a(n) _____**mnemonic**_____ to help you remember the names of the first eight Presidents: "*Will A Jolly Man Make A Jolly Visitor?*"

18. I know that they deserve to be condemned, but I can't bring myself to heap _____ obloquy _____ on them when they are in such a state of disgrace.

19. In a truly democratic society, there are no sharp differences in status and privilege between self-styled aristocrats and the _____ hoi polloi _____.

20. The situation calls for courage, in the sense of a sustained, resolute, and patient effort—not occasional feats of _____ derring-do _____.

Synonyms

*Choose the word from this unit that is **the same** or **most nearly the same** in meaning as the **boldface** word or expression in the given phrase. Write the word on the line provided.*

1. signs **indicative** of small pox — symptomatic

2. the **augury** of the oracle — divination

3. among the **related** procedures — cognate

4. suffered a torrent of **ignominy** — obloquy

5. the **indescribable** beauty of the canyons — ineffable

6. made a surprising **turnabout** — volte-face

7. wondered what all the **hoopla** was about — folderol

8. not the **cure-all** the mountebank promised — elixir

9. led the despondent explorers to a **dead end** — cul-de-sac

10. was less than an obvious **deduction** — corollary

11. spent the late hours in **deep thought** — lucubration

12. an uncalled-for, **splenetic** retort — bilious

13. the **scope** of the case before the judge — gamut

14. the **boundaries** of scientific understanding — parameter

15. a **memory aid** for recalling the rainbow's colors — mnemonic

Antonyms

*Choose the word from this unit that is **most nearly opposite** in meaning to the **boldface** word or expression in the given phrase. Write the word on the line provided.*

16. an **aversion** to the smell of cigars — affinity

17. was not the time for **timidity** — derring-do

18. considered a **dilettante** by many at the museum — pundit

19. witnessed a **poignant** performance — risible

20. a vacation spot favored by the **upper class** — hoi polloi

Choosing the Right Word

*Circle the **boldface** word that more satisfactorily completes each of the following sentences.*

1. Your irresponsible behavior has finally caught up with you; you are in a (**cul-de-sac,** **hoi polloi**) from which it will be all but impossible to extricate yourself.

2. Many sociologists believe that the high divorce rate in the United States is (**symptomatic,** **ineffable**) of basic strains and flaws in our social structure.

3. In *Inferno,* Dante introduces personages from history and mythology to portray the full (**gamut,** **folderol**) of human folly and wickedness.

4. Those remarkably accurate predictions were based not on (**derring-do,** **divination**) but on insight into human nature and the objective elements in the situation.

5. Henry had an excellent chance to make an honorable career for himself, but he seemed to have a fatal (**affinity,** **corollary**) for easy money and shady deals.

6. I knew that if I ran for public office, I would be exposed to severe criticism, but I never expected such a flood of (**obloquy,** **elixir**).

7. Is your repeated use of the expression (**cul-de-sac,** **hoi polloi**) supposed to convey the idea that you are not one of the people?

8. Only a supreme actor could express so eloquently the (**risible,** **ineffable**) quality of the "thoughts that do often lie too deep for tears."

9. We found it more difficult to master the (**mnemonic,** **parameter**) than it would have been to memorize the material to which it was keyed.

10. The advice which they offered us with such pretentious solemnity turned out to be nothing more than platitudes and (**folderol,** **elixir**).

11. No student of anthropology can fail to recognize the (**cognate,** **corollary**) elements in the cultures of societies which seem to be vastly different from one another.

12. You have had many difficulties in life, but you are helping neither yourself nor others by behaving in such a (**bilious,** **cognate**) and offensive manner.

13. It may seem to be a paradox, but I believe it is true that only a basically serious person can fully appreciate the (**risible,** **bilious**) factors in life.

14. The devastating stock market crash of 1929 surprised not only laymen, but Wall Street (**corollaries,** **pundits**) as well.

15. The first thing we must do is establish the (**parameters,** **lucubrations**) of the problem, so that we can begin to think in terms of a practical solution.

16. The pithy comments of that brilliant and delightful woman were a(n) (**elixir,** **cul-de-sac**) that we found extraordinarily exhilarating.

17. In an age of genocide, atomic weapons, and threats of ecological disaster, do you really expect a sensible person to be fascinated by such romantic tales of (**parameters,** **derring-do**)?

18. We expect to see politicians modify their points of view from time to time, but a sudden, unexpected (**cognate,** **volte-face**) by a candidate is more than we can tolerate.

19. I have listened to them state that the present situation is hopeless, but I am unwilling to accept the (**gamut,** **corollary**) that the only course open to us is surrender.

20. It is little short of incredible that all their mountainous (**lucubrations,** **divinations**) have brought forth that tiny mouse of an idea.

Vocabulary in Context

*Read the following passage, in which some of the words you have studied in this unit appear in **boldface** type. Then complete each statement given below the passage by circling the letter of the item that is **the same** or **almost the same** in meaning as the highlighted word.*

(Line)

Journalism, Anyone?

If you have a special curiosity in the world around you, in local, national, or international current events, you might want to pursue a career in journalism. Journalism jobs are to be had online, in television and radio, and, of course, in the old print stand-bys, newspapers and magazines. Through each of these
(5) media, reporters, reviewers, and editors provide the public with fresh information on a **gamut** of topics. Within the pages of almost any daily paper, one can find articles that range from the deep seriousness of the plight of earthquake victims half-way around
(10) the world to the utter **folderol** of who wore what at a society wedding.

If you have an **affinity** for the pleasures of literature, a job as a book reviewer might be just the
(15) thing. You would spend much of your time doing something you love: reading. But book reviewing, like other careers in journalism, presents certain **parameters** within which the
(20) journalists must function. Like all reporters, columnists, and magazine editors, book reviewers often have to attend to strict word limits. They must meet demanding deadlines and be

A television network's busy newsroom hums with activity round-the-clock.

(25) sure their facts are accurate. So, book reviewers need to be able to read quickly, albeit thoughtfully, and write quickly, too; they have little time to indulge in the luxury of **lucubration**.

To the professional journalist, no idea is **ineffable**. In fact, it might be said that the most important requirement asked of all journalists is to believe in the ability of
(30) words to describe, explain, and evaluate experience.

---

1. The meaning of **gamut** (line 6) is
  a. penchant   c. scolded
  (b.) range   d. sense

2. The meaning of **folderol** (line 10) is
  a. significance   c. peevishness
  b. poltroonery   (d.) nonsense

3. Affinity (line 12) most nearly means
  a. aversion   (c.) inclination
  b. elixir   d. ignominy

4. Parameters (line 19) most nearly means
  (a.) limits   c. senses
  b. tonics   d. cues

5. Lucubration (line 27) means
  a. timidity   (c.) deep thought
  b. significance   d. aversion

6. Ineffable (line 28) is best defined as
  a. droll   c. unrelated
  (b.) inexpressible   d. bilious

Definitions

Note carefully the spelling, pronunciation, part(s) of speech, and definition(s) of each of the following words. Then write the word in the blank space(s) in the illustrative sentence(s) following. Finally, study the lists of synonyms and antonyms given at the end of each entry.

1. aficionado
(ə fish yə nä′ dō)

(*n.*) an enthusiastic and usually expert follower or fan

I have been an _____ **aficionado** _____ of football since my youth.

SYNONYMS: devotee, enthusiast

2. browbeat
(braủ′ bēt)

(*v.*) to intimidate by a stern or overbearing manner; to bully

The dissatisfied customer had to _____ **browbeat** _____ the store manager into refunding his money.

SYNONYMS: cow, coerce
ANTONYMS: coax, cajole, wheedle, sweet-talk

3. commensurate
(kə men′ sə rit)

(*adj.*) equal in size, extent, duration, or importance; proportionate; measurable by the same standards

All employees got raises _____ **commensurate** _____ with their efforts.

SYNONYMS: comparable, corresponding, coordinate

4. diaphanous
(dī af′ ə nəs)

(*adj.*) very sheer and light; almost completely transparent

We were asked to use a _____ **diaphanous** _____ material like gauze to make the costumes.

SYNONYMS: translucent, gossamer
ANTONYMS: opaque, coarse, dense

5. emolument
(i mol′ yə mənt)

(*n.*) profit derived from an office or position or from employment; a fee or salary

Choosing an equitable _____ **emolument** _____ for the mayor was the latest of the city council's acts.

SYNONYMS: pay, wages, compensation

6. foray
(fôr′ ā)

(*n.*) a quick raid, especially for plunder; a venture into some field of endeavor; (*v.*) to make such a raid

The cavalry's _____ **foray** _____ behind enemy lines was a great success.

Counting on the element of surprise, the general ordered the troops to begin to _____ **foray** _____ before dawn.

SYNONYMS: (*n.*) sally, sortie
ANTONYMS: (*n.*) retreat, strategic withdrawal

7. genre
(zhän′ rə)

(*n.*) a type, class, or variety, especially a distinctive category of literary composition; a style of painting in which everyday scenes are realistically depicted

The science fiction _____**genre**_____ has produced several classics.

SYNONYMS: species, sort, school

8. homily
(hom′ ə lē)

(*n.*) a sermon stressing moral principles; a tedious moralizing lecture or discourse

The topic of this week's _____**homily**_____ is respect for diversity.

9. immure
(i myür′)

(*v.*) to enclose or confine within walls; to imprison; to seclude or isolate

The terrorist was _____**immured**_____ for life in a narrow cell.

SYNONYMS: incarcerate, mew up
ANTONYMS: release, liberate, emancipate

10. insouciant
(in sü′ sē ənt)

(*adj.*) blithely indifferent or unconcerned; carefree; happy-go-lucky

After months of worrying about the fate of his new project, the man was determined to lead a more _____**insouciant**_____ life thereafter.

SYNONYMS: nonchalant, blasé, devil-may-care
ANTONYMS: worried, careworn, agitated, distraught

11. matrix
(mā′ triks)

(*n.*) a mold; the surrounding situation or environment

Scientists discovered a tiny prehistoric creature fossilized in a _____**matrix**_____ of amber.

SYNONYMS: pattern, model

12. obsequies
(ob′ sə kwēz)

(*n.*) funeral rites or ceremonies

The nation held somber _____**obsequies**_____ for their beloved leader.

SYNONYMS: last rites, funeral services

13. panache
(pə nash′)

(*n.*) a confident and stylish manner, dash; a strikingly elaborate or colorful display

In the film *The Adventures of Robin Hood,* the actor Errol Flynn captures the _____**panache**_____ of the bandit.

SYNONYMS: style, verve, élan, éclat, flamboyance

14. persona
(pər sō′ nə)

(*n.*) a character in a novel or play; the outward character or role that a person assumes

The comic _____**persona**_____ of Charlie Chaplin is recognizable the world over.

SYNONYMS: personality, image, role

15. philippic
(fi lip′ ik)

(*n.*) a bitter verbal attack

The senator delivered a _____**philippic**_____ against the proposed law and those who supported it.

SYNONYMS: harangue, tirade, diatribe
ANTONYMS: encomium, panegyric, tribute

16. prurient
(prúr′ ē ənt)

(*adj.*) having lustful desires or interests; tending to arouse sexual desires

Considered a _____**prurient**_____ novel by some, *Ulysses* was once banned from sale in the United States.

SYNONYMS: lascivious, salacious, lewd, titillating
ANTONYMS: prudish, demure, innocent

17. sacrosanct
(sak′ rō saŋkt)

(*adj.*) very sacred or holy; inviolable; set apart or immune from questioning or attack

Members of the clergy felt privileged to be entrusted with guarding the _____**sacrosanct**_____ relic.

18. systemic
(sis tem′ ik)

(*adj.*) of or pertaining to the entire body; relating to a system or systems

The singer suffered a _____**systemic**_____ breakdown after the long and demanding season.

SYNONYMS: extensive, comprehensive, system-wide
ANTONYMS: localized, specific, isolated, confined

19. tendentious
(ten den′ shəs)

(*adj.*) intended to promote a particular point of view, doctrine, or cause; biased or partisan

The candidate's supporters heartily applauded her _____**tendentious**_____ arguments.

SYNONYM: partial
ANTONYMS: fair, impartial, equitable, disinterested

20. vicissitude
(vi sis′ ə tüd)

(*n.*) a change, variation, or alteration; (*pl.*) successive or changing phases or conditions

The inevitable _____**vicissitudes**_____ of life affect us all.

SYNONYMS: fluctuation, vacillation
ANTONYMS: sameness, evenness

Completing the Sentence

From the words for this unit, choose the one that best completes each of the following sentences. Write the word in the space provided.

1. Having been conditioned to take wealth and luxury for granted, they tended to take a(n) _____**insouciant**_____ attitude toward money, even when they had only a modest income.

2. In her speech to the entering freshman class, the dean emphasized that the benefits they derived from any course would be _____**commensurate**_____ with the effort that they devoted to it.

3. Time after time, he rose on the floor of the Senate and delivered bitter _____**philipics**_____ against the lack of effective measures against environmental pollution.

4. In my opinion, the epic poem represents the most noble and inspiring of all literary _____**genres**_____.

5. Their reverence for all creations of God was so great that, in their eyes, even the most common manifestation of nature was _____**sacrosanct**_____.

6. One of my fondest hopes is to visit Jerusalem, the city that has had a unique role in history as the _____**matrix**_____ of three great world religions.

7. It was a cat-and-mouse play about a patient detective and an aristocratic jewel thief who stole with elegance and _____**panache**_____.

8. The overbearing maitre d' _____**browbeat**_____ the diners into meekly accepting the least desirable table in the restaurant.

9. When doctors discovered the disease to be _____**systemic**_____, they held out little hope for the patient's recovery.

10. When we reflected on his long and happy life and his unmatched record of public service, we found the _____**obsequies**_____ comforting and even inspiring.

11. She claimed to be an unbiased witness, but I found her testimony to be opinionated and _____**tendentious**_____.

12. The constitution provides that the _____**emolument**_____ received by the President is to be neither increased nor decreased during his term of office.

13. You should not approach a class in sex education with such a leering and _____**prurient**_____ attitude.

14. The true test of her character will be how she is able to deal with the _____**vicissitudes**_____ of life.

15. She cannot relate to other people in a constructive way because she is _____**immured**_____ in her own prejudices and hostilities.

16. At first she showed only a mild interest in bridge, but as she played more and developed skill, she became a real _____**aficionado**_____ of the game.

17. Our troops returned from their successful _____**foray**_____ against the enemy's base in a jubilant mood.

18. The omniscient narrator is probably the most common _____persona_____ assumed by novel writers.

19. We found overwhelming beauty in the most common manifestations of nature, such as the colors of sunset, the delicate shape of a flower, or the _____diaphanous_____ wings of an insect.

20. What good does it do to regale the prisoners with _____homilies_____ about going straight if they have no chance to make an honest living when they are released?

Synonyms *Choose the word from this unit that is **the same** or **most nearly the same** in meaning as the **boldface** word or expression in the given phrase. Write the word on the line provided.*

1. a **sermon** on the value of honesty _____homily_____

2. **compensation** for the job _____emolument_____

3. the only true **enthusiast** in the room _____aficionado_____

4. envied their **nonchalant** approach _____insouciant_____

5. the **fluctuations** of the family's daily routines _____vicissitudes_____

6. was seen as **salacious** behavior _____prurient_____

7. **incarcerated** in a dungeon _____immured_____

8. let loose a searing **tirade** _____philippic_____

9. possessed a certain **flamboyance** _____panache_____

10. in the **role** of a gangster _____persona_____

11. considered to be a **sacred** right _____sacrosanct_____

12. pay **proportionate** to the task _____commensurate_____

13. a good example of that **school** of painting _____genre_____

14. used a **model** to solve the logic problem _____matrix_____

15. delivered the **last rites** _____obsequies_____

Antonyms *Choose the word from this unit that is **most nearly opposite** in meaning to the **boldface** word or expression in the given phrase. Write the word on the line provided.*

16. made of **coarse** material _____diaphanous_____

17. stunned by their **impartial** response _____tendentious_____

18. **coaxed** the players into using the new system _____browbeat_____

19. a **strategic withdrawal** under fire _____foray_____

20. reports of **localized** uprisings _____systemic_____

Choosing the Right Word

Circle the **boldface** word that more satisfactorily completes each of the following sentences.

1. I admit that you have some grounds for complaint, but those shrieks of outrage are simply not (**diaphanous, commensurate**) with having been overcharged five cents.

2. It seems incredible that a few generations ago a novel of such quality could be widely condemned as designed to appeal to (**tendentious, prurient**) interests.

3. The fact that they referred to my salary as a(n) (**panache, emolument**) did not disguise the fact that I was being woefully underpaid.

4. How can young people hope to become mature, self-reliant adults if they (**immure, foray**) themselves in a home environment that is so comfortable and protective?

5. It is often said that in Russia there are as many (**vicissitudes, aficionados**) of chess as there are of baseball or golf in the United States.

6. If the woman thinks her status as a public official renders her (**insouciant, sacrosanct**), she is in for a rude awakening.

7. The Bible reminds us that even in moments of great joy we should retain some awareness of the (**panache, vicissitudes**) and heartbreaks of life.

8. What we owe to our fallen leader is not mournful (**philippics, obsequies**) but a joyful assertion of life and a pledge to continue her work.

9. The (**matrix, persona**) that a public figure displays to the world is often quite different from the personality that he or she exhibits in private.

10. Certainly your judgment, if not your motives, must be questioned when you choose to associate yourself with an organization of that (**matrix, genre**).

11. Corot painted poetic and (**diaphanous, tendentious**) landscapes, in which even solid objects seemed to be suffused with light and movement.

12. The defense attorney claimed that the police had used scare tactics to (**browbeat, foray**) her client into a confession.

13. What gourmet feast can compare with the luscious delicacies that we consumed during our midnight (**forays, homilies**) on the well-stocked refrigerator?

14. When the results of the scholarship competition were announced, we could sense the deep disappointment beneath your (**insouciant, tendentious**) manner.

15. The commission found that police corruption was not confined to one or two isolated precincts but was (**systemic, prurient**) in nature.

16. The purpose of our policies is to develop bold new forms of international understanding and practical cooperation that can serve as the (**philippic, matrix**) for a stable peace.

17. There is no doubt of your oratorical talents, but this is a time for quiet words of reconciliation—not for thundering (**emoluments, philippics**).

18. I had hoped to hear a balanced, dispassionate discussion of this problem, but I found their approach to be distressingly one-sided and (**tendentious, sacrosanct**).

19. Young people involved in drug abuse need practical help in overcoming their addiction—not (**homilies, obsequies**) exhorting them to higher standards of behavior.

20. James Bond seems to dispose of the villains he faces with all the (**genre, panache**) of the legendary paladins of medieval romance.

*Read the following passage, in which some of the words you have studied in this unit appear in **boldface** type. Then complete each statement given below the passage by circling the letter of the item that is **the same** or **almost the same** in meaning as the highlighted word.*

Rowdy Ball

(Line)

In the last decade of the nineteenth century, **systemic** dirty play characterized American major league baseball. Players routinely spiked, tripped, and insulted opponents. But the turn of the century brought an end to what was called "rowdy ball." In the twentieth century, baseball was played more cleanly and with more strategy than ever before. (5)

The rules of professional baseball, like those of other sports, are not **sacrosanct**. Some key changes in the 1900s greatly affected the way the game was played. For the first time, foul balls were recorded as strikes. Accordingly, batting averages (10) dropped and strikeouts rose. Fielders' gloves grew in size. There followed a **commensurate** drop in errors and in runs scored. The balance of power shifted to the (15) pitchers.

A batter heads for first base in this 1887 lithograph.

In the early 1900s, team rosters were diverse. Many players were the sons of immigrants. Some were college graduates; others were (20) illiterate. Some went back to the mines or the farms in the off-season. Players had nicknames like "Wagon Tongue" and "The Flying Dutchman."

Many different **personas** shared the teams' dugouts. Although teamwork was key, not everybody on a team got along. For example, Joe Tinker and Johnny Evers, who, with Frank Chance, were the first famous double-play combination, did not get along. (25) Off the diamond, the Chicago Cubs players were enemies, but that did not affect their coordination on the field—the two worked together like a well-oiled machine.

The new rules and exciting and entertaining players drew **aficionados** of the game to the new concrete and steel stadiums. Attendance boomed. The modern age of baseball had begun. (30)

---

1. The meaning of **systemic** (line 1) is
   a. localized   c. extensive
   b. sacred   d. uncommon

2. Sacrosanct (line 7) most nearly means
   a. specific   c. reasonable
   b. inviolable   d. nonchalant

3. Commensurate (line 13) is best defined as
   a. corresponding   c. common
   b. salacious   d. partisan

4. The meaning of **personas** (line 23) is
   a. sermons   c. devotees
   b. styles   d. personalities

5. Aficionados (line 28) most nearly means
   a. officials   c. members
   b. enthusiasts   d. schools

Definitions

Note carefully the spelling, pronunciation, part(s) of speech, and definition(s) of each of the following words. Then write the word in the blank space(s) in the illustrative sentence(s) following. Finally, study the lists of synonyms and antonyms given at the end of each entry.

1. abortive
(ə bôr′ tiv)

(*adj.*) failing to accomplish an intended aim or purpose; only partially or imperfectly developed

An _____**abortive**_____ attempt to seize the throne ended badly for the participants.

SYNONYMS: miscarried, fruitless, premature
ANTONYMS: successful, realized, consummated

2. bruit
(brüt)

(*v.*) to spread news, reports, or unsubstantiated rumors

News of the company's closing and the impending job losses was immediately _____**bruited**_____ about the office.

SYNONYMS: noise abroad, broadcast, blazon
ANTONYMS: cover up, conceal, hush up

3. contumelious
(kon tü mē′ lē əs)

(*adj.*) insolent or rude in speech or behavior; insultingly abusive; humiliating

The ambassador's _____**contumelious**_____ reply was completely unexpected.

SYNONYMS: vituperative, scurrilous, excoriating
ANTONYMS: laudatory, commendatory, deferential

4. dictum
(dik′ təm)

(*n.*) a short saying; an authoritative statement

According to the _____**dictum**_____ of the critics, the play is not worth the price of admission.

SYNONYMS: maxim, precept, aphorism, axiom

5. ensconce
(en skons′)

(*v.*) to settle comfortably and firmly in position; to put or hide in a safe place

After a very long, difficult day at work, I gratefully _____**ensconced**_____ myself in my snug, warm bed.

SYNONYMS: nestle, lodge, entrench
ANTONYMS: unseat, displace, oust

6. iconoclastic
(ī kon ə klas′ tik)

(*adj.*) attacking or seeking to overthrow popular or traditional beliefs, ideas, or institutions

The writer's _____**iconoclastic**_____ opinions always seem to stir controversy.

SYNONYMS: image-breaking, irreverent, heretical
ANTONYMS: orthodox, conservative, reverent

7. in medias res
(in med' ē əs rās')

(*adv.*) in or into the middle of a plot; into the middle of things

Since this episode begins _____in medias res_____, we need to tape it and watch the earlier installments first.

8. internecine
(int ər nes' ēn)

(*adj.*) mutually destructive; characterized by great slaughter and bloodshed

An _____internecine_____ feud has existed between the clans for generations.

SYNONYMS: murderous, savage, ruinous
ANTONYMS: peaceful, harmonious, constructive

9. maladroit
(mal ə droit')

(*adj.*) lacking skill or dexterity; lacking tact, perception, or judgment

The supervisor's _____maladroit_____ interference revealed a lack of experience.

SYNONYMS: inept, awkward, clumsy, gauche
ANTONYMS: skillful, dexterous, deft, tactful

10. maudlin
(môd' lin)

(*adj.*) excessively or effusively sentimental

The tenor sang a _____maudlin_____ ballad and then a humorous ditty.

SYNONYMS: mushy, mawkish

11. modulate
(mod' yə lāt)

(*v.*) to change or vary the intensity or pitch; to temper or soften; to regulate, adjust

Asked to _____modulate_____ their voices, the choir responded adroitly.

SYNONYMS: adapt, moderate

12. portentous
(pôr ten' təs)

(*adj.*) foreshadowing an event to come; causing wonder or awe; self-consciously weighty, pompous

No one realized just how _____portentous_____ the strange events of last week would turn out to be.

SYNONYMS: foreboding, ominous, pretentious
ANTONYMS: auspicious, propitious, encouraging

13. prescience
(presh' əns)

(*n.*) knowledge of events or actions before they happen; foresight

The detectives were skeptical about the psychic's _____prescience_____ of the suspect's next crime.

SYNONYM: foreknowledge
ANTONYM: hindsight

14. quid pro quo
(kwid′ prō kwō′)

(*n.*) something given in exchange or return for something else

Before agreeing to give their support, the representatives insisted on some _____ quid pro quo _____.

SYNONYMS: swap, trade

15. salubrious
(sə lü′ brē əs)

(*adj.*) conducive to health or well-being; wholesome

Seeking the _____ salubrious _____ effects of sea air, the family headed for a shore vacation.

SYNONYMS: beneficial, healthy, invigorating
ANTONYMS: harmful, unhealthy, deleterious, noxious

16. saturnalian
(sat ər nā′ lyan)

(*adj.*) characterized by riotous or unrestrained revelry or licentiousness

The boisterously _____ saturnalian _____ spectacle was truly something to behold, even from a distance.

SYNONYMS: dissipated, debauched, orgiastic
ANTONYMS: sedate, prim, decorous, seemly

17. touchstone
(təch′ stōn)

(*n.*) a means of testing worth or genuineness

A work's popularity among succeeding generations is thought to be a _____ touchstone _____ of its merit.

SYNONYMS: criterion, yardstick, benchmark

18. traumatic
(traủ mat′ ik)

(*adj.*) so shocking to the emotions as to cause lasting and substantial psychological damage

People may feel the effects of a _____ traumatic _____ experience for years afterward.

SYNONYM: jolting
ANTONYMS: soothing, comforting, agreeable, pleasant

19. vitiate
(vish′ ē āt)

(*v.*) to weaken, debase, or corrupt; to impair the quality or value of

_____ Vitiated _____ by its lack of managerial skill, the company's fortunes went straight downhill.

SYNONYMS: degrade, undermine
ANTONYMS: purify, fortify, strengthen, enhance

20. waggish
(wag′ ish)

(*adj.*) fond of making jokes; characteristic of a joker; playfully humorous or droll

The innkeeper's _____ waggish _____ stories lifted the flagging spirits of the weary travelers.

SYNONYMS: whimsical, jocular
ANTONYMS: serious, grave, grim, dour, humorless

Completing the Sentence

From the words for this unit, choose the one that best completes each of the following sentences. Write the word in the space provided.

1. How can you expect them to cooperate with us unless they receive some reasonable _____ quid pro quo _____ for their efforts?

2. For years, Churchill's warnings about Hitler were dismissed as alarmism; only after the outbreak of World War II did people appreciate his _____ prescience _____.

3. I certainly have no intention of turning my back on them simply because it has been _____ bruited _____ about town they are involved in some sort of scandal.

4. If he would only devote more time in school to serious study and less to _____ waggish _____ pranks, his grades would probably improve.

5. All the evidence presented at such length by their lawyers does not seriously _____ vitiate _____ the case against the accused.

6. The deathbed scene might have been effective if it had been played with restraint, but their woefully ham-handed acting turned it into a(n) _____ maudlin _____ tearjerker.

7. What we are facing in this organization is not healthy competition among the executives but a(n) _____ internecine _____ struggle that will destroy the company.

8. To gain the immediate attention of the reader, the short-story writer sometimes begins a narrative _____ in medias res _____, rather than at the very beginning of events.

9. More than anything else, the ability to create distinctive characters and make them come alive on the page is the _____ touchstone _____ of a great novelist.

10. Though the critic still has nothing good to say about modern art, age and experience have somewhat _____ modulated _____ the intensity of his disapproval.

11. I was an extremely sensitive child, and the death of my beloved mother certainly had a(n) _____ traumatic _____ effect upon me.

12. If you are so _____ maladroit _____ in handling your own personal affairs, how you can presume to advise others how to manage their lives?

13. It is one thing to offer a personal opinion; it is quite another to issue a(n) _____ dictum _____ as through you were the only one with any knowledge of the subject.

14. And such are the quirks of fate that there she was, after all her mishaps and blunders, firmly _____ ensconced _____ as the president of the firm.

15. In our bored and depressed mood, her buoyant personality had a most _____ salubrious _____ effect.

16. The coach devised a clever strategy, but it proved _____ abortive _____ when our team failed to execute it properly.

17. Though the guests at the gala benefit tried to maintain an air of cheer, the _____ portentous _____ news of the international crisis hung like a pall over the gathering.

18. A group of elderly people sitting about sipping tea and discussing the weather is scarcely my idea of _____ saturnalian _____ revelry.

19. The speaker paid no attention to the _____ contumelious _____ remarks of a few hecklers in the crowd but went right on with her speech.

20. Since she thoroughly enjoys taking potshots at sacred cows, I'd describe her attitude as definitely _____ iconoclastic _____.

Synonyms

*Choose the word from this unit that is **the same** or **most nearly the same** in meaning as the **boldface** word or expression in the given phrase. Write the word on the line provided.*

1. a **beneficial** aspect of the trip — salubrious

2. would **undermine** all our achievements — vitiate

3. heard the familiar **maxim** — dictum

4. **clumsy** efforts at reconciliation — maladroit

5. a **yardstick** by which a play's success is gauged — touchstone

6. undone by a lack of **foresight** — prescience

7. one debater's **scurrilous** remarks — contumelious

8. **moderated** my tone of voice — modulated

9. **nestled** in a favorite chair — ensconced

10. thwarted by **savage** antagonisms — internecine

11. made a **premature** attempt — abortive

12. quickly **broadcast** the results — bruited

13. moved by the **sentimental** story — maudlin

14. agreed upon a reasonable **swap** — quid pro quo

15. joined the story **in the middle** — in medias res

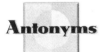

Antonyms

*Choose the word from this unit that is **most nearly opposite** in meaning to the **boldface** word or expression in the given phrase. Write the word on the line provided.*

16. their usual **sedate** behavior — saturnalian

17. the event's **propitious** beginning — portentous

18. holds **orthodox** views on the subject — iconoclastic

19. a thoroughly **agreeable** experience — traumatic

20. a **dour** group waiting at the ticket window — waggish

*Circle the **boldface** word that more satisfactorily completes each of the following sentences.*

1. With her elegance and remarkable feel for style, is it any wonder that she soon became (**modulated, ensconced**) as the arbiter of fashion?

2. Prior to the Wright brothers' first successful airplane flight in 1903, all of mankind's efforts to fly had been (**internecine, abortive**).

3. Some people seem to be natural nonconformists; for them (**prescience, iconoclasm**) is not just a mood or an affectation but a way of life.

4. Willy-nilly, parents often enter (**in medias res, waggishly**) into a quarrel between siblings, especially when lasting damage seems about to occur.

5. Historians believe that the Civil War had a collective (**traumatic, salubrious**) impact, which was not healed until a new generation had grown to maturity.

6. My plan to run in the primaries will not be diverted by the (**touchstone, dicta**) of so-called experts who assert that I have no chance of winning.

7. I felt that I had stated my case with sincerity and conviction, but my heart sank when they reacted with a (**maladroit, portentous**) silence.

8. Even the most hardened campaigner might be expected to cringe when subjected to that kind of (**maudlin, contumelious**) treatment.

9. The decline in the value of the company's stock was attributed to the fact that rumors of a contract cancellation had been widely (**bruited, vitiated**).

10. Their efforts to settle the differences between the two factions were so (**portentous, maladroit**) that what had begun as a rift became a chasm.

11. In spite of my extreme nervousness, I made every effort to (**modulate, bruit**) my voice and speak the first lines in a calm, controlled manner.

12. A rugged sense of honesty, marked by a refusal to take refuge in clever ambiguities, has been the (**touchstone, dictum**) of my career in politics.

13. Our hope for peace rests basically on the belief that the great powers now realize that warfare has become too (**internecine, saturnalian**) to risk.

14. Their cool and detached skepticism, which I would have resented under other circumstances, now struck me as a(n) (**iconoclastic, salubrious**) factor in that highly emotionalized situation.

15. When the miners arrived with all of their back pay and intent upon "having fun," our town soon took on the aspect of a frontier (**saturnalia, quid pro quo**).

16. Although those supposedly (**abortive, waggish**) remarks were dressed in the guise of humor, they betrayed a strong undertone of resentment.

17. The concessions which we are making are manifest, but I do not perceive a reasonable (**prescience, quid pro quo**) from the other side.

18. All the snide rumors that have been spread about them do not (**vitiate, ensconce**) their solid reputation for authentic kindness and decency.

19. They survived the critical years due to their uncanny (**prescience, touchstone**) which enabled them to anticipate the moves of their enemies.

20. In that situation, I don't know which was more distressing—the callous indifference of some of my "friends" or the (**maudlin, contelumious**) sympathy of others.

*Read the following passage, in which some of the words you have studied in this unit appear in **boldface** type. Then complete each statement given below the passage by circling the letter of the item that is **the same** or **almost the same** in meaning as the highlighted word.*

Someone Who Made a Difference

(Line)

Daisy Bates was born in a small Arkansas mill town in 1920. **Traumatic** experiences in her childhood could have led to a lifetime of anger. Her father, however, encouraged her to focus her energies on fighting discrimination. Bates later said this "priceless heritage" sustained her throughout her life.

(5) In 1941, Bates married L. C. Bates. Together, they published the *Arkansas State Press*, an **iconoclastic** and influential African American newspaper, which championed civil rights and attacked the abuses of segregation. The Bateses moved to Little Rock, where Bates joined the NAACP and became
(10) its state president. It was in Little Rock that Daisy Bates joined a local battle that made her famous.

Schools in the segregated South **vitiated** the education of black children.
(15) Bates herself had attended inferior schools and had used outdated books. In 1954, when the United States Supreme Court declared segregation in public schools unconstitutional, Bates led the
(20) fight to integrate the Little Rock School District. Despite threats to her safety and property, she acted as advocate for and

Daisy Bates, Thurgood Marshall, and Little Rock students at the Supreme Court, 1958

mentor to the nine students who were selected to desegregate Central High School. On September 25, 1957, federal troops sent by President Eisenhower escorted the
(25) nine students past jeering mobs and into the building. This struggle was the **touchstone** of Bates' commitment to justice and equality.

Daisy Bates devoted her life to helping African Americans achieve better lives and continually spoke out against injustice. She received more than 200 medals, citations, and other awards, and was honored by four American presidents.
(30) Daisy Bates died in Little Rock on November 4, 1999.

---

1. The meaning of **traumatic** (line 1) is
  a. memorable   c. jolting
  b. strengthened   d. regulated

2. The meaning of **iconoclastic** (line 6) is
  a. heretical   c. fruitless
  b. orthodox   d. reverent

3. Vitiated (line 14) most nearly means
  a. upgraded   c. impaired
  b. whimsical   d. sentimental

4. Touchstone (line 26) most nearly means
  a. maxim   c. jewel
  b. benchmark   d. ruination

 Internet Visit us at www.sadlier-oxford.com for interactive puzzles and games.

Analogies

In each of the following, circle the item that best completes the comparison.

See pages T38–T46 for explanations of answers.

1. obsequies is to **die** as
a. nuptials are to wed ⟵
b. philippics are to graduate
c. dicta are to divorce
d. lucubrations are to age

2. ineffable is to **express** as
a. illegible is to write
b. incalculable is to compute ⟵
c. imponderable is to deny
d. inscrutable is to puzzle

3. waggish is to **jester** as
a. mendacious is to liar ⟵
b. tendentious is to judge
c. contumelious is to diplomat
d. insouciant is to juggler

4. maudlin is to **sentiment** as
a. piquant is to flour
b. unctuous is to acid
c. saccharine is to sugar ⟵
d. acerbic is to oil

5. bilious is to **nauseate** as
a. disquieting is to elate
b. traumatic is to shock ⟵
c. benign is to alarm
d. portentous is to reassure

6. aficionado is to **enthusiastic** as
a. personal is to personable
b. braggart is to demure
c. pundit is to knowledgeable ⟵
d. craven is to valiant

7. maladroit is to **skill** as
a. sage is to wisdom
b. erudite is to knowledge
c. prestigious is to celebrity
d. feckless is to will power ⟵

8. touchstone is to **test** as
a. yardstick is to measure ⟵
b. scale is to estimate
c. gauge is to guide
d. criterion is to balance

9. sacred cow is to **sacrosanct** as
a. paper tiger is to prurient
b. red herring is to misleading ⟵
c. white elephant is to salubrious
d. lame duck is to dexterous

10. prison is to **immure** as
a. hospital is to try
b. barn is to reform
c. school is to punish
d. cemetery is to inter ⟵

Word Associations

In each of the following groups, circle the word that is best defined or suggested by the given phrase.

1. where the *Aeneid* starts
a. in medias res ⟵   b. sacrosanct   c. ensconce   d. pundit

2. Get as good as you give.
a. abortive   b. gamut   c. quid pro quo ⟵   d. prurient

3. cold springwater after a six-mile summertime jog
a. touchstone   b. matrix   c. dictum   d. elixir ⟵

4. Let me look into the crystal ball for you.
a. ensconce   b. divination ⟵   c. obsequies   d. genre

5. how a bird in a gilded cage might feel
a. prescience   b. immured ⟵   c. symptomatic   d. aficionado

6. a sudden about-face
a. volte-face ⟵   b. affinity   c. emolument   d. systemic

7. the ups and downs of life
a. maudlin   b. vitiate   (c. vicissitudes)   d. traumatic

8. How did you know that this would happen?
a. waggish   (b. prescience)   c. cognate   d. iconoclastic

9. the endless bickering that is tearing apart a family
(a. internecine)   b. bruit   c. salubrious   d. contumelious

10. see-through curtains
a. ineffable   (b. diaphanous)   c. tendentious   d. risible

11. You have to have style!
a. portentous   b. saturnalian   c. bilious   (d. panache)

12. Spring, forward; fall, back.
a. parameter   b. cul-de-sac   c. folderol   (d. mnemonic)

Choosing the Right Meaning

Read each sentence carefully. Then circle the item that best completes the statement below the sentence.

See pages T38–T46 for explanations of answers.

"The Moor replies
That he you hurt is of great fame in Cyprus,   (2)
and great affinity, and that in wholesome wisdom
He might not but refuse you." (Shakespeare, *Othello*, III, i, 43–46)   (4)

1. The phrase [**of**] **great affinity** in line 3 is used to mean
(a. widely connected)   c. much attracted
b. naturally inclined   d. very powerful

In some religions the name of the deity is considered ineffable, and believers forbear
to utter it for fear of inviting divine retribution.   (2)

2. In line 1 the word **ineffable** is used to mean
a. utterly inexpressible   c. absolutely indescribable
(b. too sacred to be spoken)   d. unknowable

They who ensconced the papyrus and leather documents now known as the Dead
Sea Scrolls could scarcely have dreamed that nearly two thousand years would   (2)
pass before the manuscripts they had hidden would see light of day once more.

3. In line 1 the word **ensconced** most nearly means
a. nestled   b. settled   c. entrenched   (d. hid)

Since the common cold is caused by a viral infection for which there is as yet no
cure, medicine can do no more than offer a symptomatic treatment of the malady.   (2)

4. The word **symptomatic** in line 2 most nearly means
a. characteristic   c. typically old-fashioned
b. indicative   (d. relating to symptoms)

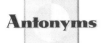

In each of the following groups, circle the word or expression that is most nearly the **opposite** of the word in **boldface** type.

1. vitiate
a. enhance
b. destroy
c. create
d. debase

2. risible
a. falling
b. slanderous
c. heartrending
d. indirect

3. cognate
a. unrelated
b. expensive
c. recent
d. weird

4. insouciant
a. open
b. distraught
c. conditional
d. guarded

5. tendentious
a. peaceful
b. disinterested
c. argumentative
d. violent

6. contumelious
a. provocative
b. complimentary
c. disdainful
d. ample

7. folderol
a. trifle
b. humor
c. sense
d. sentiment

8. portentous
a. silly
b. dispassionate
c. auspicious
d. immature

9. salubrious
a. tasty
b. hygienic
c. noxious
d. welcome

10. traumatic
a. dangerous
b. trustworthy
c. soothing
d. sage

11. abortive
a. consummated
b. untimely
c. idealistic
d. reveling

12. bilious
a. delightful
b. peevish
c. punctual
d. impoverished

13. iconoclastic
a. rational
b. conservative
c. decisive
d. aggressive

14. corollary
a. instrument
b. eve
c. axiom
d. malapropism

15. obloquy
a. confusion
b. acclaim
c. vilification
d. clarify

16. prurient
a. prudish
b. salacious
c. tiresome
d. polluted

 **Completing the Sentence**

From the following lists of words, choose the one that best completes each of the following sentences. Write the word in the space provided.

Group A

| aficionado | cognate | emolument | modulates |
| bruit | elixir | in medias res | vicissitude |

1. You have no right to change the rules ____in medias res____ just because you're losing!

2. Though modern "alchemists" continue the age-old search for the putative ____elixir____ of life, I don't think any such nostrum exists.

3. Just growing up often ____modulates____ the intensity of our reactions to things we like or dislike.

4. Unfortunately, the ____emolument____ of a college professor is almost always considerably lower than that of an executive in the business world.

5. A true ____aficionado____ of baseball can reel off the batting average of every member of the Hall of Fame.

Group B

affinity	dictum	sacrosanct	tendentious
derring-do	foray	salubrious	vitiate

1. I know that you are a highly prestigious literary critic, but I refuse to accept passively every _____ **dictum** _____ you may issue on what is or is not worth reading.

2. I can't get along with someone who is so _____ **tendentious** _____ that any opinion I may express is taken as a pretext for a full-dress argument.

3. That Errol Flynn movie on the Late Show was full of utterly incredible but delightful feats of _____ **derring-do** _____.

4. We believe in being courteous and considerate to one another, but we certainly don't regard every minor detail of etiquette and protocol as _____ **sacrosanct** _____.

5. It was only too clear that the years of power, privilege, and good living had served to _____ **vitiate** _____ his youthful idealism.

Word Families

A. On the line provided, write the word you have learned in Units 4–6 that is related to each of the following nouns.
EXAMPLE: biliousness—**bilious**

1. iconoclast, iconoclasm, icon — **iconoclastic**
2. prurience, pruriency — **prurient**
3. tendentiousness — **tendentious**
4. saturnalia — **saturnalian**
5. symptom — **symptomatic**
6. immurement — **immure**
7. modulation, modulator, modulability — **modulate**
8. ineffableness, ineffability — **ineffable**
9. insouciance — **insouciant**
10. wag, waggishness, waggery — **waggish**
11. maladroitness — **maladroit**
12. portent, portentousness — **portentous**
13. system, systemization, systematizer, systematist — **systemic**
14. risibility — **risible**

B. *On the line provided, write the word you have learned in Units 4–6 that is related to each of the following verbs.*

EXAMPLE: divine—**divination**

15. systematize, systemize _____ systemic

16. dictate _____ dictum

17. personify, personate, impersonate _____ persona

18. portend _____ portentous

19. traumatize _____ traumatic

20. abort _____ abortive

Two-Word Completions

Circle the pair of words that best complete the meaning of each of the following passages.

See pages T38–T46 for explanations of answers.

1. Though I can't say that I relish the thriller as a literary form, I'm a real
_____ of the detective _____.

  a. pundit . . . touchstone
  b. iconoclast . . . matrix
  c. aficionado . . . genre
  d. persona . . . folderol

2. In one of her more devastating _____, Dorothy Parker is reputed to have once observed that an incompetent actor's interpretation of a role ran the
_____ of emotions from A to B.

  a. dicta . . . gamut
  b. lucubrations . . . mnemonic
  c. corollaries . . . cul-de-sac
  d. homilies . . . parameters

3. Famous for his daring _____ deep behind Northern lines, J. E. B. Stuart, the South's most colorful cavalry commander, led his men on one dangerous mission after another with all the _____ and style of one of Charlemagne's legendary paladins.

  a. obsequies . . . persona
  b. emoluments . . . prescience
  c. philippics . . . derring-do
  d. forays . . . panache

4. When he realized that flattery was getting him nowhere, he attempted to
_____ me into acquiescence, but, here again, his efforts proved
_____.

  a. bruit . . . risible
  b. browbeat . . . abortive
  c. vitiate . . . tendentious
  d. modulate . . . maladroit

*Read the following passage, in which some of the words you have studied in Units 4–6 appear in **boldface** type. Then complete each statement given below the passage by circling the item that is **the same** or **almost the same** in meaning as the highlighted word.*

The Eyeglasses Mystery

(Line)

By the end of the thirteenth century, people began to see the world in a new light, for it was about that time that eyeglasses were invented. But
(5) **forays** into the question of precisely when they were invented and by whom have been inconclusive, **tendentious**, and filled with intrigue.
Researchers have put forth
(10) candidates from several European countries and China. Although the exact identity of the inventor has not as yet been established conclusively, he or she was most likely an Italian
(15) glassblower working in the 1280s. The evidence favors either Alessandro Spina or Salvino Armato, with a slight edge to Armato. Armato was an optical physicist who is believed
(20) to have contrived correcting lenses to improve his own vision.
In 1289, the Italian writer Sandro di Popozo refers to eyeglasses as having "recently been invented. . . ." Popozo
(25) writes about the advantages afforded by the lenses but never mentions the inventor's name. A second reference

appears seventeen years later in a sermon by the friar Giordano di Rivalto.
(30) In the sermon, the friar refers to the nearly 20-year-old art of making eyeglasses. He also neglects to provide us with the name of the inventor.
(35) No matter who invented them, spectacles caught on quickly. But they were not for everybody. The high cost kept them from the **hoi polloi**, and the fact that all lenses were
(40) convex made these "eye disks" "**elixirs**" for the farsighted alone. (Concave lenses, which help the nearsighted, first appeared more than a century later.) In addition, the lenses
(45) were hard to wear. The now-familiar stiff frames that loop over our ears were not developed for another 400 years.
Despite the limitations of these early eyeglasses, sales were brisk, and
(50) Italian craftspeople churned them out. The rest is history.

---

1. The meaning of **forays** (line 5) is
   a. retreats   c. attacks
   (b. ventures)   d. forages

2. Tendentious (line 8) most nearly means
   a. fair   c. impartial
   (b. partisan)   d. meaty

3. Hoi polloi (line 38) is best defined as
   a. elite   (c. masses)
   b. aristocracy   d. foreigners

4. The meaning of **elixirs** (line 41) is
   (a. cure-alls)   c. prophesies
   b. elections   d. lenses

Building with Classical Roots

gen— race, kind, class; origin, birth

This root appears in **genre**, "a type, class, or variety, especially with relation to literary composition or painting" (page 59). Some other words based on the same root are listed below.

carcinogen	**degenerate**	**generic**	**genocide**
congenital	**genealogy**	**genesis**	**homogeneous**

From the list of words above, choose the one that corresponds to each of the brief definitions below. Write the word in the blank space in the illustrative sentence below the definition.

1. creation, origin; the coming into being of something

No one is entirely sure of the _____genesis_____ of the idea that became the Internet we know today.

2. to deteriorate or decline physically or morally; exhibiting such decline; a morally degraded person

The judge condemned their _____degenerate_____ behavior by imposing a stiff sentence.

3. uniform in composition; like in nature or kind

The Latin Club is comprised of a remarkably _____homogeneous_____ group of students.

4. relating to an entire group or class; not protected by trademark, nonproprietary

We know many products by their brands but not by their _____generic_____ names.

5. cancer-causing substance

Food additives cannot be used unless they pass tests proving that they are not _____carcinogens_____ .

6. existing at birth; constituting an essential characteristic as if by birth, inherent

No amount of guidance and counseling could overcome the fact that she was simply a _____congenital_____ liar.

7. a record or account of a family's or a person's descent; lineage; the study of ancestry and family histories

Using on-line resources, he was able to trace his _____genealogy_____ back ten generations.

8. the systematic extermination of a racial, political, or cultural group

During the regime of Pol Pot (1975–1979), Khmer Rouge forces in Cambodia conducted a _____genocide_____ of unprecedented proportions.

From the list of words on page 78, choose the one that best completes each of the following sentences. Write the word in the blank space provided.

1. Rather than specify a particular brand, many physicians now prescribe less expensive _____generic_____ drugs for their patients.

2. The _____genesis_____ of Herman Melville's masterpiece *Moby Dick* lay in the author's experiences as a seaman aboard a whaling vessel.

3. The debate, which had begun as a high-minded and civil exchange of views, rapidly _____degenerated_____ into an ugly, name-calling brawl.

4. When I stumbled across an old family _____genealogy_____, I discovered that I am descended from a veteran of the Revolutionary War.

5. Consumer groups petitioned the government to ban the pesticide when it was discovered to contain a proven _____carcinogen_____.

6. The argument boiled down to a dispute over how much of one's character is _____congenital_____ and how much is acquired.

7. The designers had carefully coordinated the wallpaper, upholstery, drapes, and accessories to lend the room a _____homogeneous_____ appearance.

8. Tribal leaders branded the regime's plan to "relocate" the remaining native population as tantamount to _____genocide_____.

---

*Circle the **boldface** word that more satisfactorily completes each of the following sentences.*

1. Asbestos, once commonly used in building construction, insulation, and in making fireproof textiles, is now recognized as a powerful (**genocide, carcinogen**) and health hazard.

2. Olympic athlete Flo Hyman died at the age of 31 of a (**congenital, generic**) disorder known as Marfan syndrome.

3. An old seventeenth-century English saying compares a (**homogeneous, degenerate**) nobleman to a turnip because the only good in them is found underground.

4. Because so many records were destroyed during the Holocaust, many people with European Jewish roots remain thwarted in their efforts to compile a thorough (**genealogy, genesis**).

5. Humorist Erma Bombeck wrote that " . . . 'mother' has always been a (**degenerate, generic**) term synonymous with love, devotion, and sacrifice."

6. In Rwanda in 1994, the Hutu tried to eliminate the Tutsi in brutal (**genocide, genealogy**).

7. Some schools assign students to (**homogeneous, congenital**) classes in the belief that such groupings provide the best environment for steady progress.

8. The science of physical optics explores and analyzes the (**carcinogen, genesis**), nature, and properties of light.

Writer's Challenge

Read the following sentences, paying special attention to the words and phrases underlined. From the words in the box below, find better choices for these underlined words and phrases. Then use these choices to rewrite the sentences.

WORD BANK

affinity	diaphanous	genre	internecine	prurient
aficionado	elixir	homily	maudlin	symptomatic
bruit	foray	iconoclastic	obloquy	systemic
cognate	gamut	immure	philippic	vitiate

Futurism

1. The <u>category of composition</u> known as futurist literature sounds as though it includes science fiction and forward-looking tales of human potential.
genre

2. In fact, literary *futurism* began as an <u>heretical</u> attempt to destroy the conventions of traditional art and express the energy of early 20th-century modernism.
iconoclastic

3. Futurism began in Italy in 1909 with a <u>bitter verbal attack</u> by Filippo Marinetti. He extolled the new automotive technology, goading readers to create new forms of expression based on the dynamic beauty and power of speed.
philippic

4. Marinetti derided tradition which, he claimed, was <u>indicative</u> of the stilted and sluggish attitudes he hoped to bury beneath more vigorous modes of expression.
symptomatic

5. Futurists' <u>fondness</u> for discontinuity and shock led to experimental poetry and prose.
affinity

6. Their <u>sorties</u> into writing without the use of conventional syntax, grammar, and punctuation resulted in jumbled strings of words valued for their explosive sounds.
forays

7. Futurism's extreme views eventually became <u>mewed up and isolated</u> as other forward-looking writers, called *futurians*, made their own work widely accessible. Some well-known futurians included H. P. Lovecraft, Isaac Asimov, and Ursula LeGuin.
immured

Analogies

In each of the following, circle the item that best completes the comparison.

See pages T38–T46 for explanations of answers.

1. tearjerker is to **maudlin** as
a. opera is to prurient
b. tragedy is to risible
c. farce is to hilarious
d. satire is to heartrending

2. microcosm is to **macrocosm** as
a. plethora is to paucity
b. poltroon is to craven
c. purview is to orbit
d. parameter is to touchstone

3. salubrious is to **health** as
a. pragmatic is to validity
b. eleemosynary is to profit
c. tendentious is to justice
d. therapeutic is to recovery

4. waggish is to **laughs** as
a. risible is to yawns
b. bilious is to smiles
c. lachrymose is to tears
d. ribald is to sneers

5. philippic is to **vituperative** as
a. liturgy is to ribald
b. encomium is to complimentary
c. harangue is to restrained
d. paean is to scurrilous

6. homily is to **church** as
a. sermon is to air show
b. diatribe is to game show
c. aria is to horse show
d. monologue is to talk show

7. diaphanous is to **veils** as
a. noisome is to clouds
b. gossamer is to cobwebs
c. bulky is to showers
d. abortive is to breezes

8. klutz is to **maladroit** as
a. bigot is to intolerant
b. dynamo is to supine
c. aficionado is to blasé
d. pundit is to ignorant

9. mnemonic is to **memory** as
a. trousers are to speech
b. glasses are to vision
c. earmuffs are to movement
d. blinders are to hearing

10. insouciant is to **concern** as
a. oblivious is to consciousness
b. sanguine is to optimism
c. quizzical is to erudition
d. portentous is to intrepidity

Choosing the Right Meaning

Read each sentence carefully. Then circle the item that best completes the statement below the sentence.

See pages T38–T46 for explanations of answers.

"My brother, who despairs of ever changing our parents' hidebound views, has given up dinner-table discussions aimed at convincing them to adopt more liberal attitudes. (2)

1. In line 1 the word **hidebound** is used to mean
a. narrow-minded   b. free-wheeling   c. ribald   d. pragmatic

"These late eclipses in the sun and moon portend no good to us. Though the wisdom of nature can reason thus and thus, yet nature finds itself scourged by the sequent effects." (2)
        (Shakespeare, *King Lear*, I, ii, 103–106)

2. The word **portend** in line 1 most nearly means
a. inspire awe   b. offer   c. forebode   d. conjure

Herman Melville's masterpiece *Moby Dick* is prefaced by a sort of lexicon of etymological entries and quoted passages having to do with whales and whaling. (2)

3. The best definition for the word **lexicon** in line 1 is

a. glossary   b. dictionary   c. wordbook   (d. compendium)

I will grant that manners and mores may change with the times, but common courtesy is never effete. (2)

4. In line 2 the word **effete** is used to mean

a. exhausted   b. sterile   (c. out-of-date)   d. enfeebled

One of the great masters of genre painting is the Dutch artist Jan Vermeer, whose depictions of everyday scenes seem magically infused with light and life. (2)

5. The word **genre** in line 1 most nearly means

a. still life   (b. realist)   c. abstract   d. category

Two-Word Completions

Circle the pair of words that best complete the meaning of each of the following sentences.

See pages T38–T46 for explanations of answers.

1. In Gaetano Donizetti's famous comic opera *The* _____ *of Love*, a clever charlatan _____ an overly gullible country bumpkin into believing that a plain old bottle of Bordeaux wine is in fact a powerful love potion that will solve the poor yokel's amorous problems overnight.

a. *Mnemonic* . . . apprises   c. *Parameter* . . . browbeats
(b. *Elixir* . . . cozens)   d. *Vassal* . . . forays

2. Prudish Victorians were so offended by the _____ jokes and salacious language in some of Shakespeare's plays that they would only read his works in heavily _____ versions.

a. prurient . . . polarized   (c. ribald . . . bowdlerized)
b. risible . . . vitiated   d. ineffable . . . deracinated

3. The _____ of the forty _____ contained in *Sketches of Country Life* is truly extraordinary, and the reader is left with the distinct impression that he or she actually knows the people who are being described.

a. poltroonery . . . enclaves   c. rapacity . . . paeans
(b. verisimilitude . . . vignettes)   d. virtuosity . . . claques

4. Recently, many Christian denominations have modernized the language of the _____ that they use in their service because it had become clear that the presence of obsolete words and phrases in the traditional material tended to _____ the meaning of the rites for contemporary congregations.

a. homilies . . . bowdlerize   c. lucubrations . . . vitiate
b. obsequies . . . bruit   (d. liturgies . . . obfuscate)

Enriching Your Vocabulary

Read the passage below. Then complete the exercise at the bottom of the page.

What's in a Name?

When you don a cardigan sweater, it's unlikely that you salute James Thomas Brudenell, Seventh Earl of Cardigan (1797–1868). That British officer's title describes a style of collarless long-sleeved sweater that opens in front. Cardigan's troops wore this garment during the Crimean War. The noun "cardigan" is an example of an *eponym*—a word derived from the name of the person originally associated with the object, practice, or attitude that the word indicates.

Many eponymns enrich the English language. One example is *bowdlerize* (Unit 3). This eponym, as you may recall, comes from the name of the nineteenth century English editor who published an edition of the works of William Shakespeare in which "those words [were] omitted which [could not] with propriety be read aloud in a family." Over time, the origins of eponyms may fade from common knowledge. Did you know that graham crackers are named for Sylvester Graham, an American nutritionist who promoted the use of whole-grain flour? French acrobat Jules Leotard, the subject of the song "The Man on the Flying Trapeze," designed a tight-fitting yet flexible garment that showed off his muscles. Adolphe Sax, a Belgian instrument maker, combined the reed of a clarinet with the fingering of an oboe to form the saxophone, the instrument that bears his name to this day.

The snug-fitting leotard was designed to provide unlimited freedom of movement.

In Column A below are 8 more eponyms. With or without a dictionary, match each word with its meaning in Column B.

Column A		Column B
_g_	**1.** boycott	**a.** a traitor, turncoat or collaborator with an enemy
_d_	**2.** gerrymander	**b.** to execute illegally, usually by hanging
_b_	**3.** lynch	**c.** a fragment from a bomb, mine, or shell
_e_	**4.** maverick	**d.** to divide a region into oddly shaped electoral districts to give one party unfair advantage during an election
_a_	**5.** quisling	**e.** a nonconformist or dissenter
_h_	**6.** sandwich	**f.** hair grown in front of the ears
_c_	**7.** shrapnel	**g.** to refuse to buy, use, or deal with as a way to force the acceptance of some form of behavior; a protest
_f_	**8.** sideburns	**h.** two slices of bread with meat or other filling between them

Definitions

Note carefully the spelling, pronunciation, part(s) of speech, and definition(s) of each of the following words. Then write the word in the blank space(s) in the illustrative sentence(s) following. Finally, study the lists of synonyms and antonyms given at the end of each entry.

1. abeyance
(ə bā′ əns)

(*n.*) a state of being temporarily inactive, suspended, or set aside

The administrators and staff reluctantly agreed to hold the matter in _____ **abeyance** _____.

SYNONYMS: deferment, postponement, suspension

2. ambivalent
(am biv′ ə lənt)

(*adj.*) having opposite and conflicting feelings about someone or something

Despite their deeply _____ **ambivalent** _____ attitudes, the scientists went ahead with the program.

SYNONYMS: equivocal, ambiguous, of two minds
ANTONYMS: unequivocal, unambiguous, clear-cut

3. beleaguer
(bi lē′ gər)

(*v.*) to set upon from all sides; to surround with an army; to trouble, harass

Sherman's division arrived by train, then positioned itself to _____ **beleaguer** _____ the city's fortress.

SYNONYMS: besiege, encircle, pester

4. carte blanche
(kärt′ blänsh′)

(*n.*) full freedom or authority to act at one's own discretion

The boss gave us _____ **carte blanche** _____ in the matter of how we were going to approach the client.

SYNONYMS: blank check, free rein

5. cataclysm
(kat′ ə kliz əm)

(*n.*) a sudden, violent, or devastating upheaval; a surging flood, deluge

Diplomacy could not stop the _____ **cataclysm** _____ of World War I.

SYNONYMS: disaster, catastrophe

6. debauch
(di bôch′)

(*v.*) to corrupt morally, seduce; to indulge in dissipation; (*n.*) an act or occasion of dissipation or vice

Those who would _____ **debauch** _____ the innocent deserve our wrath.

The _____ **debauch** _____ began at midnight.

SYNONYMS: (*v.*) carouse, (*n.*) spree, orgy
ANTONYMS: (*v.*) elevate, uplift, inspire, purify

7. éclat
(ā klä')

(*n.*) dazzling or conspicuous success or acclaim; great brilliance (of performance or achievement)

Dazzled by the _____**éclat**_____ of the performance, critics heaped praise on the troupe.

SYNONYM: celebrity
ANTONYMS: dullness, insipidity, mediocrity

8. fastidious
(fa stid' ē əs)

(*adj.*) overly demanding or hard to please; excessively careful in regard to details; easily disgusted

Known for her _____**fastidious**_____ taste, the decorator was always in great demand.

SYNONYMS: precise, meticulous, exacting, finicky
ANTONYMS: careless, sloppy, messy, untidy, slovenly

9. gambol
(gam' bəl)

(*v.*) to jump or skip about playfully

The children began to _____**gambol**_____ like fawns in a meadow.

SYNONYMS: frolic, romp, cavort, caper
ANTONYMS: lumber, trudge, plod

10. imbue
(im byü')

(*v.*) to soak or stain thoroughly; to fill the mind

The celebrated teacher strove to _____**imbue**_____ her students with the desire to succeed.

SYNONYMS: infuse, instill, inculcate
ANTONYMS: remove, expunge, eradicate, erase

11. inchoate
(in kō' it)

(*adj.*) just beginning; not fully shaped or formed

At first a molten and _____**inchoate**_____ mass, it soon grew, picked up speed, and destroyed all in its path.

SYNONYMS: incipient, embryonic, rudimentary
ANTONYMS: mature, developed, complete

12. lampoon
(lam pün')

(*n.*) a malicious satire; (*v.*) to satirize, ridicule

Their _____**lampoon**_____ of his speech impediment did not amuse the dictator.

The intent was to _____**lampoon**_____ the senator.

SYNONYMS: (*n.*) burlesque; (*v.*) parody
ANTONYMS: (*n.*) compliment, flattery, homage

13. malleable
(mal' ē ə bəl)

(*adj.*) capable of being formed into different shapes; capable of being altered, adapted, or influenced

The _____**malleable**_____ minds of the young students were at the mercy of the charismatic professor.

SYNONYMS: pliable, impressionable, adaptable
ANTONYMS: rigid, inflexible, unyielding, intractable

14. nemesis
(nem′ ə sis)

(*n.*) an agent or force inflicting vengeance or punishment; retribution itself; an unbeatable rival

Calculus proved to be my _____nemesis_____.

SYNONYMS: comeuppance, avenger
ANTONYMS: guardian angel, ally, patron

15. opt
(opt)

(*v.*) to make a choice or decision

We decided to _____opt_____ for the cheaper model.

SYNONYMS: choose, select, decide

16. philistine
(fil′ i stēn)

(*adj.*) lacking in, hostile to, or smugly indifferent to cultural and artistic values or refinements; (*n.*) such a person

Their _____philistine_____ contempt for art is something the curator simply cannot abide.

The mayor is seen as a _____philistine_____ by the members of the city's arts community.

SYNONYMS: (*adj.*) boorish, lowbrow; (*n.*) yahoo
ANTONYMS: (*adj.*) refined, cultivated; (*n.*) esthete, highbrow

17. picaresque
(pik ə resk′)

(*adj.*) involving or characteristic of clever rogues or adventurers

Reviewers cited the _____picaresque_____ element in the novel as its best feature.

SYNONYMS: roguish, rascally, rakish

18. queasy
(kwē′ zē)

(*adj.*) nauseated or uneasy; causing nausea or uneasiness; troubled

The remarks gave me a _____queasy_____ feeling in the pit of my stomach.

SYNONYM: unsettled
ANTONYMS: calm, untroubled, confident

19. refractory
(ri frak′ tə rē)

(*adj.*) stubborn; hard or difficult to manage; not responsive to treatment or cure

Caring for the _____refractory_____ patient left us exhausted and drained.

SYNONYMS: unruly, disobedient, willful, mulish
ANTONYMS: docile, tractable, dutiful, obedient

20. savoir-faire
(sav wär fâr′)

(*n.*) the ability to say and do the right thing in any situation; social competence

The experienced and wily ambassador handled the delicate affair with her usual _____savoir-faire_____.

SYNONYMS: tact, finesse, suavity, sophistication
ANTONYMS: tactlessness, gaucherie, boorishness

Completing the Sentence

From the words for this unit, choose the one that best completes each of the following sentences. Write the word in the space provided.

1. You made some rather clever suggestions at the meeting, but on the whole your ideas were far too _____inchoate_____ to serve as the basis for a workable plan.

2. Perhaps once in a generation, a people is faced with a great moral crisis in which it must _____opt_____ for good or evil, war or peace, life or death.

3. Oscar's careless housekeeping and sloppy habits were an endless source of exasperation to his _____fastidious_____ roommate.

4. Should we expect the needs and purposes of a true poet to be understood by such a thoroughgoing _____philistine_____?

5. Instead of settling down to a job and a family, Tom seems to be modeling his life on the career of some rogue out of a(n) _____picaresque_____ novel.

6. How could they have _____debauched_____ themselves by joining in that obscene celebration?

7. Such capacity for growth and self-improvement can be expected only in the _____malleable_____ years of the teens and early twenties.

8. I was confident that I would do well in the scholarship examination, but my hopes were dashed by my old _____nemesis_____, mathematics.

9. Many scientists are fearful that the West Coast may someday suffer a(n) _____cataclysm_____ as violent as the earthquake that devastated San Francisco in 1906.

10. Her equivocal answers to my questions about going to college in the fall clearly revealed her _____ambivalent_____ attitude toward leaving home.

11. There are circumstances under which it is desirable to make decisions swiftly and unequivocally, but there are other cases in which it is wise to hold decisions in _____abeyance_____.

12. Though Jane's mount was as docile as a newborn lamb, mine proved to be the most _____refractory_____ animal I had ever ridden.

13. A host of creditors _____beleaguered_____ the hapless businessman with demands for payment and threats of legal action.

14. Since I had unlimited faith in their honesty and discretion, I felt no qualms about giving them _____carte blanche_____ to do whatever they thought was necessary.

15. The purpose of the course in American history is to _____imbue_____ young people with a genuine understanding and appreciation of what this country stands for.

16. The entire issue of the magazine was designed as a(n) _____lampoon_____ satirizing the follies and futilities of mass-consumption advertising.

17. The young pianist dazzled the audience with the _____éclat_____ and verve of his performance.

18. As we turned in to the ranch, we saw two young colts _____gambol_____ playfully in the open field.

19. I freely confess that just the sight of a roller coaster is enough to make me feel _____queasy_____ .

20. They showed such a deplorable lack of _____savoir-faire_____ in handling that difficult situation that they converted a mere unpleasantness into a social disaster.

Synonyms

*Choose the word from this unit that is **the same** or **most nearly the same** in meaning as the **boldface** word or expression in the given phrase. Write the word on the line provided.*

1. found the audience to be **impressionable**   malleable

2. was in its **rudimentary** form at that time   inchoate

3. welcomed the **deferment**   abeyance

4. did not participate in the **spree**   debauch

5. **instill** the troops with courage   imbue

6. a **catastrophe** never to be forgotten   cataclysm

7. a **roguish** novel of epic adventures   picaresque

8. proceeded to **ridicule** the speaker   lampoon

9. offered us **free rein**   carte blanche

10. **harass** the messenger of the bad news   beleaguer

11. took power with **acclaim**   éclat

12. **choose** for us to study abroad   opt

13. dresses in a **meticulous** manner   fastidious

14. an **equivocal** response   ambivalent

15. unappreciated by the crowd of **yahoos**   philistines

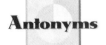

Antonyms

*Choose the word from this unit that is **most nearly opposite** in meaning to the **boldface** word or expression in the given phrase. Write the word on the line provided.*

16. approached by our **ally**   nemesis

17. is a **dutiful** employee   refractory

18. gives me a **confident** feeling   queasy

19. known for their **tactlessness**   savoir-faire

20. asked to **trudge** across the stage   gambol

Choosing the Right Word

*Circle the **boldface** word that more satisfactorily completes each of the following sentences.*

1. In spite of his courage and love of adventure, he lacks the stature of a true hero; his character might better be described as (**picaresque, abeyant**).

2. Although his poetry is somewhat crude and (**inchoate, fastidious**), it has a primitive energy and drive that many readers find extremely attractive.

3. Instead of endless lamentations about how bad things are, let us try to look realistically at the (**lampoons, options**) open to us.

4. James Thurber's stories are extremely funny, but they are also (**imbued, debauched**) with a profound sense of the pathos of the human condition.

5. Because Thurber combines humor and pathos so masterfully, we might say that the mood of his stories is (**malleable, ambivalent**).

6. Their obsession with military conquest, leading them to waste their vast resources on armaments and endless wars, proved to be their (**nemesis, gambol**).

7. Another world war would be a(n) (**éclat, cataclysm**) on so vast a scale that it is doubtful whether civilization could survive it.

8. He will never realize his full athletic potential as long as he remains (**beleaguered, opted**) by doubts about his own ability.

9. Would it not be a gross miscarriage of justice to prosecute us under a law which, for all practical purposes, has been in (**abeyance, carte blanche**) since the early years of the last century?

10. With all the misplaced confidence of inexperienced youth, I set out to make a million dollars by (**gamboling, imbuing**) in the not-so-verdant pastures of Wall Street.

11. Perhaps she felt disturbed at the prospect of having to betray her friends, but she seems to have overcome her (**queasiness, éclat**) without too much trouble.

12. Since they had always been reasonably well-behaved, I was utterly taken aback by their (**ambivalent, refractory**) behavior.

13. She was completely bewildered by the exhibition of abstract art, but, fearing to be labeled a (**lampoon, philistine**), she pretended to understand what she was looking at.

14. Perhaps you hope to divert our attention from your own misconduct by maliciously (**lampooning, gamboling**) a sincere and able public official.

15. Their (**fastidious, ambivalent**) preoccupation with minor details of style is not to be confused with a genuine feeling for language.

16. It is one thing to be open-minded and (**queasy, malleable**); it is quite another to be without fixed ideas or principles of any kind.

17. Refusing to become flustered, she handled the embarrassing situation with the finesse and (**queasiness, savoir-faire**) of a born diplomat.

18. Although we disagreed with much that you said, we could not help admiring the rhetorical brilliance and (**cataclysm, éclat**) of your writing style.

19. With plenty of free time and with an excellent library at my disposal, I gave myself up to a delightful (**cataclysm, debauch**) of reading.

20. In the last analysis all lines of authority and responsibility lead back to the President; he cannot give (**carte blanche, nemesis**) to any assistant.

*Read the following passage, in which some of the words you have studied in this unit appear in **boldface** type. Then complete each statement given below the passage by circling the letter of the item that is **the same** or **almost the same** in meaning as the highlighted word.*

A Lifelong Reformer

(Line)

The women's rights movement was an **inchoate** association of reformers when, in 1848, Elizabeth Cady Stanton (1815–1902) helped to organize the Seneca Falls Convention. A driving force behind that first women's rights convention, Stanton became the first to publicly demand the vote for women.

Stanton, who received a top-notch education at Emma Willard's Academy in Troy, (5) New York, could have chosen a life of social and leisure activities. But, instead, she married the abolitionist Henry B. Stanton, and **opted for** a life of politics and reform.

In 1851, Stanton met and formed a lifelong partnership with Susan B. Anthony, another aggressive worker for abolition and women's rights. During the Civil War, Stanton considered putting women's rights agitation in **abeyance**. But neither she nor (10) Anthony could stay inactive. They formed the National Women's Loyal League to demand the abolition of slavery. Both were disappointed when, after the war, women were still not given (15) the right to vote.

Undaunted, Stanton worked tirelessly to get legislation passed on behalf of women and to **imbue** all women with the desire for equal (20) treatment under the law. In 1869, she and Anthony founded the National Woman Suffrage Association. In

A determined woman's heritage: A young woman registers to vote.

1876, she convinced a senator to introduce a woman suffrage amendment. This amendment was finally passed in 1920. (25)

But Elizabeth Cady Stanton's interests went far beyond fighting for the right to vote. In fact, she was **beleaguered** for her views on other women's rights issues, as well as several other controversies current at the time. These views hurt her standing in the women's movement, but never for a moment slowed her work on behalf of civil rights for women. (30)

---

1. The meaning of **inchoate** (line 1) is
a. unstable
b. impressive
c. ambivalent
d. embryonic ⟵

2. Opted for (line 7) most nearly means
a. rejected
b. chose ⟵
c. neglected
d. requested

3. Abeyance (line 10) is best defined as
a. acclaim
b. parody
c. suspension ⟵
d. ambiguity

4. The meaning of **imbue** (line 19) is
a. infuse ⟵
b. expunge
c. paint
d. see

5. Beleaguered (line 27) most nearly means
a. beloved
b. flattered
c. harassed ⟵
d. corrupted

Note carefully the spelling, pronunciation, part(s) of speech, and definition(s) of each of the following words. Then write the word in the blank space(s) in the illustrative sentence(s) following. Finally, study the lists of synonyms and antonyms given at the end of each entry.

1. aberration
(ab ə rā′ shən)

(*n.*) a departure from what is proper, right, expected, or normal; a lapse from a sound mental state

In an _____ aberration _____ of judgment, the coach chose not to call a critical time-out.

SYNONYMS: deviation, anomaly, irregularity

2. ad hoc
(ad′ häk′)

(*adj.*) for this specific purpose; improvised; (*adv.*) with respect to this

An _____ ad hoc _____ committee was formed immediately.

We met, _____ ad hoc _____, to consider the issue.

SYNONYM: (*adj.*) makeshift
ANTONYMS: (*adj.*) permanent, long-standing

3. bane
(bān)

(*n.*) the source or cause of fatal injury, death, destruction, or ruin; death or ruin itself; poison

Rain, the _____ bane _____ of picnics, was forecast for the day we had scheduled ours.

SYNONYMS: spoiler, bête noire
ANTONYMS: blessing, comfort, solace, balm

4. bathos
(bā′ thos)

(*n.*) the intrusion of commonplace or trite material into a context whose tone is lofty or elevated; grossly insincere or exaggerated sentimentality;the lowest phase, nadir; an anticlimax, comedown

After wallowing in _____ bathos _____, the writer returned to her novel in earnest.

SYNONYMS: mawkishness, mush, schmaltz

5. cantankerous
(kan taŋ′ kə rəs)

(*adj.*) ill-tempered, quarrelsome; difficult to get along or deal with

The _____ cantankerous _____ machine befuddled the team of technicians assigned to repair it.

SYNONYMS: cranky, testy, peevish, irascible, ornery
ANTONYMS: good-natured, sweet-tempered, genial

6. casuistry
(kazh′ ū is trē)

(*n.*) the determination of right and wrong in questions of conduct or conscience by the application of general ethical principles; specious argument

The professor's ideas, once highly regarded, now appear to be nothing more than ingenious _____ casuistry _____.

SYNONYMS: sophistry, quibbling

7. de facto
(dē fak′ tō)

(*adj.*) actually existing or in effect, although not legally required or sanctioned; (*adv.*) in reality, actually

The dictator's wife is the _____ **de facto** _____ head of state.

It appears that, _____ **de facto** _____, the information is true.

SYNONYMS: in actuality, in point of fact
ANTONYMS: de jure, by right

8. depredation
(dep rə dā′ shən)

(*n.*) the act of preying upon or plundering

The _____ **depredation(s)** _____ of the invaders left scars that will take years to heal.

SYNONYMS: looting, pillage, outrage

9. empathy
(em′ pə thē)

(*n.*) a sympathetic understanding of or identification with the feelings, thoughts, or attitudes of someone or something else

The grandparents felt _____ **empathy** _____ for the aspirations of their grandchildren.

SYNONYMS: sympathy, compassion
ANTONYMS: insensitivity, callousness, detachment

10. harbinger
(här′ bən jər)

(*n.*) a forerunner, herald; (*v.*) to herald the approach of

Daffodils in bloom are a _____ **harbinger** _____ of spring.

Crocuses, too, _____ **harbinger** _____ the approach of spring.

SYNONYMS: (*n.*) precursor; (*v.*) presage
ANTONYMS: (*n.*) aftermath, epilogue, sequel

11. hedonism
(hē′ də niz əm)

(*n.*) the belief that the attainment of pleasure is life's chief aim; devotion to or pursuit of pleasure

A beach bum's mindless _____ **hedonism** _____ may appeal to all working people at one time or another.

SYNONYMS: pleasure seeking, sensuality, sybaritism
ANTONYMS: asceticism, puritanism, self-denial

12. lackluster
(lak′ lus tər)

(*adj.*) lacking brilliance or vitality; dull

The weary soldier's _____ **lackluster** _____ stare haunted the photographer, who captured it with her lens.

SYNONYMS: vapid, insipid, drab, flat
ANTONYMS: brilliant, radiant, dazzling

13. malcontent
(mal′ kən tent)

(*adj.*) discontented with or in open defiance of prevailing conditions; (*n.*) such a person

The _____ **malcontent** _____ transit workers went out on strike.

The angry mayor referred to the strikers as a group of vocal, lazy _____ **malcontents** _____.

SYNONYMS: (*adj.*) dissatisfied, disgruntled; (*n.*) grumbler
ANTONYMS: (*adj.*) satisfied, contented, complacent, smug

14. mellifluous
(mə lif′ lü əs)

(*adj.*) flowing sweetly or smoothly; honeyed

The folk singer's _____ **mellifluous** _____ voice appealed to young and old the world over.

SYNONYMS: euphonious, musical
ANTONYMS: shrill, strident, harsh, grating

15. nepotism
(nep′ ə tiz əm)

(*n.*) undue favoritism to or excessive patronage of one's relatives

To avoid any hint of _____ **nepotism** _____, the owner of the team refused to hire any of his relatives.

16. pander
(pan′ dər)

(*v.*) to cater to or provide satisfaction for the low tastes or vices of others; (*n.*) a person who does this

The hosts proceeded to _____ **pander** _____ to the every whim of their delighted guests.

The friend acted as a _____ **pander** _____, ferrying secret messages back and forth between them.

SYNONYMS: (*v.*) indulge; (*n.*) pimp, procurer

17. peccadillo
(pek ə dil′ ō)

(*n.*) a minor sin or offense; a trifling fault or shortcoming

If you will overlook my _____ **peccadillo** _____, I will ignore yours.

SYNONYM: indiscretion
ANTONYMS: felony, mortal sin, enormity, atrocity

18. pièce de résistance
(pē əs də rā zē stäns′)

(*n.*) the principal dish of a meal; the principal event, incident, or item; an outstanding accomplishment

The _____ **pièce de résistance** _____ of the remarkable repast was the dessert, a ten-tiered cake adorned with spun sugar.

SYNONYMS: centerpiece, chef d'oeuvre
ANTONYMS: preliminary, hors d'oeuvre

19. remand
(ri mand′)

(*v.*) to send or order back; in law, to send back to jail or to a lower court

The outlaw was _____ **remanded** _____ to the custody of the sheriff.

SYNONYMS: remit, return
ANTONYMS: forward to, send on, release

20. syndrome
(sin′ drōm)

(*n.*) a group of symptoms or signs that collectively characterize or indicate a disease, disorder, abnormality, etc.

With ubiquitous computer use, carpal tunnel has become a decidedly modern _____ **syndrome** _____.

SYNONYMS: complex, pattern

Completing the Sentence

From the words for this unit, choose the one that best completes each of the following sentences. Write the word in the space provided.

1. The pitcher's lightning fastball has proved the _____**bane**_____ of many a celebrated home-run hitter.

2. Her visits to the nursing home are motivated not by a detached sense of duty but by a genuine _____**empathy**_____ for those who are lonely.

3. Like everyone else, I was charmed by the _____**mellifluous**_____ tones of the speaker, but afterwards I could extract very little real meaning from what she said.

4. How is one to explain that strange _____**aberration**_____ from the habits and standards which he had followed for so many years?

5. I think you are showing poor judgment in condemning them so severely for what is, after all, little more than a(n) _____**peccadillo**_____.

6. Since there was no agency concerned with race relations, the Mayor created a(n) _____**ad hoc**_____ committee to deal with such matters.

7. Those cases that call for further attention will be _____**remanded**_____ to the proper agencies.

8. It was hard to believe that the eager, vibrant youth I had known was now this shabby derelict, staring into space with _____**lackluster**_____ eyes.

9. A high temperature, yellowish complexion, and general feeling of fatigue are all characteristic of the mononucleosis _____**syndrome**_____.

10. He had been happy-go-lucky as a young man, but years of disappointment and misfortune have turned him sour and _____**cantankerous**_____.

11. Would it be ungracious of me to suggest that the _____**pièce de résistance**_____ of the feast, given on the menu as "filet mignon," had the taste and texture of old shoe leather?

12. Yes, I believe in helping out relatives, but I haven't spent a lifetime building this business to make it a monument to _____**nepotism**_____.

13. Since they have followed a policy of bringing in executives and supervisors from the outside, instead of promoting from within their own ranks, the office is filled with grumbling _____**malcontents**_____.

14. Though he had embraced a creed of unabashed _____**hedonism**_____ in his youth, he ended his life among a group of ascetics living in the desert.

15. Is it too optimistic to hope that your willingness to undertake that thankless task is the _____**harbinger**_____ of a new maturity and a more responsible attitude?

16. Those sentimentalized effusions introduced a note of _____**bathos**_____ into what should have been an occasion marked by dignity and restraint.

17. Yes, you have scored a quick commercial success, but you have done it only by _____**pandering**_____ to low and depraved tastes.

18. I find myself in the position of a(n) _____ de facto _____ supervisor; now I would like to have the title, salary, and privileges that go along with the job.

19. The history of Nazi Germany and Fascist Italy teaches us that we should never let ourselves be blinded by the meretricious _____ casuistry _____ of a demagogue, no matter how appealing it may appear at first glance.

20. It took years for that country to recover from the _____ depredations _____ wrought by the Second World War and its concomitant social and economic dislocations.

Synonyms

*Choose the word from this unit that is **the same** or **most nearly the same** in meaning as the **boldface** word or expression in the given phrase. Write the word on the line provided.*

1. a **cranky** schoolmaster	cantankerous
2. serves, **in actuality**, as the chef	de facto
3. is a **herald** of the coming of winter	harbinger
4. warm weather, the **bête noire** of ski resorts	bane
5. struck me as utter **sophistry**	casuistry
6. victims of the **pillage**	depredation
7. dismissed as **schmaltz** by critics	bathos
8. seen by scientists as an **anomaly**	aberration
9. the **centerpiece** of the meal	pièce de résistance
10. committed several **indiscretions**	peccadilloes
11. **return** them to their grandparents' care	remand
12. refuses to **cater** to the criminal element	pander
13. charged with **favoritism** by his opponents	nepotism
14. completely without **compassion**	empathy
15. suffers from a recognizable **group of symptoms**	syndrome

Antonyms

*Choose the word from this unit that is **most nearly opposite** in meaning to the **boldface** word or expression in the given phrase. Write the word on the line provided.*

16. always wears a **contented** expression	malcontented
17. never experienced **self-denial**	hedonism
18. awakened by the **shrill** sound	mellifluous
19. the **long-standing** team of economists	ad hoc
20. their **dazzling** performance in the key game	lackluster

Choosing the Right Word

*Circle the **boldface** word that more satisfactorily completes each of the following sentences.*

1. Said Churchill to the British people after the Munich agreement: "We must reject these (**mellifluous, malcontent**) assurances of 'peace in our time.'"

2. With the extreme cold and the deep snows still holding on, the gradual lengthening of the days was the only (**aberration, harbinger**) of spring.

3. The negotiators agreed not to try to draw up an overall treaty but to deal with each specific problem on a(n) (**de facto, ad hoc**) basis.

4. Your efforts to prove that because "no one is perfect," all moral standards are relative and therefore meaningless, struck me as sheer (**casuistry, hedonism**).

5. In many respects it is a good movie, but sadly, the director has allowed sentiment to spill over into sentimentality, and sentimentality into (**bathos, casuistry**).

6. True, we won the game, but I think our team gave a rather (**lackluster, malcontent**) performance in beating a weak opponent by so narrow a margin.

7. "Am I to be accused of (**casuistry, nepotism**)," queried the Mayor, "just because my wife, daughter, brother, and nephew happen to be the best applicants for the jobs?"

8. A candidate for high public office should seek to debate the issues on an objective level, instead of (**remanding, pandering**) to the prejudices and misconceptions of the times.

9. The (**aberrations, depredations**) of the terrible disease could be seen only too clearly in her extreme emaciation and feebleness.

10. We learned with dismay that our application had been neither approved nor rejected, but (**pandered, remanded**) to a "higher authority for further consideration."

11. Although the law forbids residential separation of the races, we all know that a state of (**de facto, ad hoc**) segregation exists in some communities.

12. So strong is my (**empathy, casuistry**) with the poems of Robert Frost that I often feel as though I could have written them myself.

13. The car was forever breaking down, but its owner seemed to derive a sort of perverse satisfaction out of battling with the (**mellifluous, cantankerous**) old heap.

14. Then came Miss Bolton's cornet solo, which we all recognized immediately as the (**pièce de résistance, casuistry**) of that long musical evening.

15. We must not assume that their behavior, however (**aberrant, mellifluous**) by conventional standards, is a sign of mental illness.

16. The (**baneful, mellifluous**) looks which they directed at us made it only too clear that we had little hope for mercy at their hands.

17. We may find (**malcontents, hedonists**) annoying, but the fact is that they often serve as "gadflies" to bring about desirable changes.

18. How can you compare a mere social (**peccadillo, depredation**) with a misdeed that has caused such great harm to other people?

19. The (**syndrome, bathos**) of poverty, drug addiction, and crime that afflicts our cities calls for remedial action on a truly national scale.

20. In all aspects of their behavior, they showed the self-indulgence and gross indifference to others that is characteristic of the true (**malcontent, hedonist**).

Vocabulary in Context

*Read the following passage, in which some of the words you have studied in this unit appear in **boldface** type. Then complete each statement given below the passage by circling the letter of the item that is **the same** or **almost the same** in meaning as the highlighted word.*

The Great Migration

(Line)

Since the forced resettlement of Africans as slaves in the United States, migration has been a central characteristic of African American life. Before the Civil War, slaves escaped to freedom in the North. During and after it, freed blacks moved to protect their freedom. In the late 1870s, to escape the

(5) **depredations** of the Jim Crow laws, **de facto** and otherwise, more than 50,000 blacks left the South for the Midwest.

But the 1890s witnessed the beginning of the Great Migration—the mass grassroots movement

(10) of blacks from the rural South to the urban North. This lasted until the 1970s, but the single greatest period of migration was during World War I, when Northern factories needed workers desperately. During this time, 500,000 blacks left

(15) the **lackluster** economy of the South for jobs that beckoned. Although the wages they received for these semiskilled jobs were often lower than those of white workers, they were still higher than they were back home. In all, more than 6 million

(20) blacks migrated North between 1916 and 1970.

Although they left behind lynch mobs, disenfranchisement, and few opportunities to improve their quality of life, blacks who came North were not free from the degradations of

The Migration of the Negro No. 18 by Jacob Lawrence, 1941. One of 60 panels.

(25) racism, the **bane** of their existence. Although many Northerners welcomed their new neighbors with **empathy**, not all did. **Malcontents** started race riots in St. Louis, Chicago, and in other cities. In 1919 alone, there were in excess of twenty violent demonstrations. One riot in Chicago claimed the lives of thirty-eight people before the intervention of federal troops.

(30) Despite all the difficulties they encountered along the way, blacks, in reshaping their lives, have reshaped the United States and the very fabric of American society.

---

1. The meaning of **depredations** (line 5) is
a. sympathies
b. outrages
c. felonies
d. blessings

2. The meaning of **de facto** (line 5) is
a. actually existing
b. pleasure-seeking
c. de jure
d. by right

3. Lackluster (line 15) most nearly means
a. dazzling
b. hedonistic
c. flat
d. improvised

4. Bane (line 25) most nearly means
a. solace
b. comfort
c. bête noire
d. sophistry

5. Empathy (line 26) is best defined as
a. callousness
b. favoritism
c. quibbling
d. compassion

6. Malcontents (line 27) is best defined as
a. complacent people
b. disgruntled people
c. felons
d. smug people

Definitions

Note carefully the spelling, pronunciation, part(s) of speech, and definition(s) of each of the following words. Then write the word in the blank space(s) in the illustrative sentence(s) following. Finally, study the lists of synonyms and antonyms given at the end of each entry.

1. beatitude
(bē at′ ə tüd)

(*n.*) a state of perfect happiness or blessedness; a blessing

Do you think that not having to worry about money is the consummate _____**beatitude**_____ of being wealthy?

SYNONYMS: bliss, rapture
ANTONYMS: misery, despair

2. bête noire
(bet nwär′)

(*n.*) someone or something that one especially dislikes, dreads, or avoids

Spinach used to be the _____**bête noire**_____ of my diet, but that was before I tasted blood sausage.

SYNONYMS: pet peeve, bugbear, nemesis
ANTONYMS: pet, idol

3. bode
(bōd)

(*v.*) to be an omen of; to indicate by signs

With a smile that _____**bodes**_____ good news, the teacher enters the room and greets the students.

SYNONYMS: presage, augur, foreshadow

4. dank
(daŋk)

(*adj.*) unpleasantly damp or wet

The room had the _____**dank**_____ atmosphere of a wet cave.

SYNONYMS: clammy, moist, soggy
ANTONYMS: dry, arid, parched, desiccated

5. ecumenical
(ek yü men′ i kəl)

(*adj.*) worldwide or universal in influence or application

An _____**ecumenical**_____ council meets on the third Tuesday of each month.

SYNONYMS: general, comprehensive
ANTONYMS: parochial, regional, insular

6. fervid
(fər′ vid)

(*adj.*) burning with enthusiasm or zeal; extremely heated

Using _____**fervid**_____ words of praise, the coach gave the team a much-needed pep talk before the big game.

SYNONYMS: ardent, zealous, fervent, earnest
ANTONYMS: apathetic, indifferent, cool, blasé

7. fetid
(fet′ id)

(*adj.*) having an unpleasant or offensive odor

The stale, _____ **fetid** _____ air of the windowless room was an irritation to all who had to be there.

SYNONYMS: smelly, putrid, noisome, foul, malodorous
ANTONYMS: fragrant, aromatic, perfumed, sweet

8. gargantuan
(gär gan′ chū ən)

(*adj.*) of immense size, volume, or capacity; enormous, prodigious

The spirited artist had a _____ **gargantuan** _____ thirst for life.

SYNONYMS: huge, colossal, mammoth, gigantic
ANTONYMS: tiny, minuscule, infinitesimal, dwarfish

9. heyday
(hā′ dā)

(*n.*) the period of greatest power, vigor, success, or influence; the prime years

During the _____ **heyday** _____ of the clipper ship, these graceful vessels were the swiftest on the seas.

SYNONYM: golden age
ANTONYMS: formative years, twilight years, decline

10. incubus
(in′ kyə bəs)

(*n.*) a demon or evil spirit supposed to haunt human beings in their bedrooms at night; anything that oppresses or weighs upon one, like a nightmare

The young child awoke with a loud scream, claiming that a terrifying _____ **incubus** _____ had entered the room.

SYNONYMS: hobgoblin, millstone, burden

11. infrastructure
(in′ frə strək chər)

(*n.*) a basic foundation or framework; a system of public works; the resources and facilities required for an activity; permanent military installations

The city's aging _____ **infrastructure** _____ was beginning to become a problem that needed to be addressed.

SYNONYMS: base, basis, underpinning
ANTONYM: superstructure

12. inveigle
(in vā′ gəl)

(*v.*) to entice, lure, or snare by flattery or artful inducements; to obtain or acquire by artifice

The planning committee chair _____ **inveigled** _____ us to join them by promising good seats at the ceremony.

SYNONYMS: induce, beguile, cajole, wheedle

13. kudos
(kü′ dōs)

(*n.*) the acclaim, prestige, or renown that comes as a result of some action or achievement

The poet received all the _____ **kudos** _____ due a Nobel laureate.

SYNONYMS: glory, praise, accolades
ANTONYMS: boos, disapproval, condemnation

14. lagniappe
(lan′ yap)

(*n.*) an extra or unexpected gift or gratuity

To reward their loyal customers, the grateful store handed out _____<u>lagniappe</u>_____ to all the day's shoppers.

SYNONYM: bonus

15. prolix
(prō lix′)

(*adj.*) long-winded and wordy; tending to speak or write in such a way

The father of the bride regaled anyone who would listen with a _____<u>prolix</u>_____ description of the wedding.

SYNONYMS: verbose, garrulous
ANTONYMS: terse, laconic, succinct, pithy

16. protégé
(prō′ tə zhā)

(*n.*) someone whose welfare, training, or career is under the patronage of an influential person; someone under the jurisdiction of a foreign country or government

The _____<u>protégé</u>_____ of the ex-champion may one day be a champion herself.

SYNONYMS: ward, charge, disciple, trainee
ANTONYMS: sponsor, mentor, benefactor

17. prototype
(prō′ tə tīp)

(*n.*) an original pattern or model; a primitive or ancestral form

The _____<u>prototype</u>_____ of the modern detective novel is thought to be Poe's "Murders in the Rue Morgue."

SYNONYM: archetype
ANTONYMS: copy, imitation

18. sycophant
(sik′ ə fənt)

(*n.*) someone who attempts to win favors or advance him- or herself by flattery or servile behavior; a slanderer, defamer

The actor, angered by his manager's constant false flattery, called him a two-faced _____<u>sycophant</u>_____.

SYNONYMS: yes-man, toady, flunky, bootlicker

19. tautology
(tô tol′ ə jē)

(*n.*) needless repetition of an idea by using different but equivalent words; a redundancy

Filled with endless _____<u>tautologies</u>_____ and solecisms, the lengthy book is a tiresome read.

SYNONYM: pleonasm

20. truckle
(truk′ əl)

(*v.*) to yield or submit tamely or submissively

The knight would _____<u>truckle</u>_____ to no one.

SYNONYMS: kowtow, stoop, grovel
ANTONYMS: resist, defy, stand up to

Completing the Sentence

From the words for this unit, choose the one that best completes each of the following sentences. Write the word in the space provided.

1. As the _____**protégé**_____ of one of the great violinists of our times, she has had an unrivaled opportunity to develop her musical talents.

2. The memory of my ghastly blunder and of the harm it had done to innocent people weighed on my spirit like a(n) _____**incubus**_____.

3. Like most people, I enjoy flattery, but I can't be _____**inveigled**_____ into doing something that in my heart I know is wrong.

4. In the dreamy _____**beatitude**_____ of their first love, nothing I might have said would have had the slightest effect on them.

5. The speaker emphasized that in the modern world the barriers between different groups are rapidly being broken down and that we must try to think in truly _____**ecumenical**_____ terms.

6. At the risk of losing the election, I refused to _____**truckle**_____ to the fleeting passions and prejudices of a small part of the electorate.

7. In *David Copperfield*, Dickens described with heartbreaking realism the period of his own childhood that he spent working as an apprentice in a(n) _____**dank**_____ and chilly cellar.

8. May I say in all modesty that I don't deserve such _____**kudos**_____ just because I was all-state in football and led my class academically.

9. I was happy enough when she agreed to go to the prom with me, but her suggestion that we use her car was an unexpected _____**lagniappe**_____.

10. Was it just our imagination, or was the room still _____**fetid**_____ with the smell of stale cigar smoke?

11. Far better to receive sincere criticism, no matter how severe, than the groveling adulation of a(n) _____**sycophant**_____.

12. I consider the vogue use of "hopefully" illogical, inept, and pretentious; it has become my linguistic _____**bête noire**_____.

13. The atmosphere of distrust and hostility did not _____**bode**_____ well for the outcome of the peace talks.

14. To maintain that because human beings are aggressive animals, they will always be involved in conflicts seems to me a mere _____**tautology**_____.

15. The lame-duck President looked back with nostalgia on the power he had wielded during the _____**heyday**_____ of his administration.

16. It was a subject of heated debate in the early nineteenth century whether the federal government should play any part at all in building the _____**infrastructure**_____ to support the fledgling American economy.

17. I think it was terribly naive of us to expect to get a fair hearing from such _____**fervid**_____ partisans of the opposing party.

18. After I read one of your _____ **prolix** _____ and repetitive reports, I always have the feeling that you have never heard the expression "less is more."

19. In H. G. Wells's _The Time Machine_, we see the _____ **prototype** _____ of a vast number of stories and novels in the area of science fiction.

20. Falstaff is a behemoth of a man, whose _____ **gargantuan** _____ appetites, especially for sack and sleep, never seem to be satiated.

Synonyms

Choose the word from this unit that is **the same** or **most nearly the same** in meaning as the **boldface** word or expression in the given phrase. Write the word on the line provided.

1. conveyed a sense of **bliss** _____ beatitude _____

2. a **putrid** odor from the open cellar door _____ fetid _____

3. abounds in **redundancy** _____ tautology _____

4. the **model** for the house of tomorrow _____ prototype _____

5. a tottering **foundation** _____ infrastructure _____

6. many attempts to **cajole** them to join _____ inveigle _____

7. known throughout the town as a **toady** _____ sycophant _____

8. a document of **worldwide** significance _____ ecumenical _____

9. an unexpected **gratuity** _____ lagniappe _____

10. **augurs** well for the future of the franchise _____ bodes _____

11. is a **zealous** follower of the guru _____ fervid _____

12. a great champion in her **prime** _____ heyday _____

13. the **burden** of famine and disease _____ incubus _____

14. mud, the **nemesis** of a marching army _____ bête noire _____

15. while his **charge** held the sword and shield _____ protégé _____

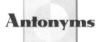

Antonyms

Choose the word from this unit that is **most nearly opposite** in meaning to the **boldface** word or expression in the given phrase. Write the word on the line provided.

16. a **minuscule** portion of food _____ gargantuan _____

17. wrote a **terse** passage _____ prolix _____

18. **stand up** to the temptation _____ truckle _____

19. the recipient of many **boos** _____ kudos _____

20. descended into the **parched** canyon _____ dank _____

Choosing the Right Word

Circle the **boldface** word that more satisfactorily completes each of the following sentences.

1. Surrounded from childhood by flattering courtiers, the monarch grew to adulthood unable to distinguish a friend from a (**beatitude, sycophant**).

2. After a long investigation, detectives arrested two con artists who had (**truckled, inveigled**) their many elderly victims into giving them their life savings.

3. His zest for life and his boundless optimism were expressed perfectly, it seemed to me, in his (**gargantuan, fetid**) laughter.

4. Leonardo da Vinci still stands out as the (**prototype, lagniappe**) of the universal genius, equally accomplished in science and in the arts.

5. My criticism of his statement is not merely that it is (**prolix, ecumenical**), but that it uses words to obscure rather than to reinforce the meaning.

6. I have no desire to be known as a nonconformist, but I am not going to allow fear of public disapproval to become my (**beatitude, bête noire**).

7. The lowering clouds and mounting winds did not (**bode, truckle**) well for our hopes for perfect beach weather.

8. When I saw the beautiful girl you had brought to the prom, I understood the reason for your smile of (**fetid, beatific**) self-satisfaction.

9. We can now recognize that many institutions that seemed, at a particular time, to be in their (**incubus, heyday**) were actually already on the decline.

10. You did nothing to help me, but now that I have achieved some success, you have the gall to claim me as your (**protégé, bête noire**).

11. Surely you can make an honest effort to please your employer without (**boding, truckling**) to the vanity of the person who pays your salary.

12. Our goal as a nation and as a society must be to free ourselves completely of the (**sycophant, incubus**) of racial prejudice.

13. When the sanitation strike continued into a second week, people began to complain about the (**fetid, prolix**) smell that hung over the sweltering city.

14. She was such a (**beatific, fervid**) supporter of the Los Angeles Dodgers that she seemed unable to speak of anything else.

15. I felt that I could not continue to live any longer in that (**dank, gargantuan**) atmosphere of prejudice and hostility.

16. I was paid generously for my work, but the kind smile and gracious words were a delightful (**lagniappe, incubus**).

17. In all the great religions, we find common standards that must be regarded as (**fervid, ecumenical**) values, equally valid at all times and in all places.

18. Scientists have for some time been correlating the functions of human consciousness with the neural (**tautology, infrastructure**) of the brain.

19. Her composition was seriously weakened by (**tautologies, kudos**) such as "an older woman who is approaching the end of her life span."

20. In the twilight of her long career, she began to receive the (**heyday, kudos**) that her brilliant but unconventional writings so richly deserved.

Vocabulary in Context

*Read the following passage, in which some of the words you have studied in this unit appear in **boldface** type. Then complete each statement given below the passage by circling the letter of the item that is **the same** or **almost the same** in meaning as the highlighted word.*

A True Patriot

(Line)

In the 1770s, American colonists faced a crisis of **gargantuan** proportions—not only were they being taxed without their consent, but British soldiers walked their streets and entered their houses. British spies sat in their taverns and listened in on conversations. Colonial governors clamped down on political activity. The problem was a big one, and to tackle it, groups of **fervid** patriots, such as the Sons of Liberty, (5) met and worked in secret. But the great distances between the villages made communication difficult and concerted action even more so.

A depiction of Paul Revere's famous midnight ride

For the most part, the leaders of the rebellion were well-heeled, well-educated aristocrats. However, (10) wealth and knowledge were not prerequisites for meaningful participation. Paul Revere, a Boston silversmith, had a typically limited colonial education. But he kept his (15) ear to the ground, and when the time came to act, he did not need to be **inveigled**.

Revere made beautiful teapots, punch bowls, and shoe buckles, but (20) the leaders of the Sons of Liberty knew this stocky tradesman as a patriot who would **truckle** to no one, least of all a British soldier or spy. They also knew that he was a superb rider.

Revere was one of the fastest of the express riders who delivered news to colonial leaders as far away as New York and Philadelphia. This **bête noire** of the (25) English army did not hesitate when his skill was needed most. On the night of April 18, 1775, he used a secret signal and muffled oars to slip past the British warship in Boston Harbor and land at Charlestown, where a horse awaited. Through the countryside he galloped, warning the colonists of the impending arrival of British troops. Paul Revere simply did what had to be done. (30)

---

1. The meaning of **gargantuan** (line 1) is
a. blissful
b. mammoth ✓
c. minuscule
d. ardent

2. Fervid (line 5) most nearly means
a. putrid
b. aromatic
c. frightened
d. zealous ✓

3. Inveigled (line 18) is best defined as
a. asked
b. paid
c. cajoled ✓
d. sponsored

4. The meaning of **truckle** (line 22) is
a. kowtow ✓
b. drive
c. chuckle
d. stand up

5. Bête noire (line 25) most nearly means
a. idol
b. pet
c. spy
d. nemesis ✓

Visit us at **www.sadlier-oxford.com**
for interactive puzzles and games.

REVIEW UNITS 7–9

Analogies

In each of the following, circle the item that best completes the comparison.

See pages T38–T46 for explanations of answers.

1. mellifluous is to **honey** as
a. unctuous is to vinegar
b. vitriolic is to acid
c. piquant is to oil
d. acerbic is to sugar

2. hedonist is to **pleasure** as
a. atheist is to honor
b. vegetarian is to meat
c. materialist is to possessions
d. misanthrope is to friends

3. satirist is to **lampoon** as
a. champion is to attack
b. eulogist is to extol
c. buttress is to undermine
d. critic is to defraud

4. curmudgeon is to **cantankerous** as
a. protégé is to intractable
b. philistine is to discriminating
c. sycophant is to obsequious
d. nepotist is to impartial

5. malcontent is to **disgruntled** as
a. virtuoso is to lackluster
b. fanatic is to fervid
c. pygmy is to gargantuan
d. slob is to fastidious

6. malleable is to **mold** as
a. ductile is to draw out
b. senile is to compress
c. tensile is to shape
d. tactile is to melt

7. highway is to **infrastructure** as
a. embargo is to trade
b. icon is to culture
c. filibuster is to legislature
d. consumer is to economy

8. inveigle is to **blandishments** as
a. coerce is to compliments
b. wheedle is to reprimands
c. intimidate is to threats
d. cajole is to rebukes

9. nemesis is to **retribution** as
a. incubus is to relief
b. bête noire is to satisfaction
c. harbinger is to death
d. bane is to ruin

10. incubus is to **oppress** as
a. pet peeve is to nettle
b. bugbear is to amuse
c. pander is to edify
d. bête noire is to delight

Word Associations

In each of the following groups, circle the word that is best defined or suggested by the given phrase.

1. You'll be the death of me yet!
a. protégé   b. nemesis   c. syndrome   d. empathy

2. how you might characterize the First World War
a. savoir-faire   b. infrastructure   c. cataclysm   d. carte blanche

3. Don't try to sweet talk me!
a. lampoon   b. bode   c. beleaguer   d. inveigle

4. something you shouldn't make a federal case of
a. debauch   b. éclat   c. syndrome   d. peccadillo

5. a behemoth of a man
a. gargantuan   b. bathos   c. lampoon   d. incubus

6. The long-winded and repetitive speech bored the entire audience.
a. ad hoc   b. inchoate   c. tautology   d. dank

7. The sight turned my stomach!
a. picaresque   b. malcontent   (c. queasy)   d. inchoate

8. They hired all of their relatives!
(a. nepotism)   b. tautology   c. hedonism   d. aberration

9. It just makes me see red!
a. debauch   b. tautology   c. kudos   (d. bête noire)

10. a crocus in early March
a. bathos   b. philistine   (c. harbinger)   d. casuistry

11. Long-lasting fatigue is one symptom of the Epstein-Barr virus.
a. tautology   (b. syndrome)   c. nepotism   d. sycophant

12. The highly touted Broadway play was less than exciting.
a. prolix   (b. lackluster)   c. dank   d. mellifluous

Choosing the Right Meaning

Read each sentence carefully. Then circle the item that best completes the statement below the sentence.

See pages T38–T46 for explanations of answers.

Because the accused was a protégé and therefore could not be tried, Federal prosecutors arranged to have him deported to his native land, there to be charged by his own government. (2)

1. The word **protégé** in line 1 is used to mean

a. trainee

b. someone enjoying
the patronage of a
powerful person

c. disciple

(d. someone under
the protection
of another government)

"Given the ghoulish zeal with which the director inflicts these scenes of mayhem and carnage on the audience," observed the critic, "this is most definitely *not* a movie recommended for the fastidious." (2)

2. In line 3 the word **fastidious** most nearly means

a. meticulous   b. finicky   (c. easily disgusted)   d. overly demanding

Medical authorities grew alarmed when the strange ailment proved refractory and, fearing an outbreak or even an epidemic, quarantined the stricken patients. (2)

3. The best definition for the word **refractory** in line 1 is

(a. untreatable)   b. unruly   c. disobedient   d. stubborn

"Our natures do pursue,
Like rats that raven down their proper bane,
A thirsty evil; and when we drink, we die." (2)
(Shakespeare, *Measure for Measure*, I, ii, 120–122)

4. The word **bane** in line 2 is used to mean

a. ruin   (b. poison)   c. death   d. destruction

Antonyms

*In each of the following groups, circle the word or expression that is most nearly the **opposite** of the word in **boldface** type.*

1. gambol
a. wager
b. trace
c. condemn
d. trudge

2. ecumenical
a. lofty
b. evasive
c. parochial
d. amateur

3. ad hoc
a. temporary
b. permanent
c. laughable
d. helpless

4. savoir-faire
a. injustice
b. tactlessness
c. profitability
d. renown

5. de facto
a. by right
b. long-standing
c. sweet tempered
d. clear-cut

6. gargantuan
a. tiny
b. summery
c. soft
d. flighty

7. malcontent
a. unruly
b. disgruntled
c. satisfied
d. fugitive

8. inchoate
a. naked
b. developed
c. conforming
d. immature

9. fastidious
a. squeamish
b. cautious
c. slovenly
d. partial

10. éclat
a. abomination
b. curiosity
c. dullness
d. rarity

11. beatitude
a. cudgel
b. ugliness
c. tension
d. despair

12. lackluster
a. distorted
b. dazzling
c. crass
d. beneficial

13. prolix
a. distant
b. verbose
c. succinct
d. tyrannical

14. imbue
a. expunge
b. lend
c. infuse
d. cancel

15. philistine
a. puny
b. foreign
c. refined
d. boorish

16. dank
a. deserted
b. arid
c. impulsive
d. soaked

Completing the Sentence

From the following list of words, choose the one that best completes each of the following sentences. Write the word in the space provided.

aberration	de facto	imbue	philistine
cataclysm	heyday	malcontent	remand

1. That one unfortunate reaction should be viewed as a(n) _____ aberration _____ rather than as an example of his customary behavior.

2. In order to avoid any further violence, the neighboring states quickly recognized the _____ de facto _____ government established by the military leaders.

3. In their _____ heyday _____ transatlantic passenger ships offered luxury unequaled on the seven seas.

4. Through examples rather than with words, the scoutmaster managed to _____ imbue _____ the troop with worthy ideas and aspirations.

5. I feel sorry for the _____ malcontents _____ who always harp on the negative rather than the positive aspects of any situation.

Interesting Derivations

From the following list of words, choose the one that best completes each of the sentences below. Write the word in the space provided.

ecumenical	inchoate	nemesis	picaresque
gargantuan	kudos	nepotism	prolix

1. Since, throughout history, powerful leaders have tended to favor their relatives and close personal friends, it is not surprising to find that the word ____**nepotism**____ comes from the Latin word for "nephew."

2. A bit of British university slang, derived from the Greek word for "glory" or "honor," is preserved in the English word ____**kudos**____.

3. The adjective ____**ecumenical**____ comes from the Greek word meaning "encompassing all of the known world."

4. The English adjective ____**picaresque**____ is derived from the Spanish noun meaning "rascal" or "rogue."

5. The name of the "hero" of François Rabelais's famous novel, a character with an astounding capacity for food and pleasure, is the source of the English adjective ____**gargantuan**____.

Word Families

A. *On the line provided, write the word you have learned in Units 7–9 that is related to each of the following nouns.*

EXAMPLE: cantankerousness—**cantankerous**

1. ecumenics — **ecumenical**

2. ambivalence — **ambivalent**

3. fastidiousness — **fastidious**

4. malleability, malleableness — **malleable**

5. queasiness — **queasy**

6. refractoriness — **refractory**

7. prolixity — **prolix**

8. inveiglement, inveigler — **inveigle**

9. fetidness — **fetid**

10. dankness — **dank**

11. lampooner, lampoonery — **lampoon**

12. philistia, philistinism — **philistine**

13. aberrant — **aberration**

14. debauchee, debauchery — **debauch**

15. hedonist — **hedonism**

16. casuist — **casuistry**

B. *On the line provided, write the word you have learned in Units 7–9 that is related to each of the following verbs.*
EXAMPLE: depredate—**depredation**

17. empathize   empathy

18. boding   bode

19. beatify   beatitude

20. optimize   opt

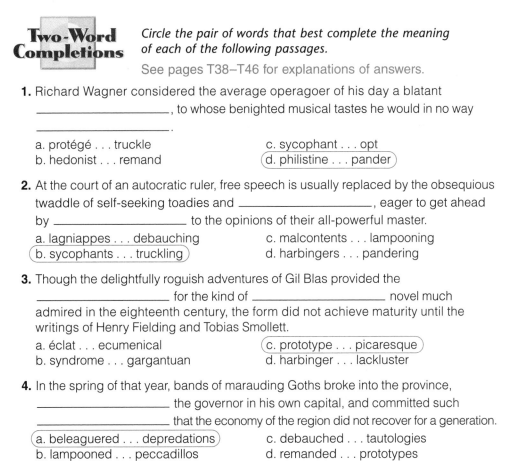

Two-Word Completions

Circle the pair of words that best complete the meaning of each of the following passages.

See pages T38–T46 for explanations of answers.

1. Richard Wagner considered the average operagoer of his day a blatant
_____, to whose benighted musical tastes he would in no way
_____.
   a. protégé . . . truckle
   b. hedonist . . . remand
   c. sycophant . . . opt
   d. philistine . . . pander

2. At the court of an autocratic ruler, free speech is usually replaced by the obsequious twaddle of self-seeking toadies and _____, eager to get ahead by _____ to the opinions of their all-powerful master.
   a. lagniappes . . . debauching
   b. sycophants . . . truckling
   c. malcontents . . . lampooning
   d. harbingers . . . pandering

3. Though the delightfully roguish adventures of Gil Blas provided the _____ for the kind of _____ novel much admired in the eighteenth century, the form did not achieve maturity until the writings of Henry Fielding and Tobias Smollett.
   a. éclat . . . ecumenical
   b. syndrome . . . gargantuan
   c. prototype . . . picaresque
   d. harbinger . . . lackluster

4. In the spring of that year, bands of marauding Goths broke into the province, _____ the governor in his own capital, and committed such _____ that the economy of the region did not recover for a generation.
   a. beleaguered . . . depredations
   b. lampooned . . . peccadillos
   c. debauched . . . tautologies
   d. remanded . . . prototypes

Read the following passage, in which some of the words you have studied in Units 7–9 appear in **boldface** type. Then complete each statement given below the passage by circling the item that is **the same** or **almost the same** in meaning as the highlighted word.

An Essential Yet Overlooked Innovation

(Line)

In a list of the world's significant historical technological advances, one that surely deserves **ecumenical** support for inclusion is the sewer.

(5) **Kudos** to the ancient engineers who worked on the age-old problem of waste disposal—imagine if they had not!

Today, an effective sewage system is a key feature of the **infrastructure**
(10) of any city, large or small. But this was not always the case. One of the earliest attempts at a sewage system that improved upon the impractical practice of hauling away waste and
(15) dumping it elsewhere, took place about 5,000 years ago in the Orkney Islands, off the coast of Scotland. Archaeologists have discovered evidence of stone-lined drains leading
(20) from small rooms in houses, going underground. These **harbingers** of future sewers emptied into the sea through nearby cliffs.

At about the same time, in the
(25) larger cities of the Indus Valley, engineers were dealing with the same issue, albeit on a grander scale. There, in what is now India and Pakistan, they built networks of
(30) brick drains along the streets. Sewage ran from rooms in houses into underground U-shaped drains.

More than 2,000 years later, sewage disposal methods had
(35) gained little in sophistication. For example, in the **heyday** of the great Athenian civilization, sewage pipes from houses emptied directly into cesspools in the streets. Private
(40) contractors cleaned the foul mess.

Systems improved with the Romans, four centuries later. Emperor Augustus enclosed the massive *Cloaca Maxima*, an
(45) enormous brick sewage tunnel that passed right through the center of the city. This structure, big enough for a chariot to pass through, was one of many the Romans built
(50) throughout their empire. Never **ambivalent** about the importance of cleanliness, the Romans used their engineering skill to meet their sanitation needs.

1. The meaning of **ecumenical** (line 3) is
a. regional
b. worldwide
c. local
d. religious

2. **Kudos** (line 5) most nearly means
a. accolades
b. boos
c. disapproval
d. jobs

3. **Infrastructure** (line 9) is best defined as
a. superstructure
b. foundation
c. suburbs
d. government

4. The meaning of **harbingers** (line 21) is
a. copies
b. patterns
c. messengers
d. precursors

5. **Heyday** (line 36) most nearly means
a. decline
b. harvest time
c. prime
d. beginning

6. **Ambivalent** (line 51) is best defined as
a. unequivocal
b. clear-cut
c. equivocal
d. meticulous

Building with Classical Roots

mal—bad, ill

This root appears in **malcontent** (page 92), which means "one who is dissatisfied with conditions." Some other words based on the same root are listed below.

maladapted	malfeasance	malfunction	malingerer
malaise	malformation	malice	malodorous

From the list of words above, choose the one that corresponds to each of the brief definitions below. Write the word in the blank space in the illustrative sentence below the definition.

1. unsuited or poorly suited for a particular purpose or situation

The storage area was large enough, but it was _____maladapted_____ for use as a classroom.

2. wrongdoing or misconduct in public office

The politician was accused of _____malfeasance_____ when the crooked scheme became public.

3. one who pretends to be ill in order to escape duty or work

He was fired from the squad because he proved to be a shiftless _____malingerer_____.

4. an abnormal or faulty bodily structure or part

Ravages of disease caused an unsightly _____malformation_____ of the patient's face.

5. having a bad odor; ill-smelling; highly improper

To my sensibilities, all blue-veined cheeses are unbearably _____malodorous_____.

6. a failure to operate correctly or in a normal manner; to operate poorly or imperfectly

Radio contact was lost for over an hour due to a technical _____malfunction_____.

7. a desire to cause harm or suffering; deep-seated ill will

Legally, murder is distinguished from manslaughter by the element of _____malice_____ aforethought.

8. a vague feeling of physical or mental discomfort

For no evident reason, she was too beset by _____malaise_____ to attend class.

From the list of words above, choose the one that best completes each of the following sentences. Write the word in the blank space provided.

1. The _____malfunction_____ of a simple switching device set off a chain reaction that culminated in a complete power failure.

2. The woman's delicate constitution and refined sensibility were _____maladapted_____ to the rough-and-tumble life of the frontier.

3. The review panel found the department head guilty of _____malfeasance_____ in handling the funds for public housing.

4. Who has not suffered that indefinable sense of _____malaise_____ that so often accompanies the onset of the flu?

5. A _____malodorous_____ vapor seemed to waft from the fetid bog.

6. Advances in reconstructive surgery now permit doctors to correct many _____malformations_____ that once were untreatable.

7. Lincoln believed that national unity could never be restored if the South were treated with _____malice_____ rather than magnanimity.

8. The new captain personally visited the ship's sickbay to make sure that no _____malingerers_____ were being harbored there.

---

*Circle the **boldface** word that more satisfactorily completes each of the following sentences.*

1. The convertible two-seater sports car is (**maladapted,** **malodorous**) to the rugged, steep, and icy back roads of the Canadian Rockies.

2. Sociologists posit that the (**malice,** **malaise**) that makes some Americans feel depressed might lift if those people would become more involved in community activities.

3. A (**malingerer,** **malfunction**) in the fresh-air circulation system of the office building led the health inspector to evacuate all interior offices that lack windows.

4. Due to an unusual (**malfeasance,** **malformation**) of the retina in my left eye, my vision cannot be adequately corrected by glasses or by contact lenses.

5. When it is roasted, the edible but (**malodorous,** **maladapted**) seed of the female ginkgo tree is considered a seasonal delicacy in Japan and China.

6. A (**malingerer,** **malfunction**) in a closely-knit group may escape criticism at first, but will one day be exposed and reviled as the weak link in an otherwise effective team.

7. Bees do not sting out of (**malaise,** **malice**) toward their victims; rather, they sting to survive.

8. The tenacious work of two investigative reporters led to dramatic revelations about the treasurer's (**malformation,** **malfeasance**) with the company's finances.

Writer's Challenge

Read the following sentences, paying special attention to the words and phrases underlined. From the words in the box below, find better choices for these underlined words and phrases. Then use these choices to rewrite the sentences.

WORD BANK

aberration	cantankerous	fervid	nemesis	savoir-faire
ambivalent	de facto	fetid	opt	sycophant
bane	depredation	lackluster	pander	tautology
beleaguer	éclat	malcontent	prolix	truckle

Stand Watie: One Last Stand

1. Opposite and conflicting responses to Stand Watie were common in his lifetime (1806–1871), yet this Cherokee leader developed a legendary reputation.
Ambivalent

2. Born into a prominent Cherokee family in Georgia, Watie's views on tribal politics were burning with enthusiasm, but sometimes at odds with those of other Cherokee leaders.
fervid

3. When the Civil War broke out in 1861, Watie made the choice to support the Confederacy, and joined as a lieutenant.
opted

4. Watie's cavalry regiment, the Cherokee Mounted Rifles, attacked supply trains with zeal, soon becoming the bête noir of Federal forces in parts of the West.
bane

5. Successful preying upon and plundering of the enemy by his regiment helped Stand Watie rise to brigadier general, the only Native American ever to achieve that rank.
depredation

6. On June 25, 1865, two months after Lee surrendered to Grant at Appomattox, Stand Watie finally saw that he had no other choice but to submit tamely to Union authority; thus he became the last Confederate general to lay down his sword.
truckle

Analogies

In each of the following, circle the item that best completes the comparison.

See pages T38–T46 for explanations of answers.

1. bilious is to **queasy** as
a. quizzical is to content
b. contumelious is to elated
c. portentous is to alarmed
d. ambivalent is to sleepy

2. midget is to **minuscule** as
a. fait accompli is to abortive
b. dictum is to risible
c. volte-face is to waggish
d. colossus is to gargantuan

3. tautology is to **redundant** as
a. lampoon is to prolix
b. vignette is to noisome
c. homily is to incoherent
d. solecism is to erroneous

4. prude is to **fastidious** as
a. philistine is to crass
b. prodigy is to lackluster
c. incubus is to prurient
d. hedonist is to malcontent

5. bathos is to **maudlin** as
a. obloquy is to complimentary
b. empathy is to callous
c. persiflage is to picaresque
d. casuistry is to specious

6. inchoate is to **form** as
a. ineffable is to size
b. chimerical is to substance
c. ecumenical is to scope
d. sacrosanct is to duration

7. inveigle is to **flattery** as
a. cozen is to encouragement
b. browbeat is to intimidation
c. reassure is to censure
d. cajole is to criticism

8. mule is to **refractory** as
a. pig is to indolent
b. horse is to iconoclastic
c. fox is to maladroit
d. elephant is to oblivious

9. virtuoso is to **éclat** as
a. gallant is to panache
b. proselyte is to insouciance
c. harbinger is to verisimilitude
d. klutz is to tact

10. aficionado is to **fervid** as
a. pundit is to apathetic
b. sycophant is to caustic
c. connoisseur is to discriminating
d. pessimist is to sanguine

Choosing the Right Meaning

Read each sentence carefully. Then circle the item that best completes the statement below the sentence.

See pages T38–T46 for explanations of answers.

Besides inventing the lens that bears his name, French physicist Augustin-Jean Fresnel (1788–1827) investigated the laws governing the interference of polarized light. (2)

1. The word **polarized** in line 3 is used to mean
a. physically alienated
b. vibrating in a pattern
c. evenly split
d. completely estranged

The summer saw hundreds of volunteers in towns along the rain-swollen Mississippi work around-the-clock, shoring up river levees with sandbags in a desperate effort to hold back the cataclysm. (2)

2. In line 3 the word **cataclysm** most nearly means
a. deluge
b. upheaval
c. catastrophe
d. disaster

"He had often noticed that six months' oblivion amounts to newspaper death, and that resurrection is rare. Nothing is easier, if a man wants it, than rest, profound as the grave." (Henry Adams, *The Education of Henry Adams*) (2)

3. In line 1 the word **oblivion** is used to mean

a. forgetfulness   b. unawareness   (c. being forgotten)   d. insensibility

Beleaguered by American and French forces, Lord Cornwallis surrendered his encircled army to George Washington at Yorktown in October 1781. (2)

4. The best definition for the word **Beleaguered** in line 1 is

a. Outnumbered   b. Troubled   c. Defeated   (d. Surrounded)

When joke after joke met with dead silence, the comedian began seriously to doubt whether the audience was at all risible. (2)

5. The word **risible** in line 2 most nearly means

a. laughable   b. ludicrous   c. droll   (d. inclined to laugh)

Two-Word Completions

Circle the pair of words that best complete the meaning of each of the following sentences.

See pages T38–T46 for explanations of answers.

1. Because her work flouted the canons of classical ballet, Isadora Duncan soon came to be regarded as an artistic _____ to whom nothing was _____.

a. poltroon . . . ambivalent
b. aficionado . . . internecine
c. persona . . . cognate
(d. iconoclast . . . sacrosanct)

2. Though King Edward VII is often pictured as an effete _____, with appetites as _____ as his physique, he was an intelligent, perceptive observer of the European scene.

(a. hedonist . . . gargantuan)
b. harbinger . . . fetid
c. pundit . . . philistine
d. mountebank . . . dank

3. "You may consider me a narrow-minded prude," I replied, "but I can see no redeeming social or artistic value in this book. Indeed, it appears to _____ exclusively to the _____ interests of the reader."

a. inveigle . . . bibulous
b. condescend . . . eleemosynary
(c. pander . . . prurient)
d. opt . . . philistine

4. Boss Tweed and his Tammany Hall cronies were as _____ as hungry sharks; their _____ on New York's treasury left the city in severe financial straits.

a. supine . . . aberrations
(b. rapacious . . . depredations)
c. effete . . . peccadilloes
d. maladroit . . . lucubrations

5. Though he is somewhat awkward and _____, he handled that ticklish social problem with all the _____ of a born diplomat.

a. lackluster . . . folderol
b. queasy . . . gamut
c. mellifluous . . . prescience
(d. maladroit . . . savoir-faire)

Read the passage below. Then complete the exercise at the bottom of the page.

Borrowed Words

"The traitor calmly sipped coffee on the veranda." The preceding sentence, which most English-speakers can readily comprehend, includes words borrowed from French (*traiteur*), Latin (*calma*), Arabic (*qahwa*), and Hindi (*varanda*). One of the beauties of English is its flexibility to incorporate words from many sources. Most people know the powerful influence that Greek and Latin have had on English. But English has also made use of words from many other parts of the world.

As *borrowed* (or *guest*) *words* enter English from other languages, they often undergo modification, especially when their original language has a different alphabet. In some cases, spelling oddities, such as the *b* in *debt* (from Latin, *debitum*), signal the remnants of a word's origin. A borrowed word in Unit 4 is *pundit*, from the Hindi *pandit*. World War II soldiers brought home the Chinese term *gung ho*, which means

"enthusiastically dedicated." Russian has lent us the word *mammoth* (from *mamot*), which means "huge." Turkish has given us the term *yogurt* (from *yoghurt*). Farsi—the language of Iran—has donated the word *shawl* (*shal*). Bantu, an African language, is the source of the noun *banjo* (from *mbanza*). Arawak, a Caribbean tongue, shares with us *iguana* (from *iwana*); and Wolof, a language of Senegal, contributes *banana*.

The common green iguana is found from Mexico southward to Brazil.

In Column A below are 8 more words borrowed from various languages. With or without a dictionary, match each word with its meaning in Column B.

Column A	Column B
<u>h</u> **1.** amok (amuck)	**a.** unintelligible or incomprehensible language; complicated and seemingly purposeless activity (from Mandingo)
<u>d</u> **2.** boomerang	
<u>f</u> **3.** caucus	**b.** to express respect, submission; to show servile deference (from Chinese)
<u>b</u> **4.** kowtow	
<u>g</u> **5.** mufti	**c.** a prohibition excluding something from use or mention; forbidden (from Tongan)
<u>a</u> **6.** mumbo jumbo	
<u>c</u> **7.** taboo	**d.** a flat, curved stick that returns when thrown (from Dharuk)
<u>e</u> **8.** tycoon	
	e. a powerful, highly successful business person (from Japanese)
	f. a closed meeting of members of a political party (from Algonquian)
	g. civilian dress, especially when worn by someone who usually wears a uniform (from Arabic)
	h. in a frenzy of violence; in a blind, undisciplined manner (from Malay)

Definitions

Note carefully the spelling, pronunciation, part(s) of speech, and definition(s) of each of the following words. Then write the word in the blank space(s) in the illustrative sentence(s) following. Finally, study the lists of synonyms and antonyms given at the end of each entry.

1. acumen
(a kyü′ mən)

(*n.*) keenness of insight; quickness or accuracy of judgment

Stars who enjoy long careers generally choose their roles with remarkable _____ **acumen** _____ .

SYNONYMS: perspicacity, shrewdness, acuity
ANTONYMS: ignorance, stupidity, obtuseness

2. adjudicate
(ə jüd′ i kāt)

(*v.*) to act as judge in a matter; to settle through the use of a judge or legal tribunal

An arbitrator may sometimes _____ **adjudicate** _____ a civil suit involving a relatively small sum of money.

SYNONYMS: arbitrate, referee, mediate

3. anachronism
(ə nak′ rə niz əm)

(*n.*) a chronological misplacing of events, objects, customs, or persons in regard to each other

To avoid introducing _____ **anachronisms** _____ into their work, authors of historical novels must do painstaking research.

SYNONYM: chronological error

4. apocryphal
(ə pok′ rə fəl)

(*adj.*) of doubtful or questionable authenticity

Although his tales of youthful derring-do are probably _____ **apocryphal** _____ , they are very entertaining.

SYNONYMS: fictitious, mythical, spurious, bogus
ANTONYMS: authentic, genuine, true

5. disparity
(dis par′ ə tē)

(*n.*) a difference or inequality in age, rank, degree, amount, or quality; a dissimilarity, unlikeness

The growing _____ **disparity** _____ between the rich and the poor is a matter of grave concern.

SYNONYMS: discrepancy, incongruity
ANTONYMS: similarity, likeness, congruity

6. dissimulate
(di sim′ yə lāt)

(*v.*) to hide or disguise one's true thoughts, feelings, or intentions

In awkward social situations, it is sometimes more courteous to _____ **dissimulate** _____ than to be straightforward.

SYNONYMS: dissemble, pretend, misrepresent
ANTONYM: reveal

7. empirical
(em pir′ i kəl)

(*adj.*) derived from, dependent upon, or guided by practical experience, observation, or experiment, rather than by theory; so verifiable

The compilation of _____ empirical _____ data is an essential part of sound scientific research.

SYNONYMS: observed, experiential, pragmatic
ANTONYMS: theoretical, hypothetical, conjectural

8. flamboyant
(flam boi′ ənt)

(*adj.*) highly elaborate or ornate; vividly colored; strikingly brilliant or bold

We were dazzled by the _____ flamboyant _____ plumage of the birds in the tropical rain forest.

SYNONYMS: showy, ostentatious, florid
ANTONYMS: staid, sedate, decorous, seemly, sober

9. fulsome
(fùl′ səm)

(*adj.*) offensively insincere or excessive; disgusting, sickening

It is best to take the _____ fulsome _____ praise that appears in movie ads with a grain of salt.

SYNONYMS: inordinate, repulsive
ANTONYMS: understated, muted, restrained, agreeable

10. immolate
(im′ ə lāt)

(*v.*) to kill as a sacrifice, especially by fire; to destroy or renounce for the sake of another

When the Aztecs took captives, they enslaved some and _____ immolated _____ others.

SYNONYMS: slay, kill
ANTONYMS: save, rescue, preserve

11. imperceptible
(im pər sep′ tə bəl)

(*adj.*) extremely slight; incapable of being perceived by the senses or the mind

When two candidates agree on most issues, voters may find the differences between them _____ imperceptible _____.

SYNONYMS: minimal, undetectable
ANTONYMS: conspicuous, noticeable, flagrant

12. lackey
(lak′ ē)

(*n.*) a uniformed male servant; a servile follower

A wealthy Victorian household generally included numerous maids, _____ lackeys _____, and other domestics.

SYNONYMS: footman, toady, flunky, hanger-on
ANTONYMS: lord, liege, employer, boss

13. liaison
(lē′ ə zon)

(*n.*) the contact or means of communication between groups; someone acting as such a contact; any close relationship; a thickening or binding agent used in cooking

Block associations serve as _____ liaisons _____ between neighborhoods and city governments.

SYNONYMS: intermediary, channel

14. monolithic
(mon ə lith′ ik)

(*adj.*) characterized by massiveness, solidity, and total uniformity

The government buildings in the state's capital can best be described as _____ monolithic _____ in style.
SYNONYMS: undifferentiated, massive, dense
ANTONYMS: diversified, variform, multifarious

15. mot juste
(mō zhüst')

(*n.*) the most suitable or exact word or expression

The erudite film and theater critic always managed to find the _____ mot juste _____ to sum up her opinion.
SYNONYM: right word
ANTONYMS: misnomer, misusage, malapropism

16. nihilism
(nī' əl iz əm)

(*n.*) a total rejection of existing laws, institutions, and moral values; extreme radicalism

Those who rebel against the restraints imposed by society may be attracted to _____ nihilism _____.
ANTONYM: conservatism

17. patrician
(pə trish' ən)

(*n.*) a member of the ruling class; a person of high or noble rank or of prominent social standing; (*adj.*) belonging to, befitting, or characteristic of such a person

Though her origins were humble, she had the assurance and bearing of a _____ patrician _____.

Many scions of _____ patrician _____ families feel obliged to choose a life of public service.
SYNONYMS: (*n.*) aristocrat, peer, noble; (*adj.*) highborn
ANTONYMS: (*n.*) peasant, commoner, plebeian

18. propitiate
(prō pish' ē āt)

(*v.*) to make someone or something favorably inclined toward oneself; to conciliate, satisfy, or appease

Many ancient peoples practiced rituals involving offerings and sacrifices to _____ propitiate _____ their gods.
SYNONYMS: placate, mollify
ANTONYMS: estrange, alienate, provoke, annoy

19. sic
(sik)

(*adv.*) thus so; intentionally written so

The American poet e.e. cummings [_____ sic _____] paid close attention to the way his poems looked when set in type.

20. sublimate
(səb' lə māt)

(*v.*) to redirect the energy of a biological or instinctual impulse into a higher or more acceptable channel

If we are to live in harmony with one another, we must learn to _____ sublimate _____ our aggressive impulses.
SYNONYMS: rechannel, elevate

Completing the Sentence

From the words for this unit, choose the one that best completes each of the following sentences. Write the word in the space provided.

1. The company's profits increased remarkably last year, thanks mainly to the new president's exceptional business _____**acumen**_____.

2. Although these stories have been widely accepted for many years, we now have ample evidence to show that they are completely _____**apocryphal**_____.

3. Then she leaned toward me and said confidingly, "Between you and I [_____**sic**_____], I didn't believe a word he said."

4. As the duke's coach drew up, two _____**lackeys**_____ in splendid livery stepped forth to open the carriage door.

5. The fate of individuals accused of war crimes may be _____**adjudicated**_____ by an international court.

6. The able auctioneer acknowledged bids from the audience that were so discreet as to be _____**imperceptible**_____ to the untrained eye.

7. What a shock it was for her to discover the unworthiness of the cause for which she had _____**immolated**_____ her youth, her talents, and her hopes of happiness.

8. We need not try actively to _____**propitiate**_____ the opponents of our candidate, but we can certainly take reasonable precautions to avoid antagonizing them.

9. During the campaign in West Virginia in 1861, Robert E. Lee acted as the _____**liaison**_____ between the commanders of the two independent Confederate brigades operating in the area.

10. Though I believed their promises at first, I soon came to realize the great _____**disparity**_____ between their words and their deeds.

11. It is one thing to spin out ingenious theories; it is quite another to find _____**empirical**_____ confirmation for them.

12. I know you're trying to curry favor with the boss, but must you greet each and every one of his bright ideas with such _____**fulsome**_____ flattery?

13. In calling them "stinkers," I may not have been too refined; but in view of their disgraceful conduct, I think I applied the _____**mot juste**_____.

14. The aggressive drive can be channeled into antisocial forms of behavior or _____**sublimated**_____ into loftier, more worthwhile endeavors.

15. A major political party in the United States represents a coalition of many different views and interests, rather than a(n) _____**monolithic**_____ structure.

16. His efforts to _____**dissimulate**_____ his feelings of inadequacy by pretending to be bored and indifferent are a sign of immaturity.

17. Having the Civil War general sign documents with a ballpoint pen struck me as the most ludicrous _____**anachronism**_____ in the whole miniseries.

18. During the early years of the Roman Republic, plebeians vied bitterly with _____ patricians _____ for political dominance.

19. Their blanket rejection of the standards and values on which our society is founded seems to be little short of senseless _____ nihilism _____ .

20. One would expect such _____ flamboyant _____ behavior from an attention-seeking celebrity, not from a normally shy, unassuming person.

Synonyms *Choose the word from this unit that is **the same** or **most nearly the same** in meaning as the **boldface** word or expression in the given phrase. Write the word on the line provided.*

1. letters that proved to be **spurious** _____ apocryphal _____

2. based on **experiential** evidence _____ empirical _____

3. surrounded by **flunkies** _____ lackeys _____

4. sustained **minimal** damage _____ imperceptible _____

5. learned to **rechannel** their impulses _____ sublimate _____

6. known for wearing **showy** outfits _____ flamboyant _____

7. has a tendency to **dissemble** _____ dissimulate _____

8. sought to **placate** their supervisor _____ propitiate _____

9. embarrassed by the **inordinate** thanks _____ fulsome _____

10. a group of **undifferentiated** structures _____ monolithic _____

11. called to **mediate** the dispute _____ adjudicate _____

12. an **intermediary** we can rely on _____ liaison _____

13. said it was a pitty [**thus so**] _____ sic _____

14. sought the **right word** with which to end the speech _____ mot juste _____

15. filled with **chronological errors** _____ anachronisms _____

Antonyms *Choose the word from this unit that is **most nearly opposite** in meaning to the **boldface** word or expression in the given phrase. Write the word on the line provided.*

16. descended from **peasants** _____ patricians _____

17. acted with surprising **ignorance** _____ acumen _____

18. a group that espouses **conservatism** _____ nihilism _____

19. a plan to **rescue** the hostages _____ immolate _____

20. the **similarities** between their stories _____ disparities _____

Choosing the Right Word

*Circle the **boldface** word that more satisfactorily completes each of the following sentences.*

1. The main character in the comedy is a bumbling inventor who has accidentally transported himself into the past, there to suffer the misadventures of a hapless (**lackey, anachronism**).

2. When you say that your rival has a talent for (**disparity, dissimulation**), what you really mean is that he is an out-and-out phony.

3. The story about Bunker Hill and "Don't fire until you see the whites of their eyes" may be (**monolithic, apocryphal**), but I like it, and I'm going to continue believing it.

4. While I agree that there are imperfections in our society, I simple cannot accept your (**imperceptible, nihilistic**) belief that the entire heritage of the past must be discarded.

5. There seemed no point in the author's gratuitous use of such (**fulsome, apocryphal**) language other than to offend the taste of the reader.

6. She is so concerned with words that she seems to think the only thing that is needed to deal with a problem is to find the (**mot juste, anachronism**) to describe it.

7. There is probably nothing worse than having (**patrician, apocryphal**) tastes on an income better suited to the lifestyle of a pauper.

8. People who engage in self-destructive behavior seem to have a desire to (**propitiate, immolate**) themselves.

9. There is often a (**liaison, disparity**) between what people aspire to do and what they are equipped to do by natural endowment and training.

10. It's no wonder he's got such a swelled head when all those (**patricians, lackeys**) that tag along after him do nothing but sing his praises.

11. Those solemn religious ceremonies are intended to protect the tribe from disasters by (**propitiating, adjudicating**) the gods who control natural phenomena.

12. Some psychologists theorize that genius in any field represents a special kind of (**immolation, sublimation**) of capacities, drives, and needs that are in all of us.

13. American voters may be amused by a (**patrician, flamboyant**) personality, but they seem to prefer more sober types when making their choice for high public office.

14. Because deadly carbon monoxide gas can be neither seen nor smelled, its presence is practically (**empirical, imperceptible**).

15. In a campaign speech the candidate said, "My opponent has flaunted (**[sic], mot juste**) all of the principles of sound fiscal management."

16. We are not suggesting that students should run the school, but we believe that the administration should maintain a (**nihilism, liaison**) with the students.

17. No country can survive the combined threat of foreign invasion and domestic insurrection unless it is governed by leaders possessing extraordinary political (**acumen, disparity**).

18. Though Plato's approach to philosophy often seems somewhat mystical, Aristotle's is decidedly (**empirical, fulsome**).

19. In a pluralistic democracy, such as the United States, there is little chance that a (**flamboyant, monolithic**) public opinion will ever develop on any controversial issue.

20. When a small sum is involved, the cost of (**adjudication, dissimulation**) can exceed the amount of the award.

*Read the following passage, in which some of the words you have studied in this unit appear in **boldface** type. Then complete each statement given below the passage by circling the letter of the item that is **the same** or **almost the same** in meaning as the highlighted word.*

(Line)

Who Got Here First?

Who were the first Americans? Where did they come from, and how and when did they get here? For a long time, the archaeological community accepted a seemingly **monolithic** body of **empirical** evidence supporting the theory that the earliest Americans were Siberian hunters who crossed the dry
(5) land bridge at the Bering Strait at the close of the last ice age, around 11,500 years ago. This conclusion was based on unique stone projectile points found near Clovis, New Mexico, which date from that time.

Now, however, a growing body of evidence
(10) presents certain **disparities** that cast doubt upon this theory. Recent discoveries indicate that the first Americans may have arrived much earlier, by different routes, and from different parts of the world.

(15) Primarily responsible for the change in thinking are two intriguing finds: a pre-Clovis camp in Monte Verde, Chile, and a male skeleton found in Washington State that bears little resemblance to the skeletons of Siberian
(20) origin. These discoveries, and those of pre-Clovis artifacts found in several eastern states, have given rise to new theories.

One theory attempts to explain the early dates of the Chilean site by suggesting that people
(25) migrated down the Pacific coast in skin-covered

Pre-Clovis wooden digging stick, about 12,230 years old, found at Monte Verde

boats. Another tries to explain the early dates of the East Coast sites by suggesting that early Europeans sailed close to the coasts of Greenland and Iceland to cross the North Atlantic. A third theory proposes that people from Southeast Asia went to Australia first and then crossed the Pacific to South America.

(30) Some of these new theories may eventually prove to be **apocryphal**. But the ongoing debate is lively and sometimes heated. It is an exciting time indeed to be an archaeologist.

---

1. The meaning of **monolithic** (line 3) is
a. diversified   c. genuine
(b.) massive   d. suspicious

2. Empirical (line 3) most nearly means
a. statistical   c. circumstantial
b. theoretical   (d.) observed

3. Disparities (line 10) is best defined as
(a.) incongruities   c. similarities
b. indications   d. details

4. The meaning of **apocryphal** (line 30) is
a. ridiculous   (c.) bogus
b. authentic   d. intriguing

Definitions

Note carefully the spelling, pronunciation, part(s) of speech, and definition(s) of each of the following words. Then write the word in the blank space(s) in the illustrative sentence(s) following. Finally, study the lists of synonyms and antonyms given at the end of each entry.

1. apostate
(ə pos′ tāt)

(*n.*) one who forsakes his or her religion, party, or cause

A politician who switches parties can expect to be denounced by former allies as an _____**apostate**_____.

SYNONYMS: renegade, defector, turncoat
ANTONYMS: true believer, loyalist

2. bravado
(brə vä′ dō)

(*n.*) a display of false or assumed courage

The challenger's boast that he would knock the champ out in the first round was sheer _____**bravado**_____.

SYNONYMS: swagger, bluster, braggadocio
ANTONYMS: mettle, bravery, pluck

3. consensus
(kən sen′ səs)

(*n.*) a collective or general agreement of opinion, feeling, or thinking

After an unusually contentious debate, the council finally reached a _____**consensus**_____.

SYNONYMS: unanimity, concord, accord, harmony
ANTONYMS: dissension, discord, disagreement

4. constrict
(kən strikt′)

(*v.*) to make smaller or narrower, draw together, squeeze; to stop or cause to falter

An accident or road repairs can _____**constrict**_____ the flow of traffic on a busy highway.

SYNONYMS: contract, curb, restrain
ANTONYMS: enlarge, dilate, expand

5. dichotomy
(dī kot′ ə mē)

(*n.*) a division into two contradictory or mutually exclusive parts; a branching or forking in an ancestral line

Many of the world's great works of literature examine the _____**dichotomy**_____ between good and evil.

SYNONYMS: schism, division, bifurcation
ANTONYMS: uniformity, oneness

6. effusive
(i fyü′ siv)

(*adj.*) highly demonstrative; unrestrained

I received such an _____**effusive**_____ welcome from my hosts that I felt like the party's guest of honor.

SYNONYMS: gushy, lavish
ANTONYMS: restrained, reserved, muted, subdued

7. euphoria
(yü fôr′ ē ə)

(*n.*) a feeling of great happiness or well-being, often with no objective basis

It is perfectly normal for a person who wins the lottery to feel an initial surge of _____**euphoria**_____.

SYNONYMS: elation, bliss, ecstasy, rapture
ANTONYMS: melancholy, depression, gloom

8. gothic
(goth′ ik)

(*adj.*) characterized by or emphasizing a gloomy setting and grotesque or violent events; such a literary or artistic style; a type of medieval architecture

In many a _____**gothic**_____ novel, the life of the brooding protagonist is blighted by a dark secret.

SYNONYMS: sinister, eerie

9. impasse
(im′ pas)

(*n.*) a dead end; a position from which there is no escape; a problem to which there is no solution

When negotiations reached an _____**impasse**_____, the workers went out on strike.

SYNONYMS: deadlock, standoff, stalemate

10. lugubrious
(lù gü′ brē əs)

(*adj.*) sad, mournful, or gloomy, especially to an exaggerated or ludicrous degree

The clown's _____**lugubrious**_____ face, complete with a painted teardrop, never fails to make the audience laugh.

SYNONYMS: doleful, melancholy, dismal, dolorous
ANTONYMS: merry, jovial, hilarious, funny

11. metamorphosis
(met ə môr′ fə sis)

(*n.*) a complete transformation, as if by magic

The beauty makeovers that we sometimes see on talk shows are a kind of _____**metamorphosis**_____.

SYNONYMS: change, makeover

12. mystique
(mi stēk′)

(*n.*) an aura or attitude of mystery or veneration surrounding something or someone

A _____**mystique**_____ still clings to some of the great movie stars of the past.

SYNONYMS: charisma

13. non sequitur
(non sek′ wi tər)

(*n.*) an inference or conclusion that does not follow logically from the facts or premises

When it was the next debater's turn, he confounded us with an argument undermined by _____**non sequiturs**_____.

SYNONYMS: illogical reference, unsound conclusion

14. parlous
(pär' ləs)

(*adj.*) full of danger or risk, perilous

In a televised speech, the president warned the nation that it faced _____ parlous _____ times.

SYNONTMS: hazardous, risky, dangerous
ANTONYMS: safe, secure, risk-free

15. punctilio
(pəŋk til' ē ō)

(*n.*) a minute detail of conduct or procedure; an instant of time

The mark of a true perfectionist is the need to check each and every _____ punctilio _____ personally.

SYNONYMS: fine point, nicety

16. quagmire
(kwag' mīr)

(*n.*) soft, soggy mud or slush; a difficult or entrapping situation

After a week of heavy rain, the farmer's fields were reduced to a _____ quagmire _____.

SYNONYMS: fen, marsh, bog, morass
ANTONYMS: bedrock, solid footing, terra firma

17. quixotic
(kwik sot' ik)

(*adj.*) extravagantly or romantically idealistic; visionary without regard to practical considerations

Utopian fiction presents _____ quixotic _____ fantasies of ideal social orders.

SYNONYMS: fanciful, impractical, utopian
ANTONYMS: realistic, down-to-earth, pragmatic

18. raconteur
(rak on tər')

(*n.*) a person who tells stories and anecdotes with great skill

The author, a noted _____ raconteur _____, was much sought after as a dinner party guest.

SYNONYMS: storyteller, anecdotist

19. sine qua non
(sin ə kwä nōn')

(*n.*) an essential or indispensable element or condition

The _____ sine qua non _____ for a successful paty is a group of interesting and sociable guests.

SYNONYMS: necessity, requisite, desideratum

20. vendetta
(ven det' ə)

(*n.*) a prolonged feud, often between two families, characterized by retaliatory acts of revenge; any act motivated by vengeance

The two novelists, once good friends, have been carrying on a literary _____ vendetta _____ for more than two decades.

SYNONYMS: blood feud, rivalry

Completing the Sentence

From the words for this unit, choose the one that best completes each of the following sentences. Write the word in the space provided.

1. Every great president must combine various roles—the practical politician, the masterful intellectual, the tough administrator, the persuasive advocate—and at least a touch of the _____ **quixotic** _____ visionary.

2. Although it may be true that hard work does not guarantee success, it is certainly a(n) _____ **sine qua non** _____ for doing well in any endeavor.

3. His challenge to fight was pure _____ **bravado** _____; inwardly he hoped that no one would take him on.

4. It took Rome centuries to achieve the miraculous _____ **metamorphosis** _____ from a minor city-state on the banks of the Tiber to the leading power in the Mediterranean world.

5. One look at the coach's _____ **lugubrious** _____ expression, and I knew that all our misgivings about the outcome of the game had been borne out.

6. Modern military power requires great industrial resources, but to conclude from this that industrialized nations are inherently militaristic is a _____ **non sequitur** _____.

7. To achieve an hourglass figure, fashionable ladies of the nineteenth century employed tight-fitting corsets to _____ **constrict** _____ their waistlines.

8. Hemingway's *Death in the Afternoon* offers a rare insight into the _____ **mystique** _____ of the bullring and the attitudes that surround that ancient blood sport.

9. Not until later did I realize that their _____ **effusive** _____ expressions of interest in our welfare were insincere and self-serving.

10. The police investigation established that the victim was not an innocent bystander but the target of a gangland _____ **vendetta** _____.

11. When he came to the throne, Julian the _____ **Apostate** _____ renounced Christianity and began a vigorous campaign to reestablish paganism as the official religion of the Roman Empire.

12. You cannot duck your responsibility for negotiating an agreement simply by announcing that you have reached a hopeless _____ **impasse** _____.

13. As the disappointing results of the poll filtered in, the candidate sank into a(n) _____ **quagmire** _____ of doubts about the future.

14. Each episode in the silent-movie serial *The Perils of Pauline* ended with the heroine facing another _____ **parlous** _____ predicament.

15. The mood of _____ **euphoria** _____ brought about by our extraordinary good fortune caused us to relax our usual alertness.

16. Though everyone in our club agreed that we had a problem, there was no group _____ **consensus** _____ on how to solve it.

17. The rugged landscape, with the severe vertical lines of the mountains in the background, lent an air of _____ **gothic** _____ gloom to the entire scene.

18. How can you concern yourself with the _____ **punctilio** _____ of protocol when your whole world is collapsing about your ears?

19. The speakers said that they could see little hope for world peace unless something could be done to bridge the _____ **dichotomy** _____ between the "have" and the "have-not" nations.

20. The man was a skilled _____ **raconteur** _____ whose repertory of amusing anecdotes was seemingly inexhaustible.

Synonyms

*Choose the word from this unit that is **the same** or **most nearly the same** in meaning as the **boldface** word or expression in the given phrase. Write the word on the line provided.*

1. attend to each **fine point** myself — punctilio

2. **fanciful** plans for solving the problem — quixotic

3. an extremely **risky** undertaking — parlous

4. unable to break the **deadlock** — impasse

5. the glaring **division** between wealth and poverty — dichotomy

6. waged a **blood feud** for generations — vendetta

7. an **eerie** story of betrayal and madness — gothic

8. heaped **lavish** praise upon the performance — effusive

9. a **storyteller** without equal — raconteur

10. was not deceived by my opponent's **bluster** — bravado

11. stuck in the **bog** — quagmire

12. has a certain **charisma** — mystique

13. a **requisite** for good health — sine qua non

14. underwent a truly remarkable **transformation** — metamorphosis

15. a series of **unsound conclusions** — non sequiturs

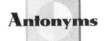

Antonyms

*Choose the word from this unit that is **most nearly opposite** in meaning to the **boldface** word or expression in the given phrase. Write the word on the line provided.*

16. overcome by **melancholy** when I heard the news — euphoria

17. a meeting that ended in **discord** — consensus

18. sang a **merry** ballad — lugubrious

19. caused the vessels to **dilate** — constrict

20. has a reputation for being a **loyalist** — apostate

Choosing the Right Word

*Circle the **boldface** word that more satisfactorily completes each of the following sentences.*

1. Even though their son had abandoned the religion in which he had been brought up, his parents never thought of him as an (**apostate,** impasse).

2. I wanted a direct, factual explanation of what had happened, but all I got was emotional (**effusions,** quagmires) describing in painful detail how much they had suffered.

3. For a long time we lived under the illusion that "everything would come out all right," but inevitably we arrived at the (vendetta, **impasse**) where we had to face realities.

4. Our thesis was that at this stage in their history, Americans must eschew the (sine qua non, **mystique**) of force and violence and develop new ideals of social cooperation.

5. Their analysis of the problem seemed to me extremely fallacious—full of false assumptions, dubious generalizations, and (constrictions, **non sequiturs**).

6. There are times when I like to read a (**gothic,** parlous) tale of gloomy castles, mysterious strangers, and unhappy romances.

7. Space suits are designed to afford astronauts maximum protection without unduly (**constricting,** dichotomizing) their freedom of movement.

8. Perhaps her volunteering to undertake the mission was mere (**bravado,** consensus), but the fact remains that she did accomplish everything that was expected of her.

9. As we learned to understand each other's needs and aspirations, a sort of unspoken (**consensus,** impasse) developed that enabled us to work together harmoniously.

10. It is impossible for me to convey the intensity of emotion that I felt at that (lugubrious, **euphoric**) moment when I learned I had won the scholarship.

11. There is no point in trying to decide exactly which of the factors is most important for victory in the election; every one of them is a (non sequitur, **sine qua non**).

12. The ordeal of the Civil War (apostasized, **metamorphosed**) Lincoln from an obscure small-town lawyer into a historical personality of universal appeal.

13. Does it seem paradoxical that like many other great comedians, she goes about with a characteristically (**lugubrious,** quixotic) expression on her face?

14. Despite the grave risks that the rescue attempt would entail, there was no shortage of volunteers for the (**parlous,** effusive) undertaking.

15. Very few of the world's problems can be understood in terms of a simple (euphoria, **dichotomy**) of right and wrong.

16. The new assistant dean's adherence to every (mystique, **punctilio**) in the Student Code alienated both the faculty and the student body.

17. In *Romeo and Juliet*, the hero's tragic death comes as the result of a long-standing (**vendetta,** bravado) between his family and Juliet's.

18. Though your efforts to enact a program of ecological reform in the face of strong opposition were (**quixotic,** gothic) and doomed to failure, they were inspiring.

19. It's laughable of you to think that you are an accomplished (**raconteur,** apostate) just because you have memorized an assortment of feeble old jokes.

20. Involvement in the long war in Vietnam led the United States into a (consensus, **quagmire**) from which it was extremely difficult to withdraw.

Vocabulary in Context

*Read the following passage, in which some of the words you have studied in this unit appear in **boldface** type. Then complete each statement given below the passage by circling the letter of the item that is **the same** or **almost the same** in meaning as the highlighted word.*

The Erie Canal

(Line)

Skeptics called the idea **quixotic**. Critics called it "Clinton's big ditch." But DeWitt Clinton, the governor of New York, ignored them all. He successfully pushed for building a canal that would connect New York City with the Great Lakes.

Construction began in 1817. Despite predictions that the canal would prove to be a **quagmire**, the project proceeded smoothly. Parts of the Erie Canal were (5) operating as early as 1820. When it was fully completed in 1825, at a cost of $7 million, the canal linked the Hudson River with Buffalo on Lake Erie. The waterway was 40 feet wide, 4 feet (10) deep, and 363 miles long— 335 miles longer than any other canal in the country.

Euphoria greeted the canal's completion. (15) Celebrations took place in New York City and Buffalo. River towns boomed. Goods from the South and West could be shipped (20)

Boats were drawn along the Erie Canal by horses on the towpath.

east faster and cheaper than ever before. And as quickly and inexpensively as the canal brought western goods east, it took immigrants west to the frontier. Only the canal's width and depth **constricted** traffic, but these dimensions were soon increased. The Erie Canal was a huge success, and New York City emerged as the port through which every major trade route passed. (25)

The sharp drop in travel times and in costs quickly got the attention of government officials. The **consensus** was that canal building was in order, and by 1849, 3300 miles of canals crossed the Northeast and Midwest. But a new, faster, and cheaper form of transportation was on the rise: the railroad. The heyday of canals was over. (30)

---

1. The meaning of **quixotic** (line 1) is
a. impractical   c. difficult
b. pragmatic   d. costly

2. Quagmire (line 5) most nearly means
a. bonanza   c. morass
b. mistake   d. bore

3. Euphoria (line 14) is best defined as
a. depression   c. elation
b. annoyance   d. fear

4. The meaning of **constricted** (line 23) is
a. expanded   c. slowed
b. policed   d. restrained

5. Consensus (line 27) most nearly means
a. agreement   c. discord
b. decision   d. proposal

Note carefully the spelling, pronunciation, part(s) of speech, and definition(s) of each of the following words. Then write the word in the blank space(s) in the illustrative sentence(s) following. Finally, study the lists of synonyms and antonyms given at the end of each entry.

Definitions

1. apposite
(ap′ ə zit)

(*adj.*) appropriate; suitable; apt

I did my best to give an _____**apposite**_____ answer to each of the interviewer's questions.

SYNONYMS: relevant, pertinent, material, germane
ANTONYMS: irrelevant, immaterial, inappropriate

2. augur
(ô′ ger)

(*n.*) a prophet or seer; (*v.*) to predict, foreshadow

The old man who lived alone in the forest was believed by the villagers to be a(n) _____**augur**_____.

The news did not _____**augur**_____ well for the health of the economy in the short term.

SYNONYMS: (*n.*) oracle; (*v.*) bode

3. bilk
(bilk)

(*v.*) to defraud, cheat, or swindle; to evade payment of; to frustrate, thwart

There will always be people who are only too ready to _____**bilk**_____ credulous individuals.

SYNONYMS: dupe, cozen

4. charisma
(kə riz′ mə)

(*n.*) the special personal magnetism that makes an individual exceptionally appealing to other people; a divinely bestowed gift or power

According to leading pundits, the dynamic young politician has the _____**charisma**_____ of a born leader.

SYNONYMS: appeal, charm, mystique

5. debilitate
(di bil′ ə tāt)

(*v.*) to make weak or feeble

Illness _____**debilitated**_____ the patient so severely that she was no longer able to perform even the simplest everyday chores.

SYNONYMS: enervate, sap, exhaust, enfeeble
ANTONYMS: strengthen, fortify, invigorate

6. execrable
(ek′ si krə bəl)

(*adj.*) utterly detestable, hateful, or abhorrent; extremely inferior

The crude and _____**execrable**_____ behavior of a few individuals spoiled the evening for the rest of us.

SYNONYMS: odious, abominable, reprehensible
ANTONYMS: commendable, praiseworthy, meritorious

7. impinge
(im pinj′)

(v.) to strike against or collide with violently; to encroach or obtrude upon; to make an impression upon

Political forces sometimes _____**impinge**_____ on our everyday lives.

SYNONYMS: horn in, affect

8. labyrinth
(lab′ ə rinth)

(n.) a bewildering maze; any confusing or complicated situation

I quickly lost my way as I wandered through the old city's _____**labyrinth**_____ of winding streets.

SYNONYMS: tangle, mystery, enigma

9. narcissism
(när′ sə siz əm)

(n.) excessive self-love; absorption in oneself

Because of her _____**narcissism**_____, she was completely unwilling to listen to other people's opinions.

SYNONYMS: egotism, conceit, vanity, amour propre

10. niggardly
(nig′ ərd lē)

(adj.) stingy; meanly small or insufficient

The old miser was as _____**niggardly**_____ with his advice as he was with his money.

SYNONYMS: tightfisted, penny-pinching, mean
ANTONYMS: generous, bountiful, magnanimous

11. pastiche
(pas tēsh′)

(n.) a dramatic, musical, or literary work made up of bits and pieces from other sources; a hodgepodge

The figure skater performed to a _____**pastiche**_____ of melodies from *Carmen*.

SYNONYMS: medley, patchwork, melange, potpourri

12. precarious
(pri kâr′ ē əs)

(adj.) very uncertain or unsure; dangerous or risky

A long period of unemployment left my friend in a financially _____**precarious**_____ position.

SYNONYMS: perilous, dubious, ticklish
ANTONYMS: secure, safe, sturdy, firm

13. rapport
(ra pôr′)

(n.) a close and harmonious relationship

The players in a chamber music ensemble need to develop an excellent _____**rapport**_____.

SYNONYMS: bond, tie, affinity, understanding

14. utilitarian
(yü til ə târ′ ē ən)

(adj.) stressing practicality over other considerations; relating to the belief that what is good or desirable is determined purely by its usefulness

The layout and organization of the busy restaurant's small kitchen were strictly _____**utilitarian**_____.

SYNONYMS: practical, functional, pragmatic
ANTONYMS: nonfunctional, ornamental, decorative

15. vacuous
(vak' yü əs)

(*adj.*) devoid of matter, substance, or meaning; lacking ideas or intelligence; purposeless

From the _____ **vacuous** _____ expression on your face, no one would guess that you have such a sharp mind.

SYNONYMS: inane, insipid, fatuous, void, empty
ANTONYMS: incisive, trenchant, perceptive, intelligent

16. vagary
(vā' gə rē)

(*n.*) an unpredictable, erratic, or seemingly purposeless action, occurrence, or notion

Who can explain the _____ **vagaries** _____ of the world of high fashion?

SYNONYMS: caprice, whim, quirk

17. viable
(vī' ə bəl)

(*adj.*) capable of living or developing under normal circumstances

The mayor announced a _____ **viable** _____ plan to reduce traffic in the downtown business district.

SYNONYMS: practicable, workable, feasible
ANTONYMS: impracticable, unworkable, unfeasible

18. xenophobia
(zen ə fō' bē ə)

(*n.*) undue or unreasonable fear, hatred, or contempt of foreigners or strangers or of what is foreign or strange

It is sad when people who themselves were once newcomers to a land are blinded by _____ **xenophobia** _____ .

SYNONYMS: provinciality, parochialism, chauvinism

19. zany
(zā' nē)

(*adj.*) clownish or funny in a crazy, bizarre, or ludicrous way; (*n.*) one who plays the clown

Who doesn't love the _____ **zany** _____ antics of the Marx brothers?

In every sitcom, there is a goofy character who can best be described as a _____ **zany** _____ .

SYNONYMS: (*adj.*) comical, daffy; (*n.*) buffoon
ANTONYMS: (*adj.*) sedate, decorous, prim, sober, grave

20. zealot
(zel' ət)

(*n.*) a fanatical partisan; an ardent follower

When it comes to our school's hockey team, my brother can best be described as a _____ **zealot** _____ .

SYNONYMS: fanatic, extremist

Completing the Sentence

From the words for this unit, choose the one that best completes each of the following sentences. Write the word in the space provided.

1. Only after living and working in Washington for many years were we able to find our way through the vast _____**labyrinth**_____ of government departments and agencies.

2. When we asked the climbers why they wanted to scale the mountain, they gave the _____**apposite**_____ reply, "Because it's there."

3. His _____**vacuous**_____ remarks revealed how little he really knew about political economy.

4. Since the play is essentially a(n) _____**pastiche**_____ of devices and ideas drawn from many different sources, it lacks the consistency and cohesiveness of the writer's other works.

5. "Any organization that is able to survive and prosper in these trying times has indeed proven itself _____**viable**_____," she observed.

6. Instead of sentimentalizing about the passing of rural America, we must work to achieve an effective _____**rapport**_____ with our modern urban environment.

7. Luxury and self-indulgence _____**debilitated**_____ the once vigorous Roman people and led to the fall of the empire.

8. Some leaders have such great personal _____**charisma**_____ that they inspire an attitude akin to religious veneration in their followers.

9. Our party can use the support of ardent young _____**zealots**_____, but we also need the help of older and cooler heads.

10. We recognize the need for vigorous criticism in a political campaign, but we will certainly not tolerate that kind of _____**execrable**_____ character assassination.

11. Attacked from all sides by superior forces, the army found itself in a(n) _____**precarious**_____, if not totally untenable, position.

12. Although I am not one of the more prosperous members of the community, my contributions to charity are by no means _____**niggardly**_____.

13. We cannot say with any confidence how long this trip will take us because our progress is dependent upon the _____**vagaries**_____ of the weather.

14. Oscar Wilde's famous epigram that "Self-love is the beginning of a life-long romance" is a clever comment on _____**narcissism**_____.

15. Only later did we come to realize that there was a serious purpose behind his apparently frivolous remarks and _____**zany**_____ behavior.

16. I cannot accept a purely _____**utilitarian**_____ view of life that ignores such aspects of human experience as beauty, love, and humor.

17. By filing false claims over a period of many years, the pair attempted to _____**bilk**_____ the insurance company of large sums of money.

18. As I lay there, drifting off to sleep, suddenly the sound of a very loud, very raucous, and very obnoxious television commercial _____**impinged**_____ on my ears.

19. The fumble by our quarterback on the opening kickoff, followed by a 15-yard penalty against us, did not _____**augur**_____ well for our team.

20. Their consistent attitude of hostility toward any cultural tradition different from their own cannot be excused by calling it _____**xenophobia**_____ .

Synonyms

*Choose the word from this unit that is **the same** or **most nearly the same** in meaning as the **boldface** word or expression in the given phrase. Write the word on the line provided.*

1. a **patchwork** of other people's ideas — pastiche

2. results that **bode** well for our success — augur

3. **duped** the unsuspecting couple — bilked

4. subject to the **whims** of fortune — vagaries

5. has a reputation as a **fanatic** — zealot

6. could never be accused of **egotism** — narcissism

7. a disease that **enfeebles** those who contract it — debilitates

8. **relevant** to the matter being discussed — apposite

9. **obtrudes** on the rights of others — impinges

10. denounced their **odious** behavior — execrable

11. a **tangle** of rules and regulations — labyrinth

12. friends who have a unique **bond** — rapport

13. possesses undeniable **charm** — charisma

14. a strictly **functional** design — utilitarian

15. criticized the politician's **chauvinism** — xenophobia

Antonyms

*Choose the word from this unit that is **most nearly opposite** in meaning to the **boldface** word or expression in the given phrase. Write the word on the line provided.*

16. received a **generous** bequest — niggardly

17. concluded that the idea was **impracticable** — viable

18. surprised by her **decorous** behavior — zany

19. the commentator's **trenchant** remarks — vacuous

20. found ourselves in a **secure** position — precarious

Choosing the Right Word

Circle the **boldface** word that more satisfactorily completes each of the following sentences.

1. Because the speaker before me had defined the topic so narrowly, I had to revise my notes so that only (**apposite, precarious**) data remained.

2. His idea of (**zany, zealous**) behavior at a party is to wear a lampshade as if it were a hat.

3. Every president of our country should renew our determination to create a more (**precarious, viable**) political and social structure for the future.

4. Anyone who spends so many hours a day primping and preening in front of a mirror can only be considered a blatant (**narcissist, zealot**).

5. Although I had no desire to wander through a strange town on foot, I was reluctant to trust my person to the (**vagaries, rapports**) of those wild cab drivers.

6. Even while stressing, as we must, (**utilitarian, narcissistic**) goals, we cannot afford to ignore ethical and aesthetic values.

7. Education is a living process that requires above all a close (**charisma, rapport**) between teacher and student.

8. In condemning their (**apposite, execrable**) conduct, let us not assume that we ourselves are completely free of blame.

9. Their optimism is so unwavering and so all-encompassing that bad news simply fails to (**impinge, bilk**) on their confidence.

10. The disease had such a(n) (**debilitating, execrable**) effect upon her constitution that she was unable to return to work for almost a year.

11. How can you be so easily impressed by those (**vacuous, niggardly**) generalizations and clichés?

12. Succeeding in business is comparable, not to advancing along a straight line, but rather to finding one's way through an uncharted, (**labyrinthine, apposite**) passage.

13. It was the function of a Roman (**augur, zany**) to divine the will of the gods through the interpretation of various natural phenomena, including the flight of birds.

14. I have no sympathy for those who have allowed themselves to be (**impinged, bilked**) by such an obvious get-rich-quick scheme.

15. What we need now is not (**utilitarian, charismatic**) leadership, however inspiring, but steady, modest, and down-to-earth assistance in defining and achieving our goals.

16. True patriotism is a positive attitude, as contrasted with the negative orientation of (**charisma, xenophobia**).

17. When I had lived only a short time in that godforsaken part of the world, I began to realize just how (**vacuous, niggardly**) Nature could sometimes be in bestowing her bounty.

18. With so many rival claimants actively engaged in trying to depose him, the monarch knew that his hold on the throne was at best (**viable, precarious**).

19. A true work of art must be an integrated whole rather than a (**vagary, pastiche**) of discrete or incongruous elements.

20. Your (**xenophobic, zealous**) enthusiasm must be matched by training and discipline if you are to achieve anything worthwhile.

Vocabulary in Context

*Read the following passage, in which some of the words you have studied in this unit appear in **boldface** type. Then complete each statement given below the passage by circling the letter of the item that is **the same** or **almost the same** in meaning as the highlighted word.*

America's Game

(Line)

American football, like soccer and rugby, has its roots in a rough-and-tumble village-against-village game played in the Middle Ages. By the late nineteenth century, football began to look like the game we know today. The system of measured yardage and downs was introduced in 1882. A forward pass was first thrown in the early

(5) twentieth century. The first intercollegiate game was played in 1869, and professional teams were formed in the 1890s. By 1900, football was the country's most popular intercollegiate sport. With popularity, however, came controversy. There was widespread outrage over the game's

(10) violence. Even President Theodore Roosevelt called for change. To answer critics, university presidents formed the National Collegiate Athletic Association in 1906. This group established **viable** rules

(15) to decrease the violence.

Rival high school teams vie for a chance to compete for the state championship.

In the second half of the twentieth century, professional football's popularity soared, primarily because of television coverage. Electronic scoreboards,

(20) halftime extravaganzas, and sophisticated promotional techniques have broadened the game's appeal and made it even more of a spectacle. The Super Bowl, which determines the professional championship, is perhaps the country's most

(25) watched single athletic event, and college bowls are perennial favorites.

Football today is a big business. Its participants can enjoy huge financial rewards. But it remains a **precarious** game to play. Serious injuries can be as close as the next snap of the ball. Nevertheless, the game is played better than ever, and the players are bigger, stronger, and faster than ever.

(30) Many people complain that football has become too commercial. Many remain disturbed by its aggressiveness and the "win at all costs" approach of coaches and players. Nonetheless, the game continues to gain in popularity. Indeed, football has **impinged** upon baseball's claim as America's pastime. For football fans, after all, it's the game that counts, not the sport's **vagaries** or dangers.

---

1. The meaning of **viable** (line 14) is
a. feasible
b. stringent
c. unworkable
d. simple

2. Precarious (line 27) most nearly means
a. safe
b. enjoyable
c. risky
d. difficult

3. Impinged (line 33) is best defined as
a. stumbled
b. frowned
c. called
d. encroached

4. The meaning of **vagaries** (line 34) is
a. rules
b. quirks
c. scandals
d. finances

REVIEW UNITS 10–12

 Visit us at www.sadlier-oxford.com for interactive puzzles and games.

Analogies In each of the following, circle the item that best completes the comparison.

See pages T38–T46 for explanations of answers.

1. imperceptible is to **notice** as
a. intangible is to touch
b. insoluble is to discern
c. invisible is to sense
d. invariable is to foresee

2. gullible is to **bilk** as
a. valiant is to cow
b. confident is to perturb
c. docile is to lead
d. affluent is to impoverish

3. immolate is to **fire** as
a. pulverize is to dust
b. incinerate is to ashes
c. debilitate is to air
d. inundate is to water

4. xenophobe is to **strangers** as
a. miser is to money
b. narcissist is to self
c. misogynist is to women
d. glutton is to food

5. astute is to **acumen** as
a. indigent is to wealth
b. diplomatic is to tact
c. clumsy is to skill
d. vacuous is to intelligence

6. clown is to **zany** as
a. zealot is to patrician
b. showoff is to flamboyant
c. jester is to lugubrious
d. spy is to effusive

7. niggardly is to **tight fist** as
a. liberal is to open hand
b. quixotic is to green thumb
c. ethical is to light finger
d. execrable is to itching palm

8. parlous is to **danger** as
a. monolithic is to variety
b. precarious is to insecurity
c. fulsome is to restraint
d. quixotic is to practicality

9. judge is to **adjudicate** as
a. lawyer is to propitiate
b. bodyguard is to guide
c. doctor is to sublimate
d. champion is to defend

10. mot juste is to **apposite** as
a. non sequitur is to illogical
b. anachronism is to timely
c. malapropism is to accurate
d. sine qua non is to optional

Word Associations In each of the following groups, circle the word that is best defined or suggested by the given phrase.

1. wrapped in a mystery
a. dichotomy   b. charisma   c. mystique   d. impasse

2. "It seems like they've known each other forever!"
a. narcissism   b. rapport   c. quagmire   d. acumen

3. a magical transformation
a. metamorphosis   b. xenophobia   c. vagary   d. augur

4. an unpredictable event
a. vagary   b. bravado   c. xenophobia   d. vendetta

5. an official representing the local union at national headquarters
a. anachronism   b. consensus   c. liaison   d. apostate

6. a maze of underground passageways
a. consensus   b. labyrinth   c. non sequitur   d. punctilio

7. a bit of this and a bit of that
   a. nihilism   b. apostate   c. metamorphosis   (d. pastiche)

8. a novel abounding in blood, violence, and weird happenings
   a. fulsome   b. apocryphal   (c. gothic)   d. viable

9. a statement that is not logical
   (a. non sequitur)   b. sine qua non   c. mot juste   d. metamorphosis

10. reminiscent of the Oracle at Delphi
   a. punctilio   (b. augur)   c. patrician   d. lackey

11. a born storyteller
   a. charisma   b. dichotomy   c. bravado   (d. raconteur)

12. personal magnetism
   a. quixotic   b. disparity   c. euphoria   (d. charisma)

13. "Foreigners, go home!"
   (a. xenophobia)   b. impasse   c. narcissism   d. raconteur

Choosing the Right Meaning   *Read each sentence carefully. Then circle the item that best completes the statement below the sentence.*

See pages T38–T46 for explanations of answers.

As we drove into the storm we were greeted by a staccato drumming produced by marble-size hailstones impinging upon the rooftop of the car.   (2)

   1. In line 2 the phrase **impinging upon** most nearly means
     a. obtruding upon   b. encroaching upon   c. effecting   (d. striking)

Cosmologists who subscribe to the big bang theory believe that the explosion from which the universe emerged occurred at least 10 billion years ago but lasted only a punctilio.   (2)

   2. The best definition for the word **punctilio** in line 3 is
     a. nicety   b. fine point   c. detail   (d. instant)

Any chef who would venture to cook Asian dishes must be sure to have a supply of cornstarch, which is employed as a liaison in the preparation of many common sauces.   (2)

   3. The word **liaison** in line 2 is used to mean
     a. intermediary   b. channel   (c. thickener)   d. contact

A genealogy of the American Whig party would show a final dichotomy in the 1850s, one branch merging with the newly formed Republican party, the other with the soon-to-be-extinct Know-Nothing party.   (2)

   4. In line 1 the word **dichotomy** is used to mean
     (a. forking)   b. schism   c. bifurcation   d. union

Antonyms

*In each of the following groups, circle the word or expression that is most nearly the **opposite** of the word in **boldface** type.*

1. vacuous
a. incisive
b. cool
c. decisive
d. elderly

2. dissimulate
a. reveal
b. misrepresent
c. organize
d. disrupt

3. flamboyant
a. staid
b. obnoxious
c. harmless
d. immense

4. acumen
a. verbosity
b. sharpness
c. artfulness
d. obtuseness

5. constrict
a. reject
b. disturb
c. expand
d. divide

6. mot juste
a. harangue
b. benefit
c. malapropism
d. desideratum

7. consensus
a. survey
b. agreement
c. beginning
d. disagreement

8. quagmire
a. morass
b. defeat
c. bedrock
d. detour

9. debilitate
a. invigorate
b. enervate
c. remit
d. injure

10. zany
a. daffy
b. impromptu
c. decorous
d. complicated

11. monolithic
a. old-fashioned
b. trite
c. energetic
d. diversified

12. lugubrious
a. melancholy
b. hilarious
c. temporary
d. drowsy

13. niggardly
a. grasping
b. generous
c. uncomfortable
d. pensive

14. execrable
a. commendable
b. intentional
c. indisposed
d. intense

15. viable
a. wordy
b. truthful
c. unworkable
d. practical

16. fulsome
a. repulsive
b. enjoyable
c. complete
d. restrained

17. disparity
a. flaw
b. similarity
c. fusion
d. rationality

18. apposite
a. irrelevant
b. meek
c. mutual
d. similar

19. euphoria
a. charisma
b. narcissism
c. pastiche
d. melancholy

20. bravado
a. vigilance
b. kindness
c. bravery
d. swagger

Completing the Sentence

From the following list of words, choose the one that best completes each of the following sentences. Write the word in the space provided.

apocryphal   disparity   narcissism   quagmire
apposite   empirical   pastiche   raconteur

1. It is sometimes very difficult to tell where self-confidence leaves off and
_____narcissism_____ begins.

2. A _____pastiche_____ of old plots and new scandals, this soap opera has little chance of catching on with the viewing public.

3. My hypothesis is based solely on the _____empirical_____ data collected by reliable observers.

4. I was not pleased to learn that "Washington and the Cherry Tree" is a(n) _____apocryphal_____ story.

5. The wily politician hoped to avoid the _____quagmire_____ of controversial social issues in which his opponent had become inextricably mired.

Interesting Derivations

From the following list of words, choose the one that best completes each of the sentences below. Write the word in the space provided.

apostate	gothic	patrician	zany
augur	labyrinth	quixotic	zealot

1. The name applied to members of a radical, aggressive, and fanatically patriotic Jewish sect in first-century Palestine is the source of the English noun _____zealot_____.

2. The name of the barbarous and fearful Germanic tribe that suddenly swooped down on the Roman Empire during the third century A.D. is still preserved in the English adjective _____gothic_____.

3. The name of the elaborate complex of passageways and corridors built to house the Minotaur, the Cretan monster eventually slain by Theseus, gives us the English noun _____labyrinth_____.

4. *Gianni (Johnny),* the name usually given to one of the clowns or buffoons in the Italian *commedia dell'arte,* is probably the basis for the English adjective _____zany_____.

5. The name of the hero of Cervantes' famous novel, who was inspired by lofty but quite unobtainable goals, is the source of the English adjective _____quixotic_____.

Word Families

A. *On the line provided, write the word you have learned in Units 10–12 that is related to each of the following nouns.*

EXAMPLE: empiricist—**empirical**

1. apocrypha, apocryphalness	apocryphal
2. debilitation	debilitate
3. constriction, constrictor	constrict
4. viability	viable
5. monolith	monolithic
6. sublimation	sublimate
7. adjudication	adjudicate
8. precariousness	precarious
9. quixotism, quixotry	quixotic
10. impassibility	impasse
11. lugubriousness	lugubrious

12. disparateness ___disparity___

13. niggard ___niggardly___

14. nihilist ___nihilism___

15. impingement ___impinge___

B. *On the line provided, write the word you have learned in Units 10–12 that is related to each of the following verbs.*

EXAMPLE: metamorphose—**metamorphosis**

16. dichotomize ___dichotomy___

17. execrate ___execrable___

18. utilize ___utilitarian___

19. effuse ___effusive___

20. perceive ___imperceptible___

 **Two-Word Completions**

Circle the pair of words that best complete the meaning of each of the following passages.

See pages T38–T46 for explanations of answers.

1. When the representatives of labor and management found that they had reached a hopeless _____ in the negotiations for a new contract, they called in an outside mediator to help break the deadlock and _____ the dispute.
   a. liaison . . . impinge
   b. consensus . . . debilitate
   c. rapport . . . dissimulate
   d. impasse . . . adjudicate ⟵

2. As her _____ lover Aeneas fled her embraces in search of his destiny on the wild and desolate shores of Italy, distraught Queen Dido _____ herself on a huge pyre atop the highest building in Carthage.
   a. apocryphal . . . bilked
   b. fulsome . . . debilitated
   c. apostate . . . immolated ⟵
   d. execrable . . . adjudicated

3. Throughout the 18th and 19th centuries the great _____ houses of England were staffed by armies of servants and _____, but today it is impossible for a duke or earl to keep such a sizable domestic staff.
   a. patrician . . . lackeys ⟵
   b. monolithic . . . apostates
   c. gothic . . . zealots
   d. utilitarian . . . raconteurs

4. Some anecdotes about historical figures are clearly _____ because they contain _____ and other improbable elements that show the stories were written at a much later date.
   a. empirical . . . disparities
   b. apocryphal . . . anachronisms ⟵
   c. utilitarian . . . dichotomies
   d. apposite . . . non sequiturs

Read the following passage, in which some of the words you have studied in Units 10–12 appear in **boldface** type. Then complete each statement given below the passage by circling the item that is *the same* or *almost the same* in meaning as the highlighted word.

Humble Beginnings

(Line)

When Henry Hudson returned to Amsterdam in 1610, he informed investors that he had not found a river passage to the Pacific. But he did
(5) report that he sailed into a huge, deep harbor surrounded by rich land, a **sine qua non** for a fur-trading enterprise. Dutch merchants wasted no time. They sent six ships there in
(10) less than two years. Thus, the great city of New York began as a minor trading outpost in the vast Dutch mercantile empire.

For a small country, the Netherlands
(15) had big plans—all bottom-line oriented. It already had holdings in Asia, Africa, and South America. For the Dutch, the New Netherlands colony, headquartered at the foot of
(20) Manhattan, was a venture launched solely to make money for investors. It was managed by the Dutch West India Company. Peter Minuit arrived there to govern in 1626. He quickly
(25) "bought" the island from the Native Americans for goods worth about 60 guilders.

The colony grew slowly, settled by **patricians** through a system whereby
(30) land was deeded to them in return for bringing new settlers. The Dutch traded with the Native Americans, often **bilked** them, and made no effort to understand them. Worse, albeit
(35) inadvertently, they passed on diseases to which the Native Americans had no resistance.

Manhattan became a cosmopolitan place, home to some 2,000 people
(40) of many backgrounds and religions. But the Dutch forts were weak and no match for the four English warships that sailed into the harbor in 1664. The colony changed hands, becoming the
(45) property of the Duke of York, brother to King Charles II. Changes due to the takeover were largely **imperceptible**. The colony, now called New York, kept its multicultural identity, and
(50) continued to prosper. Although Dutch control lasted but forty years, its impact on the growth of New York as a commercial and cultural center is undeniable.

---

1. The meaning of **sine qua non** (line 7) is
  a. task
  (b. requisite)
  c. plan
  d. transformation

2. Patricians (line 29) most nearly means
  a. peasants
  b. farmers
  c. commoners
  (d. aristocrats)

3. Bilked (line 33) most nearly means
  (a. swindled)
  b. laughed at
  c. frustrated
  d. charmed

4. Imperceptible (line 47) is best defined as
  a. immediate
  (b. undetectable)
  c. obvious
  d. flagrant

chron—time

This Greek root appears in **anachronism** (page 117), which means "a misplacing in time of events, objects, customs, or persons in regard to each other." Some other words based on the same root are listed below.

chronically	**chronicler**	**chronology**	**crony**
chronicle	**chronological**	**chronometer**	**cronyism**

From the list of words above, choose the one that corresponds to each of the brief definitions below. Write the word in the blank space in the illustrative sentence below the definition.

1. arranged in order of time or occurrence; relating to or in keeping with the ordering of events in time

This discography is a ____chronological____ listing of all of the composer's recorded works.

2. one who writes or keeps a record of historical events

That magazine has long been regarded as an astute ____chronicler____ of fashion.

3. the determination of dates or of the sequence of events; the sequential ordering of dates and events; such a list or table

The CD-ROM provides an accurate ____chronology____ of key battles of the last century.

4. an exceptionally accurate clock, watch, or other timepiece

The marine biologist especially values her underwater ____chronometer____ when she dives.

5. a close friend or companion, chum

They planned an outing at the beach as a casual reunion of their old school ____cronies____.

6. constantly, habitually, over a prolonged period

Despite his responsibility as recording secretary, he is ____chronically____ late for meetings.

7. a record of historical events presented in order of occurrence; to make or keep such a record

Anne Frank's poignant ____chronicle____ of her years in hiding in an Amsterdam attic during World War II has been translated into scores of languages.

8. favoritism shown to old friends or companions in official or political appointments

The search committee accused the dean of ____cronyism____ in his recent appointments.

From the list of words on page 144, choose the one that best completes each of the following sentences. Write the word in the space provided.

1. Hopelessly poor and _____**chronically**_____ ill, the wretched man despaired of ever finding relief from his persistent suffering.

2. The retired senator enjoyed nothing more than to swap stories with a group of his old _____**cronies**_____.

3. The _____**chronometer**_____ was guaranteed not to deviate more than five seconds from the correct time over the course of a year.

4. Historians like Tacitus and Gibbon do not merely _____**chronicle**_____ events, but interpret their meaning and importance as well.

5. Students were given a list of important events in American history and asked to arrange them in correct _____**chronological**_____ order.

6. A Benedictine monk, whom we now call the Venerable Bede, was an important _____**chronicler**_____ of Christianity's growth in Anglo-Saxon England.

7. Police detectives drew up a _____**chronology**_____ to show in proper sequence the events leading up to the crime.

8. When the governor began to fill key administration posts with his old business pals, the press accused him of _____**cronyism**_____.

---

*Circle the **boldface** word that more satisfactorily completes each of the following sentences.*

1. Writers must decide whether to organize the facts in a paragraph in order of importance, in compare-and-contrast order, or in (**chronological,** **chronic**) order.

2. The patient's hospital chart includes a highly detailed (**chronometer,** **chronology**) of her responses to the prescribed course of treatment.

3. Most (**chronometers,** **chronicles**) rely on the vibrations of a quartz crystal to control the rate at which the time-indicating display moves.

4. I hadn't wanted to attend my twenty-fifth high school reunion, but when I reminisced with my old (**chroniclers,** **cronies**) at the dinner, I was really glad I had come.

5. After Olaudah Equiano bought his freedom, he became a (**cronyism,** **chronicler**) of his experiences; his 1789 autobiography was one of the first slave narratives written in English.

6. The Sirens, the Cyclops, and the other mythical beings in Homer's ancient (**cronyism,** **chronicle**) of Ulysses' adventures continue to inspire writers and filmmakers.

7. If the appointee, a longtime friend of the governor, is indeed highly qualified, is the accusation of (**cronyism,** **chronicles**) really justified?

8. The (**chronically,** **chronologically**) love-struck teen devours romance novels and listens to albums of dreamy music.

Writer's Challenge

Read the following sentences, paying special attention to the words and phrases underlined. From the words in the box below, find better choices for these underlined words and phrases. Then use these choices to rewrite the sentences.

WORD BANK				
acumen	dissimulate	execrable	precarious	rapport
anachronism	effusive	fulsome	quagmire	sine qua non
bravado	empirical	impasse	quixotic	utilitarian
consensus	euphoria	impinge	raconteur	vacuous

Mr. Eiffel's Tower

1. Today, there is almost universal general agreement that the Eiffel Tower is one of the world's most recognizable and beloved structures.
consensus
_____

2. The plan Gustave Eiffel submitted for the Paris Exposition of 1889 was unanimously chosen to commemorate the centennial of the French Revolution. His perspicacity in structural engineering led to radical ideas for a 985-foot iron tower—then the tallest structure in the world.
acumen
_____

3. Praise for the tower was lavish and unrestrained from many quarters. But 300 prominent intellectuals signed a strongly worded petition urging a halt to construction of Eiffel's "useless . . . monstrous tower."
effusive
_____

4. Some opponents felt that the tower was abominable and utterly detestable, and that it would scare birds away.
execrable
_____

5. Others complained that its structure would be extremely perilous and risky and that it resembled "a mast of iron gymnasium apparatus," a "metallic carcass," and "a truly tragic street lamp."
precarious
_____

6. But when it opened to the public in 1889, Eiffel's grand tower became a magnet for tourists and Parisians alike, whose delight verged on bliss and rapture at the sight of the city in all its beauty far below them.
euphoria
_____

Analogies

In each of the following, circle the item that best completes the comparison.

See pages T38–T46 for explanations of answers.

1. rogue is to **picaresque** as
a. mnemonic is to allegorical
b. incubus is to gothic
c. apostate is to epistolary
d. pundit is to historical

2. augur is to **birds** as
a. necromancer is to tea leaves
b. medium is to tarot cards
c. haruspex is to entrails
d. mountebank is to poltergeists

3. dichotomy is to **two** as
a. disparity is to four
b. liaison is to five
c. affinity is to three
d. consensus is to one

4. anachronism is to **time** as
a. malapropism is to tone
b. neologism is to structure
c. solecism is to grammar
d. spoonerism is to accent

5. raconteur is to **anecdotes** as
a. nitwit is to dictums
b. scholar is to tautologies
c. encomiast is to philippics
d. moralist is to homilies

6. quixotic is to **chimerical** as
a. lugubrious is to lachrymose
b. fastidious is to malcontent
c. minuscule is to gargantuan
d. dank is to mellifluous

7. beatitude is to **blissful** as
a. euphoria is to ecstatic
b. despair is to fervid
c. apathy is to disinterested
d. composure is to distraught

8. quagmire is to **morass** as
a. heyday is to decline
b. kudos is to obloquy
c. bane is to nemesis
d. pundit is to proselyte

9. showoff is to **flamboyant** as
a. nihilist is to hidebound
b. apostate is to loyal
c. poltroon is to valiant
d. skinflint is to niggardly

10. patrician is to **aristocracy** as
a. philistine is to bourgeoisie
b. plebeian is to hoi polloi
c. utilitarian is to proletariat
d. sycophant is to elite

Choosing the Right Meaning

Read each sentence carefully. Then circle the item that best completes the statement below the sentence.

See pages T38–T46 for explanations of answers.

The fighting at the Sunken Road during the Battle of Antietam was so sanguine that the site afterward came to be known as Bloody Lane. (2)

1. The word **sanguine** in line 1 most nearly means
a. flushed   b. bloody   c. confident   d. optimistic

The man whom Edgar Allan Poe appointed his literary executor proved to be a malicious sycophant whose baseless slanders gave rise to myths about Poe that have endured to this day. (2)

2. In line 2 the word **sycophant** is used to mean
a. defamer   b. toady   c. flatterer   d. yes-man

Gradually, we came to see that the champion's every move, though apparently vacuous, was in fact in furtherance of a grand design. (2)

3. The word **vacuous** in line 2 most nearly means

   a. void   b. fatuous   c. inane   (d. purposeless)

"People in those old times had convictions; we moderns only have opinions, and it takes more than a mere opinion to erect a Gothic cathedral." (2)
   (Heinrich Heine, *The French Stage*)

4. The best definition of the word **Gothic** in line 2 is

   a. grotesque   b. sinister   c. gloomy   (d. medieval-style)

In certain cultures shamans are believed to possess a sort of charisma that permits them to heal the sick and even communicate with the spirits of the dead. (2)

5. In line 1 the word **charisma** is used to mean

   a. personal magnetism   (c. divine gift)
   b. charm   d. mystique

Two-Word Completions

Circle the pair of words that best complete the meaning of each of the following sentences.

See pages T38–T46 for explanations of answers.

1. Many 18th-century composers merely sketched out the broad outlines of a piece of music and left the details to the taste and discretion of the individual performer. Though this system of composition gives the artist considerable latitude for choice within the _____ of the composer's style, it by no means gives him or her _____ to change the basic structure, design, or mood of the work.

   a. purview . . . pièce de résistance   c. lexicon . . . fait accompli
   (b. parameters . . . carte blanche)   d. matrix . . . mot juste

2. Though human sacrifice was more or less unknown to the Greeks and Romans of ancient times, many of the barbarian tribes along the borders of the classical world customarily _____ their angry gods by _____ prisoners of war or other captives on huge pyres erected in sacred groves or other such places.

   a. bruited . . . debauching   c. cozened . . . deracinating
   b. lampooned . . . bowdlerizing   (d. propitiated . . . immolating)

3. Although one of the most learned men of his time, François Rabelais is best known as a(n) _____, under the broad, earthy, and often _____ humor of whose tales lie serious discussions of education, politics, religion, and philosophy.

   (a. raconteur . . . ribald)   c. homilist . . . maladroit
   b. polemicist . . . supine   d. virtuoso . . . tendentious

4. When they're in their cups, some of the _____ denizens of the local pub become pugnacious, others become sleepy, and still others become teary-eyed and _____.

   a. hidebound . . . effusive   (c. bibulous . . . maudlin)
   b. bilious . . . waggish   d. malleable . . . contumelious

Enriching Your Vocabulary

Read the passage below. Then complete the exercise at the bottom of the page.

Loanwords from Greek

The Greek language has the longest history among the languages currently spoken in Europe. Throughout its evolution from the fourteenth century B.C. to the present, Greek has developed many words and word parts that English has borrowed to form a vast store of words. In fact, the word *etymology*—the study of word origins—is itself from the Greek *etumologia,* meaning "the true sense of the word."

You may never have studied Greek, visited Greece, or even tasted Greek food. Still, you undoubtedly know quite a few loanwords from that language. In Unit 9, you studied the word *kudos,* meaning "acclaim." *Hedonism* (Unit 8), or "the pursuit of pleasure," comes directly from *hedone,* the Greek word for pleasure. Have you ever experienced a feeling of *euphoria* (Unit 11)? If so, you used a Greek loanword to describe that heady sensation of well-being.

The Greek alphabet is different from the English one. For this reason, some English words derived from Greek exhibit particular spelling traits. For example, consider English words that use the prefix *psych-,* from the Greek word *psyche,* meaning "soul" or "mind." In the word *psychology,* the *p* is silent and the *ch* has a hard /**k**/ sound. Both of these spelling features are consistent with the word's Greek origin.

Psyche Riding a Camel. Bas relief, ca. first century B.C.–third century A.D.

In Column A below are 6 more loanwords from Greek. With or without a dictionary, match each word with its meaning in Column B.

Column A

e	**1.** aroma
b	**2.** catastrophe
f	**3.** catharsis
a	**4.** climax
c	**5.** hubris
d	**6.** phenomenon

Column B

a. the point of greatest intensity in a series of events; to reach or bring about such a point (Greek meaning: *ladder*)

b. a great calamity; total failure; sudden violent change (Greek meaning: *overturning, ruin*)

c. excessive pride, arrogance, or self-confidence (Greek meaning: *insolence, outrage*)

d. any occurrence or fact perceptible to the senses; a marvel; a paragon (Greek meaning: *that which appears*)

e. a pleasant odor that is characteristic of something (Greek meaning: *spice*)

f. a purification or eradication; a figurative release of tension or the emotions (Greek meaning: *purging*)

Definitions

Note carefully the spelling, pronunciation, part(s) of speech, and definition(s) of each of the following words. Then write the word in the blank space(s) in the illustrative sentence(s) following. Finally, study the lists of synonyms and antonyms given at the end of each entry.

1. accolade
(ak′ ə lād)

(*n.*) praise or approval; a ceremonial embrace or greeting

The playwright enjoyed the _____ **accolades** _____ of both the theater critics and the public.

SYNONYMS: kudos, acclaim, cheers, plaudits
ANTONYMS: boos, disapproval, censure, criticism

2. acerbity
(ə sər′ bə tē)

(*n.*) sourness or bitterness of taste; harshness or severity of manner or expression

Offended by the _____ **acerbity** _____ of the director's remarks, the actor stormed out of the rehearsal.

SYNONYMS: acidity, astringency, mordancy, asperity
ANTONYMS: blandness, mellowness, mildness

3. attrition
(ə trish′ ən)

(*n.*) the process of wearing down by friction or gradual impairment

After many losses due to _____ **attrition** _____, the weakened army sought an end to hostilities.

SYNONYMS: abrasion, erosion, exhaustion, reduction
ANTONYMS: augmentation, proliferation, enlargement

4. bromide
(brō′ mīd)

(*n.*) a trite or commonplace remark; a tiresome or boring person; a sedative

The usual _____ **bromides** _____ offered by politicians may please crowds but won't solve the nation's problems.

SYNONYMS: cliché, platitude

5. chauvinist
(shō′ və nist)

(*adj.*) extravagantly patriotic; blindly devoted to a cause; (*n.*) such a person

During wartime, some newspapers may take an extremely _____ **chauvinist** _____ stance in their editorials.

Denying that he is a male _____ **chauvinist** _____, the senator cited his record of support for equal rights for women.

SYNONYMS: (*n.*) superpatriot, flag-waver, jingoist

6. chronic
(kron′ ik)

(*adj.*) continuing over a long period of time or recurring often

The president set up a blue-ribbon committee to look into the problem of _____ **chronic** _____ unemployment.

SYNONYMS: recurrent, persistent, inveterate, habitual
ANTONYMS: transitory, transient, sporadic

7. expound
(ek spaùnd')

(*v.*) to explain in detail

The students listened attentively as their physics professor
_____**expounded**_____ upon the new theory.

SYNONYMS: elucidate, explicate, delineate

8. factionalism
(fak' shən əl iz əm)

(*n.*) party strife and intrigue

Because of bitter _____**factionalism**_____ in both houses
of Congress, no legislation of consequence was passed.

SYNONYMS: infighting, dissension
ANTONYMS: unanimity, harmony, agreement, consensus

9. immaculate
(i mak' yə lit)

(*adj.*) spotless; without blemish or fault

After I finished washing and waxing my parent's white car, it
was as _____**immaculate**_____ as new-fallen snow.

SYNONYMS: unsoiled, impeccable
ANTONYMS: blemished, tarnished, stained, sullied

10. imprecation
(im prə kā' shən)

(*n.*) a curse; the act of cursing

When I found myself stuck in a traffic jam, I could not stop
myself from muttering a few _____**imprecations**_____.

SYNONYMS: execration, malediction
ANTONYMS: blessing, benediction

11. ineluctable
(in i lək' tə bəl)

(*adj.*) not able to be avoided, changed, or overcome

Two of life's _____**ineluctable**_____ facts are
death and taxes.

SYNONYMS: unavoidable, inescapable, inevitable
ANTONYMS: avoidable, escapable, reversible, revocable

12. mercurial
(mər kyùr' ē əl)

(*adj.*) characterized by rapid and unpredictable changes of
mood; fickle or inconstant

The temperamental diva is perhaps even more famous for her
_____**mercurial**_____ behavior than for her voice.

SYNONYMS: erratic, flighty, capricious, volatile
ANTONYMS: phlegmatic, sluggish, constant, steady

13. palliate
(pal' ē āt)

(*v.*) to make less serious or severe by glossing over; to relieve
without actually curing, mitigate

A few new laws may _____**palliate**_____ the
ills that plague our society but will not eradicate them.

SYNONYMS: alleviate, extenuate
ANTONYMS: intensify, magnify, aggravate

14. protocol
(prō' tə kôl)

(*n.*) customs and regulations dealing with official behavior and etiquette, as in a court or among diplomats; a type of international agreement; a memorandum, official account, or record

A breach of _____**protocol**_____ at a summit meeting of world leaders can have serious consequences.

SYNONYMS: code of conduct, minutes

15. resplendent
(ri splen' dənt)

(*adj.*) shining or gleaming brilliantly; splendid or magnificent

The knights, clad in _____**resplendent**_____ armor, rode forth to engage the foe.

SYNONYMS: radiant, dazzling, glorious
ANTONYMS: dull, drab, lusterless

16. stigmatize
(stig' mə tīz)

(*v.*) to brand or mark as in some way discreditable, disgraceful, or ignominious

People sometimes _____**stigmatize**_____ innocent children because of their parents' misdeeds.

SYNONYMS: sully, taint, disgrace
ANTONYMS: whitewash, laud, extol

17. sub rosa
(səb rō' zə)

(*adv.*) in secret; confidentially; privately; (*adj.*) secretive

An unnamed White House source passed crucial information to reporters _____**sub rosa**_____.

At a series of _____**sub rosa**_____ meetings, the dissenting shareholders planned their next move.

SYNONYMS: (*adv.*) secretly, covertly, stealthily, furtively
ANTONYMS: (*adv.*) overtly, openly

18. vainglory
(vān' glô rē)

(*n.*) excessive pride in and boastfulness about one's own accomplishments or qualities; a vain show or display

With insufferable _____**vainglory**_____ the young tennis star taunted his opponent after each winning point.

SYNONYMS: vanity, conceit, swagger, pretentiousness
ANTONYMS: humility, modesty, diffidence

19. vestige
(ves' tij)

(*n.*) a trace or visible evidence of something that once existed but now is lost or vanished

The spectacular ruins of the ancient temple are the last _____**vestiges**_____ of a once-mighty civilization.

SYNONYMS: artifact, relic, remains

20. volition
(vō lish' ən)

(*n.*) the power to choose, will, or decide; the act of choosing, willing, or deciding

Ignoring all my relatives' warnings, I chose the perilous course of my own _____**volition**_____.

SYNONYMS: free will, choice
ANTONYMS: coercion, compulsion, duress

Completing the Sentence

From the words for this unit, choose the one that best completes each of the following sentences. Write the word in the space provided.

1. Isn't there truly an element of pathos in the certain knowledge that the _____**vainglory**_____ and overconfidence of our youth will be laid low by "the slings and arrows of outrageous fortune"?

2. You may be scornful about matters of "mere _____**protocol**_____," as you call it, but you will soon learn that *how* things are done is often as important as *what* is done.

3. The steady and quiet devotion of people who truly love their country is very different from the noisy fulminations of mindless _____**chauvinists**_____.

4. Despite the heat and the dirt of a summer day in the city, he managed somehow to look cool and _____**immaculate**_____.

5. The Founding Fathers warned that without an overriding sense of national purpose, this country could be torn apart by _____**factionalism**_____.

6. His personality was so _____**mercurial**_____ that we never knew on any given occasion how he would react.

7. Shall I be modest and say that I simply do not deserve these extravagant _____**accolades**_____, or shall I be honest and admit that I do?

8. Have we reached the stage where anyone who refuses to go along with the majority is to be _____**stigmatized**_____ as a malcontent?

9. In spite of her advanced age and illness, one could still recognize the _____**vestiges**_____ of her once ravishing beauty.

10. In an influential book published in 1936, the economist John M. Keynes _____**expounded**_____ his theory of the causes of economic collapse.

11. It was a bitter experience to have to leave the village in disgrace, followed by the jeers and _____**imprecations**_____ of people I had tried to help.

12. Why is it that so many theater critics are noted for the trenchancy of their perceptions and the _____**acerbity**_____ of their wit?

13. Since we cannot overcome the enemy by direct attack, we will wage a war of _____**attrition**_____ against them.

14. No one suggested that I take algebra in my freshman year; I decided to do it purely of my own _____**volition**_____.

15. The agreements that had been concluded _____**sub rosa**_____ by the leaders of both parties aroused a storm of protest when they were finally made public.

16. G. B. Shaw's remark to the effect that "youth is wasted on the young" may be, as you say, an old _____**bromide**_____, but it is also profoundly true.

17. Over the years she has tried many different remedies to relieve the pain caused by her _____**chronic**_____ arthritis.

18. Many a time-honored home remedy may indeed _____palliate_____ the symptoms of a disease but do little or nothing to cure it.

19. In the innocent glow of youth and inexperience, we simply assumed that we would be able to avoid the _____ineluctable_____ consequences of our own folly.

20. _____Resplendent_____ in her first evening gown and her first professional hairdo, she waited impatiently for her date to escort her to the dance.

Synonyms

*Choose the word from this unit that is **the same** or **most nearly the same** in meaning as the **boldface** word or expression in the given phrase. Write the word on the line provided.*

1. preserved the **relics** of an ancient culture _____vestiges_____

2. used one **cliché** after another _____bromide_____

3. a tirade filled with **maledictions** _____imprecations_____

4. acted of their own **free will** _____volition_____

5. **disgraced** because of past mistakes _____stigmatized_____

6. an **impeccable** record of service _____immaculate_____

7. asked to **explicate** the meaning of the poem _____expound_____

8. accused the candidate of being a **jingoist** _____chauvinist_____

9. an organization riven by **dissension** _____factionalism_____

10. known as a **flighty** individual _____mercurial_____

11. ranks depleted by **exhaustion** _____attrition_____

12. behaved with outrageous **conceit** _____vainglory_____

13. the **inescapable** ravages of time _____ineluctable_____

14. helps to **alleviate** the patient's discomfort _____palliate_____

15. fully complied with the **code of conduct** _____protocol_____

Antonyms

*Choose the word from this unit that is **most nearly opposite** in meaning to the **boldface** word or expression in the given phrase. Write the word on the line provided.*

16. the unexpected **mildness** of the coach's remarks _____acerbity_____

17. accepted the **criticism** with good grace _____accolade_____

18. suffers from **sporadic** depression _____chronic_____

19. discussed the matter **openly** _____sub rosa_____

20. clad in **drab** garments _____resplendent_____

Choosing the Right Word

*Circle the **boldface** word that more satisfactorily completes each of the following sentences.*

1. Beneath the (**volition, acerbity**) of their criticism, we recognized a sincere desire to help us solve our problems.

2. My brother's (**chronic, resplendent**) tardiness is constantly getting him into trouble at school.

3. Letting the grim facts speak for themselves, the doctor explained quietly the (**ineluctable, immaculate**) tragedy that results from drug abuse.

4. We spent most of the evening listening to her (**palliate, expound**) on her views on all sorts of interesting subjects.

5. Critics who bestow their (**stigma, accolades**) too easily may gain some quick popularity, but they will soon lose their credibility and influence.

6. Our party can resist the attacks of its enemies from the outside, but it may fall victim to the erosion of (**bromide, factionalism**) from within.

7. His claim to be the "greatest pole-vaulter in the world" would indeed have seemed outrageously (**sub rosa, vainglorious**) if it were not for the fact that he went ahead and proved it.

8. We sought desperately for some new forms of amusement to (**palliate, expound**) the boredom of those endless summer afternoons.

9. George Washington's (**immaculate, mercurial**) reputation as a dedicated patriot has been an inspiration to many generations of Americans.

10. Because the difficulty of the subject matter increases rapidly as the term proceeds, mathematics and physics courses have a high rate of student (**attrition, vainglory**).

11. Although she emphasizes that she was the helpless victim of bad luck, one can recognize the effects of her own (**imprecation, volition**) in bringing about her downfall.

12. In the light of the lessons of history, I am skeptical about the value of any diplomatic conferences held (**sub rosa, ineluctably**).

13. We are all eager to avoid the (**accolade, stigma**) of being prejudiced at the same time that we may be unwilling to purge ourselves of our biases.

14. Although he saw himself as a wit, a bon vivant, and a man-about-town, everyone else regarded him as a hopeless (**factionalism, bromide**).

15. The small bone at the base of the spinal column in humans is thought by biologists to be the (**vestige, accolade**) of a tail.

16. They preceded her to the table, not because (**volition, protocol**) required it, but because they were eager to get at the food.

17. "My country, right or wrong" expresses (**chauvinism, attrition**) in its most common form.

18. Though they are twins, one of them has a highly (**mercurial, vestigial**) temperament, while the other is stolid and reserved.

19. Your threats and (**imprecations, protocols**) leave me unimpressed because I know that your words will not be followed by deeds.

20. His talents, which had seemed so (**vestigial, resplendent**) in his youth, now struck us as unimpressive and even pathetic.

Vocabulary in Context

*Read the following passage, in which some of the words you have studied in this unit appear in **boldface** type. Then complete each statement given below the passage by circling the letter of the item that is **the same** or **almost the same** in meaning as the highlighted word.*

Canyon of Mysteries

(Line)

U.S. Army surveyors made an astonishing discovery when, in 1848, they rode into a deserted canyon in what is now western New Mexico. All around them they saw massive multistory sandstone buildings. They had discovered the center of the vanished Anasazi culture of Chaco Canyon, home to perhaps 5000 people in the early twelfth century. *Anasazi* is a Navajo word meaning "ancient ones" or "ancient (5) strangers." No one knows what these remarkable people called themselves.

The Anasazi left no written records behind. Yet much can be learned about them from the **vestiges** of the **resplendent** structures and the system of roads they built, and from

objects and petroglyphs (rock carvings) found at the large number of archaeological sites (10) located in and around the canyon.

The people of Chaco were highly skilled stonemasons. They erected so-called great houses that rose as high as four stories and contained hundreds of rooms and numerous (15) ceremonial chambers called *kivas*. They constructed hundreds of miles of straight roads over uneven terrain. These roads linked some seventy-five outlying settlements to the hub at Chaco. And they did all this (20) without metal tools or the wheel.

The Chacoans found ways to channel water to their land. This enabled them to **palliate** to some extent the difficulties of

Remains of multistory Anasazi dwelling at Chaco Canyon

living in such a harsh and unpredictable climate. But despite such efforts and (25) ceremonies to bring the rains, they found themselves facing **chronic** drought. A prolonged period of scant rainfall beginning around 1130 sent the Chacoan culture into an **ineluctable** decline. By the middle of the century, the great dwellings and little towns were deserted. No one knows where the Anasazi went.

---

1. The meaning of **vestiges** (line 8) is
   a. drawings
   c. remains
   b. photos
   d. ruins

2. Resplendent (line 8) most nearly means
   a. elaborate
   c. unusual
   b. large
   d. magnificent

3. Palliate (line 24) is best defined as
   a. mitigate
   c. aggravate
   b. avoid
   d. analyze

4. The meaning of **chronic** (line 26) is
   a. sporadic
   c. ruinous
   b. moderate
   d. persistent

5. Ineluctable (line 28) most nearly means
   a. swift
   c. reversible
   b. inevitable
   d. unexpected

 **Definitions**

Note carefully the spelling, pronunciation, part(s) of speech, and definition(s) of each of the following words. Then write the word in the blank space(s) in the illustrative sentence(s) following. Finally, study the lists of synonyms and antonyms given at the end of each entry.

1. accoutrements
(ə kü' trə mənts)

(*n., pl.*) accessory items of clothing or equipment; a soldier's outfit, usually not including arms or clothing; trappings

When the new administration took office, it was accorded all the _____**accoutrements**_____ of power.

SYNONYMS: gear, equipage, appurtenances

2. apogee
(ap' ə jē)

(*n.*) the point in the orbit of a heavenly body or artificial satellite farthest from the earth; the farthest or highest point

Many people consider the works of Michelangelo to represent the _____**apogee**_____ of Renaissance art.

SYNONYMS: zenith, apex, summit, pinnacle
ANTONYMS: nadir, bottom, pits, perigee

3. apropos
(ap rə pō')

(*adj.*) appropriate, opportune; (*adv.*) relevantly; incidentally, by the way; speaking of

When choosing a greeting card, I look for the one that is most _____**apropos**_____ to the occasion.

_____**Apropos**_____ of your plans for the summer, where are you going to spend your vacation?

SYNONYMS: (*adj.*) pertinent, germane, apposite, relevant
ANTONYMS: (*adj.*) irrelevant, inappropriate, immaterial

4. bicker
(bik' ər)

(*v.*) to engage in a petty or peevish dispute; to move or run rapidly, rush; to flicker, quiver

If we _____**bicker**_____ over every minor detail, we'll never get the job done.

SYNONYMS: squabble, wrangle, quarrel, plash
ANTONYMS: concur, agree, acquiesce

5. coalesce
(kō ə les')

(*v.*) to blend together or fuse so as to form one body or substance

Many small tributaries _____**coalesce**_____ to form the mighty Amazon River.

SYNONYMS: amalgamate, merge, combine, unite
ANTONYMS: scatter, diffuse, separate

6. contretemps
(kon' trə tän)

(*n.*) an inopportune or embarrassing occurrence; a mishap

I believe in taking life's _____**contretemps**_____ in my stride rather than making a fuss over them.

SYNONYMS: blunder, mischance, faux pas, gaffe

7. convolution
(kon və lü' shən)

(*n.*) a rolling up, coiling, or twisting together; a sinuous folding or design

Becase of its many _____**convolutions**_____ , San Francisco's Lombard Street is called "the crookedest street in the world."

SYNONYMS: twist, turn, complication

8. cull
(kəl)

(*v.*) to pick out or select; to gather or collect

I will _____**cull**_____ pertinent quotations from my research to illustrate the point of my paper.

SYNONYMS: glean, choose, pluck

9. disparate
(dis par' ət) *or*
(dis' pər it)

(*adj.*) completely distinct or different; entirely dissimilar

Despite our _____**disparate**_____ backgrounds and life experiences, we have remained the best of friends.

SYNONYM: divergent
ANTONYMS: similar, homogeneous, uniform

10. dogmatic
(dôg mat' ik)

(*adj.*) certain of the truth of one's own ideas; inclined to state opinions as if they were indisputable facts

People who are _____**dogmatic**_____ are unlikely to have much tolerance for views that differ from their own.

SYNONYMS: opinionated, doctrinaire, authoritarian
ANTONYMS: open-minded, disinterested, dispassionate

11. licentious
(lī sen' shəs)

(*adj.*) morally or sexually unrestrained; having no regard for accepted rules, customs, or laws

In *The Lives of the Caesars* the biographer Suetonius describes the emperor Caligula's _____**licentious**_____ behavior.

SYNONYMS: wanton, dissolute, lascivious
ANTONYMS: chaste, modest, restrained, prudish

12. mete
(mēt)

(*v.*) to distribute or apportion by or as if by measure; to allot

Part of the job of being a parent is the responsibility to _____**mete**_____ out suitable punishment when a child misbehaves.

SYNONYMS: assign, parcel out

13. noxious
(nok' shəs)

(*adj.*) harmful to physical health or morals

Firefighters wear respirator masks to protect them from smoke and _____**noxious**_____ fumes.

SYNONYMS: pernicious, noisome, deleterious, toxic
ANTONYMS: wholesome, salubrious, beneficial

14. polemic
(pə lem′ ik)

(*n.*) an aggressive attack on or refutation of a specific opinion or doctrine

The columnist was known for his _____**polemics**_____ against those at the opposite end of the political spectrum.

SYNONYMS: diatribe, controversy

15. populous
(pop′ yə ləs)

(*adj.*) full of people; filled to capacity; densely populated; having a large population

Millions of people along the _____**populous**_____ Atlantic Coast fled inland as the hurricane approached.

SYNONYMS: crowded, teeming, swarming
ANTONYMS: uninhabited, unpeopled, deserted, barren

16. probity
(prō′ bə tē)

(*n.*) complete and confirmed honesty; total integrity

We should demand that our elected officals conduct themselves with the utmost _____**probity**_____.

SYNONYMS: uprightness, rectitude
ANTONYMS: corruption, venality, immorality, iniquity

17. repartee
(rep ər tē′)

(*n.*) a swift, witty reply; conversation full of such remarks; skill in making such replies or conversation

The writers who made up the famous Algonquin Roundtable were celebrated for their sparkling _____**repartee**_____.

SYNONYMS: retort, comeback, banter, verbal sparring

18. supervene
(sü pər vēn′)

(*v.*) to take place or occur as something additional or unexpected; to follow immediately after

Events that none of us could have foreseen in our wildest imaginings _____**supervened**_____ to blight our hopes.

SYNONYMS: ensue, succeed
ANTONYMS: precede, antecede

19. truncate
(trən′ kāt)

(*v.*) to shorten by or as if by cutting off, lop

A family emergency forced us to _____**truncate**_____ our summer vacation.

SYNONYMS: trim, abbreviate, curtail
ANTONYMS: lengthen, elongate, extend, protract

20. unimpeachable
(ən im pē′ chə bəl)

(*adj.*) beyond doubt or reproach; unquestionable

The members of the jury found the testimony of the key prosecution witness to be _____**unimpeachable**_____.

SYNONYMS: irreproachable, irrefutable, unassailable
ANTONYMS: questionable, debatable, dubious

Completing the Sentence

From the words for this unit, choose the one that best completes each of the following sentences. Write the word in the space provided.

1. Our purpose is to help people in trouble, not to _____ **mete** _____ out justice like a court of law.

2. After the noisy excitement of the big party, the eerie silence that suddenly _____ **supervened** _____ seemed unnatural and difficult to accept.

3. They possess the kind of unshakable _____ **probity** _____ that not only precludes lying but also requires them to express the truth, no matter what.

4. Although the author's conclusions are open to debate, the scholarship upon which they are based is _____ **unimpeachable** _____ .

5. How can we continue to live in this _____ **noxious** _____ atmosphere of suspicion and hatred?

6. Though her career in the movies had many ups and downs over the years, it reached its _____ **apogee** _____ when she won an Academy Award.

7. I hate to _____ **bicker** _____ with you over the cost of a few gallons of gasoline, but I have to because I don't have a dime to spare.

8. The report was not an impartial assessment of the problems we face; it was an intemperate _____ **polemic** _____ .

9. Although the premier enjoyed all the _____ **accoutrements** _____ of high office, in practice he was merely a figurehead who wielded very little power.

10. Does "artistic freedom" justify the making of a movie that is deliberately vulgar and _____ **licentious** _____ in the hope of cashing in at the box office?

11. From the vast mass of unsolicited manuscripts, the editor _____ **culled** _____ the few that might be considered for publication.

12. It was absolutely impossible to follow the _____ **convolutions** _____ of the man's tortuous reasoning as he desperately tried to prove his point.

13. Five minutes after arriving at the dance, I upset the punch bowl—the first of many _____ **contretemps** _____ that made the evening a nightmare.

14. Their respective talents seemed to _____ **coalesce** _____ so that they developed into a well-rounded and highly productive team.

15. True, you did reply to the wisecrack, but I hardly regard "Sez you!" as an outstanding example of devastating _____ **repartee** _____ .

16. Problems such as overcrowding, traffic congestion, and air pollution are more common in big cities than they are in less _____ **populous** _____ areas.

17. _____ **Apropos** _____ of your remarks on the probable effect of the law, may I quote from the column of a well-known political commentator?

18. The lower end of the ridge had been somewhat ____truncated____ by the action of glacial erosion many thousands of years ago.

19. There are so many ____disparate____ elements in her personality that I find it difficult to tell you what kind of person she is.

20. You can't hope to hold a fruitful conversation if you are so ____dogmatic____ that you issue pronouncements instead of offering opinions.

Synonyms

*Choose the word from this unit that is **the same** or **most nearly the same** in meaning as the **boldface** word or expression in the given phrase. Write the word on the line provided.*

1. a hiker's **gear** — accoutrements

2. earned them a reputation for **rectitude** — probity

3. accepted responsibility for the **blunder** — contretemps

4. began to **squabble** as soon as we sat down — bicker

5. unprepared for the disaster that **ensued** — supervened

6. too **opinionated** to be reasoned with — dogmatic

7. disgusted by their **wanton** behavior — licentious

8. amused by their **verbal sparring** — repartee

9. **gleaned** a few key ideas from the article — culled

10. **assign** punishments to the guilty parties — mete out

11. **combine** to form a united front — coalesce

12. forced to **curtail** their stay — truncate

13. the **toxic** effects of air pollution — noxious

14. delivered a **diatribe** against her opponent — polemic

15. one unexpected **complication** after another — convolution

Antonyms

*Choose the word from this unit that is **most nearly opposite** in meaning to the **boldface** word or expression in the given phrase. Write the word on the line provided.*

16. a person of **questionable** character — unimpeachable

17. responses that are **inappropriate** — apropos

18. the **nadir** of the president's popularity rating — apogee

19. come from **similar** backgrounds — disparate

20. visited **uninhabited** islands — populous

Choosing the Right Word

*Circle the **boldface** word that more satisfactorily completes each of the following sentences.*

1. Abraham Lincoln warned that the (**convolutions, dogmas**) of the quiet past were inadequate to the needs of the stormy present.

2. From the roots of ancient prejudices, there grew the (**disparate, noxious**) plants of racial and religious hatreds.

3. The route of the army's retreat was littered with the discarded (**polemics, accoutrements**) of war.

4. We are all imperfect creatures, and none of us has been divinely ordained to (**cull, mete**) out punishment to others for their transgressions.

5. (**Repartee, Supervention**) has been likened to a sort of verbal fencing, with the more skillful contestants driving home their weapons for the kill.

6. Los Angeles recently supplanted Chicago as the second most (**populous, unimpeachable**) city in the United States.

7. Instead of taking a fresh look at the situation, they were satisfied to refute their opponents by repeating old and weary (**polemics, accoutrements**).

8. I had hoped for some understanding and generosity of spirit, not this endless (**bickering, repartee**) over petty details.

9. When we least expected it, a crucial event (**coalesced, supervened**) that changed the outcome of our project.

10. If you are to get along in polite society, you must learn that a remark that is factually true is not necessarily (**populous, apropos**).

11. We must not close our eyes to the flagrant (**disparities, contretemps**) between what our society aspires to be and what it actually is.

12. What they described as a new spirit of freedom and vigorous originality seemed to me mere (**accoutrements, licentiousness**).

13. I agree that it is a very good book, but it is a gross exaggeration to say that it represents the (**apogee, convolution**) of the development of the American novel.

14. "Unless the various factions put aside their differences and (**coalesce, supervene**) into a unified force, we will get absolutely nowhere," I said.

15. Even the most relentless investigations by our political opponents could uncover no evidence that challenged our reputation for (**dogmatism, probity**).

16. We expected a simple explanation, but what we got was an involved rationalization, full of all kinds of strange (**contretemps, convolutions**).

17. The reporter assured her boss that the charges contained in her story were based on information from a(n) (**unimpeachable, noxious**) source.

18. How do you expect to deal with the inevitable problems of life if you raise every (**repartee, contretemps**) to the level of a major tragedy?

19. I have neither the time nor the inclination to plough through those long, dreary books in the hope of (**meting, culling**) a few interesting passages.

20. Because the original article was too long for our needs, we published it in a somewhat (**coalesced, truncated**) form.

Vocabulary in Context

*Read the following passage, in which some of the words you have studied in this unit appear in **boldface** type. Then complete each statement given below the passage by circling the letter of the item that is **the same** or **almost the same** in meaning as the highlighted word.*

Tough Times

(Line)

During the Great Depression, life was especially hard for those living in the panhandle regions of Texas and Oklahoma and in some parts of neighboring states. A severe drought began in 1931 and lasted until 1939. For decades, grasslands had been plowed and planted with wheat; other areas had been

(5) overgrazed. There was nothing to hold the parched soil in place. The consequences were devastating. Powerful winds blew across the land, sweeping up the loose topsoil into great, rolling clouds of dust that people called "black

(10) blizzards." Acres of farmland and pastures were destroyed, and cattle died by the thousands. Banks foreclosed mortgages on farm after farm. The area became known as the Dust Bowl.

More than two million of the region's inhabitants

(15) were forced to leave their homes. These people, mostly dispossessed farmers, piled their meager belongings into their cars and trucks and headed west in the largest migration in American history. Many went to California, hoping to find work in the

(20) state's orchards and cotton fields, but their hopes for a fresh start were cruelly **truncated**. Instead of opportunities, they found squalid, **populous** labor

Dorothea Lange's camera captured the suffering of migrant workers.

camps crammed with poor, desperate migrants like themselves. Living conditions in the camps were **noxious**. There was no sanitation or electricity, and outbreaks of

(25) diseases such as typhoid, smallpox, and tuberculosis were common. People **bickered** and competed for the few low-paying jobs the larger growers made available. It was a terrible time indeed.

Some of America's finest artists chronicled the suffering of the migrants during these terrible years. John Steinbeck's novels, Woody Guthrie's songs, and Dorothea

(30) Lange's photographs poignantly captured the human drama of the Dust Bowl era.

---

1. The meaning of **truncated** (line 21) is
a. mocked
b. curtailed
c. protracted
d. revised

2. Populous (line 22) most nearly means
a. deserted
b. makeshift
c. filthy
d. teeming

3. Noxious (line 24) is best defined as
a. pernicious
b. repugnant
c. salubrious
d. dangerous

4. The meaning of **bickered** (line 26) is
a. languished
b. quarreled
c. joked
d. schemed

Definitions

Note carefully the spelling, pronunciation, part(s) of speech, and definition(s) of each of the following words. Then write the word in the blank space(s) in the illustrative sentence(s) following. Finally, study the lists of synonyms and antonyms given at the end of each entry.

1. adumbrate
(ad' əm brāt)

(*v.*) to outline or sketch broadly; to foreshadow or prefigure; to disclose partially

Writers often _____**adumbrate**_____ key ideas right away and then elaborate on them later.
SYNONYM: indicate

2. apotheosis
(ə poth ē ō' sis)

(*n.*) the elevation of a person to a divine rank or status; the glorification of a person as an ideal; a glorified ideal

Medieval knights were fierce warriors, but in literature they are presented as the _____**apotheosis**_____ of chivalry.
SYNONYM: deification

3. ascetic
(ə set' ik)

(*adj.*) practicing strict self-denial for the sake of personal or spiritual discipline; (*n.*) one who leads a life of self-discipline, especially to express religious devotion

Some artists and writers may find it beneficial to lead an _____**ascetic**_____ life free of distractions.

The life of an _____**ascetic**_____ repays the sacrifice of wordly things with profound spiritual rewards.
SYNONYMS: (*adj.*) austere, spartan; (*n.*) celibate
ANTONYMS: (*adj.*) wanton, dissolute; (*n.*) hedonist

4. bauble
(bô' bəl)

(*n.*) a small, showy ornament of little value or use

I found a rather valuable piece of vintage costume jewelry among the _____**baubles**_____ at the yard sale.
SYNONYMS: trifle, gewgaw, knickknack, bagatelle
ANTONYMS: gem, precious jewel, treasure

5. beguile
(bi gīl')

(*v.*) to mislead or deceive; to cheat; to divert; to cause to vanish unnoticed

Many travelers choose to _____**beguile**_____ away the long hours of a journey with an absorbing book.
SYNONYMS: delude, dupe, lure, while away

6. burgeon
(bər' jən)

(*v.*) to put forth new buds, leaves, or greenery; to develop rapidly or suddenly

Though it was still winter according to the calendar, our garden _____**burgeoned**_____ in the warm, sunny weather.
SYNONYMS: sprout, blossom, bloom, flourish
ANTONYMS: atrophy, wither, shrivel, diminish

7. complement
(kom′ plə mənt)

(*n.*) something that completes a whole; the quantity or number needed to make up a whole; the full number or allowance; (*v.*) to complete

The full _____**complement**_____ of dignitaries was present for the president's State of the Union Address.

She chose a hat that _____**complements**_____ her new outfit.

SYNONYMS: (*n.*) balance; (*v.*) round out

8. contumacious
(kon tü mā′ shəs)

(*adj.*) obstinately or willfully disobedient; openly rebellious

Teenagers who are eager to assert their independence may become quite _____**contumacious**_____ at times.

SYNONYMS: impudent, unruly, defiant, refractory
ANTONYMS: docile, meek, deferential, cooperative

9. curmudgeon
(kər məj′ ən)

(*n.*) an irascible, churlish person

No matter how hard we try, nothing we do seems to please our _____**curmudgeon**_____ of a boss.

SYNONYMS: grouch, crank, sorehead, churl

10. didactic
(dī dak′ tik)

(*adj.*) intended to instruct, especially morally; inclined to moralize too much

At its best, children's literature teaches values, making it _____**didactic**_____ as well as entertaining.

SYNONYMS: educational, instructional, moralistic

11. disingenuous
(dis in jen′ yü əs)

(*adj.*) lacking in sincerity or candor

_____**Disingenuous**_____ individuals sometimes betray themselves in the very act of trying to appear sincere.

SYNONYMS: artful, sly, two-faced, insincere
ANTONYMS: candid, frank, artless, sincere

12. exculpate
(ek′ skəl pāt)

(*v.*) to clear of guilt or blame

"I will present irrefutable evidence," the lawyer declared, "that will _____**exculpate**_____ my client."

SYNONYMS: absolve, exonerate, acquit
ANTONYMS: convict, condemn

13. faux pas
(fō pä′)

(*n.*) a slip in manners or conduct; a social blunder

No sooner had I arrived at the party than I embarrassed myself by committing a dreadful _____**faux pas**_____.

SYNONYMS: indiscretion, gaffe
ANTONYMS: coup, tour de force

14. fulminate
(fulʹ mə nāt)

(v.) to denounce or condemn vehemently; to explode, detonate
The senator proceeded to _____ fulminate _____
against foreign commitments and entanglements.
SYNONYMS: rail, inveigh
ANTONYMS: praise, applaud, commend, extol

15. fustian
(fəsʹ chən)

(n.) inflated or pretentious language in speech or writing; a cloth made of cotton and flax
Although the politician's speech was filled with bombast and
_____ fustian _____, it was devoid of substance.
SYNONYMS: rant, claptrap, bombast, grandiloquence

16. hauteur
(hô tûrʹ)

(n.) haughtiness of bearing or attitude
His cold _____ hauteur _____ and disdainful
attitude made him extremely unpopular with his colleagues.
SYNONYMS: conceit, superciliousness, snobbishness
ANTONYMS: modesty, humility, diffidence, mousiness

17. inhibit
(in hibʹ it)

(v.) to restrain or hold back; to hinder or arrest; to prohibit
Poor eating habits may _____ inhibit _____ a
young person's physical development.
SYNONYMS: repress, check, suppress
ANTONYMS: foster, promote, expedite, facilitate

18. jeremiad
(jer ə mīʹ əd)

(n.) an elaborate or prolonged lamentation; any tale of woe
When asked about their sad plights, talk show guests often
launch into tearful _____ jeremiads _____.
ANTONYMS: paean, song of praise

19. opportunist
(op ər tüʹ nist)

(n.) one who makes a practice of taking advantage of circumstances to further his or her own self-interest, regardless of principles or ultimate consequences
_____ Opportunists _____ tend to treat those who are
not useful to them with callous indifference.
SYNONYMS: self-seeker, exploiter

20. unconscionable
(ən konʹ shən ə bəl)

(adj.) not guided or restrained by conscience, prudence, or reason; unscrupulous; immoderate
Top management's looting of the employees' retirement fund
can only be described as _____ unconscionable _____.
SYNONYMS: unjustifiable, indefensible, unforgivable
ANTONYMS: justifiable, reasonable, honorable

Completing the Sentence

From the words for this unit, choose the one that best completes each of the following sentences. Write the word in the space provided.

1. What at first appeared to be no more than a rather favorable opinion of himself has _____**burgeoned**_____ into a seemingly unlimited conceit.

2. Her standards of proper behavior are so demanding that she regards every minor _____**faux pas**_____ as an unforgivable social offense.

3. In a rather silly painting called *The* _____**Apotheosis**_____ *of Homer*, the artist attempts to show the blind poet's reception among the gods.

4. I wonder how many people have been taken in by those silly TV ads that attempt to pass off worthless _____**baubles**_____ as valuable jewelry.

5. The editorial argues that the crime-fighting situation cannot improve until the police department receives its full _____**complement**_____ of personnel.

6. How could a person of your knowledge and experience allow yourself to be _____**beguiled**_____ by vague promises and empty reassurances?

7. While two of the accused were indicted on conspiracy charges, the third was eventually _____**exculpated**_____ of any involvement in the plot.

8. It is often more effective to offer a few just words of criticism than to _____**fulminate**_____ long and loud against those who offend us.

9. Because there was no time to go into elaborate details, all that we could do was to _____**adumbrate**_____ the general features of the plan.

10. Instead of simply stating his case, he launched into an emotional appeal whose language degenerated into mere _____**fustian**_____ and bombast.

11. I won't go into that shop because the snooty salespeople treat me with the _____**hauteur**_____ and disdain of aristocrats dealing with their lackeys.

12. Successful politicians must be alert to take advantage of every favorable circumstance, but if they are no more than _____**opportunists**_____, it is hard to see how they will ever accomplish anything worthwhile.

13. After his conversion, the young man renounced his former profligacy and dissipation to lead the life of a(n) _____**ascetic**_____.

14. I find it impossible to understand how the world can stand idly by while _____**unconscionable**_____ acts of cruelty are being committed daily.

15. Though your unwillingness to make me a small loan is disappointing, what infuriates me is your _____**disingenuous**_____ explanation that it is "for my own good."

16. At first we thought that he was just pretending to be surly, but later we discovered that he really was a(n) _____**curmudgeon**_____.

17. What we need in this situation is not a lugubrious _____**jeremiad**_____ cataloging our troubles but a workable plan for improvements.

18. The chairman of the Senate committee angrily threatened the witness with contempt charges because of her _____contumacious_____ attitude.

19. For the eighteenth-century moralist, art and literature had an essentially _____didactic_____ purpose; they should teach as well as entertain.

20. We all have aggressive impulses, but in most cases our early training and conditioning tend to _____inhibit_____ the open expression of them.

Synonyms

*Choose the word from this unit that is **the same** or **most nearly the same** in meaning as the **boldface** word or expression in the given phrase. Write the word on the line provided.*

1. mocked the orator's **grandiloquence** _____fustian_____

2. led an **austere** existence _____ascetic_____

3. **misled** unwary customers with vague promises _____beguiled_____

4. **rounded out** the meal perfectly _____complemented_____

5. **outlined** their plans at a press conference _____adumbrated_____

6. committed one **gaffe** after another _____faux pas_____

7. will **exonerate** them without further ado _____exculpate_____

8. the **deification** of the emperor _____apotheosis_____

9. **flourished** in that mild climate _____burgeoned_____

10. **rails** against the government's policies _____fulminates_____

11. **knicknacks** that have great sentimental value _____baubles_____

12. has a reputation for being a **grouch** _____curmudgeon_____

13. listened patiently to my friend's **tale of woe** _____jeremiad_____

14. dismissed as **moralistic** by most literary critics _____didactic_____

15. regaded as a ruthless **exploiter** _____opportunist_____

Antonyms

*Choose the word from this unit that is **most nearly opposite** in meaning to the **boldface** word or expression in the given phrase. Write the word on the line provided.*

16. a group of **docile** individuals _____contumacious_____

17. considered their actions **justifiable** _____unconscionable_____

18. gave a **sincere** answer to the question _____disingenuous_____

19. surprised by the celebrity's **diffidence** _____hauteur_____

20. conditions that **foster** economic growth _____inhibit_____

Choosing the Right Word

*Circle the **boldface** word that more satisfactorily completes each of the following sentences.*

1. When you have been guilty of rude conduct, don't try to minimize your guilt by referring to the incident as a mere (**jeremiad, faux pas**).

2. You are too young to understand how the trials of life can transform a happy-go-lucky youth into a solitary (**bauble, curmudgeon**).

3. The situation was rapidly becoming intolerable because some of the club members were not merely uncooperative but positively (**contumacious, opportunist**).

4. You have written a(n) (**didactic, unconscionable**) novel with a wealth of authentic documentation, but you have forgotten to entertain your readers.

5. (**Beguiled, Burgeoned**) by high-pressure sales talk, I bought a car that I did not need, could not afford, and did not even know how to drive.

6. The author found it ironic that the novel he had tossed off in his youth as a mere (**bauble, complement**) came to be viewed as his masterpiece.

7. The aim of the new biography was to (**exculpate, inhibit**) its subject of charges that previous biographers had wrongfully pressed against him.

8. What is the basis for your statement that advertising costs account for an (**ascetic, unconscionable**) part of the retail price of many products?

9. Many historians believe those apparently minor incidents (**adumbrated, exculpated**) the great revolutionary uprising that occurred a few years later.

10. In a democracy we have no need to disguise the human failings of our leaders; we can respect them without (**beguiling, apotheosizing**) them.

11. The candidates underrate the electorate if they think they can win votes with that kind of antiquated (**curmudgeon, fustian**).

12. What disappointed me was not so much your failure to complete the job but your (**didactic, disingenuous**) efforts to avoid all responsibility for the debacle.

13. Even the innate talents of a Mozart or an Einstein cannot (**fulminate, burgeon**) unless the environment is favorable to their growth.

14. Unlike the Athenians, who delighted in luxury, the Spartans espoused the virtue of (**ascetic, fustian**) simplicity.

15. The speaker referred scornfully to the "hysterical (**jeremiads, hauteurs**) of the ecologists," but I believe that they are warning us of real dangers.

16. I must say that I agree with their (**inhibitions, fulminations**) against those who deface our public buildings with unsightly graffiti.

17. They make an excellent team because his deftness in handling people effectively (**complements, adumbrates**) her remarkable executive abilities.

18. When I asked him if he could dance, he looked at me with supreme (**disingenuousness, hauteur**) and said, "Could Caruso sing?"

19. Your tactics prove that you are not just an (**opportunist, apotheosis**) but someone with a ruthless disregard for others.

20. Since you are usually a rather boisterous person, I was surprised by your (**ascetic, inhibited**) behavior at the party.

Read the following passage, in which some of the words you have studied in this unit appear in **boldface** type. Then complete each statement given below the passage by circling the letter of the item that is **the same** or **almost the same** in meaning as the highlighted word.

Genius Rediscovered

(Line)

Zora Neale Hurston, folklorist, novelist, and anthropologist, once said that "the world is to the strong." She did not let anything **inhibit** her talent and ambition. Young Zora was raised in Eatonville, Florida, the first incorporated black community in America. Life in Eatonville had a profound impact on her character and her writing. The town was self-sufficient and largely free of racial prejudice. (5) African American culture thrived there.

Hurston attended Howard University and published her first story in the school's literary magazine in 1921. In 1925, she moved to New York City. There the outspoken and spirited Zora became a part of the flourishing Harlem Renaissance. She studied anthropology at Barnard College on a scholarship, concentrating on (10) African American folklore. In 1929, she returned to the South to do field research.

Hurston spent six years listening and learning. Her research provided her with material for a number of folklore collections, (15) beginning with *Mules and Men* (1935). She also continued to write fiction, publishing her most famous novel, *Their Eyes Were Watching God*, in 1938. Hurston's works are rich portrayals of life in black communities and capture the (20) authentic dialect of the people who lived in them. Although she broke new ground in the field of ethnography by employing literary techniques, little of her output was appreciated during her lifetime. Hurston's writing style (25)

Zora Neale Hurston (1891–1960)

disturbed many of her contemporaries. They **fulminated** against her re-creation of the oral culture and dismissed her writings as reactionary. The novelist Richard Wright likened her portrayals of African Americans to minstrel shows.

After her death, however, her talents were reassessed. Writers such as Alice Walker praised her as a pioneer. A new generation of readers and critics **exculpated** Hurston (30) of the charge that her work was offensive, and her reputation **burgeoned**. Many of her works now appear in literature texts and in anthologies of African American writings.

---

1. The meaning of **inhibit** (line 2) is
  a. conceal   c. shape
  b. restrain   d. foster

2. Fulminated (line 26) most nearly means
  a. demonstrated   c. railed
  b. argued   d. voted

3. Exculpated (line 30) is best defined as
  a. exonerated   c. accused
  b. condemned   d. indicted

4. The meaning of **burgeoned** (line 31) is
  a. flourished   c. grew
  b. stagnated   d. diminished

Visit us at **www.sadlier-oxford.com** for interactive puzzles and games.

REVIEW UNITS 13–15

Analogies

In each of the following, circle the item that best completes the comparison.

See pages T38–T46 for explanations of answers.

1. immaculate is to **blemish** as
a. imperfect is to flaw
b. impeccable is to fault
c. imperative is to spot
d. impassive is to taint

2. didactic is to **teach** as
a. monitory is to warn
b. monetary is to profit
c. mandatory is to amuse
d. minatory is to encourage

3. mercurial is to **quicksilver** as
a. contumacious is to oil
b. saccharine is to flour
c. acerbic is to sugar
d. phlegmatic is to molasses

4. vestigial is to **trace** as
a. rudimentary is to beginning
b. inchoate is to conclusion
c. prehensile is to grasp
d. consummate is to embryo

5. unimpeachable is to **question** as
a. inviolable is to revere
b. unconscionable is to perform
c. ineluctable is to avoid
d. incalculable is to enjoy

6. braggart is to **vainglory** as
a. turncoat is to fidelity
b. showoff is to ostentation
c. opportunist is to volition
d. spoilsport is to factionalism

7. apotheosize is to **god** as
a. lionize is to villain
b. personify is to celebrity
c. vilify is to hero
d. ostracize is to pariah

8. repartee is to **scintillating** as
a. fustian is to restrained
b. bickering is to petty
c. bromide is to novel
d. fulmination is to generous

9. jeremiad is to **dolorous** as
a. diatribe is to complimentary
b. polemic is to bellicose
c. encomium is to vituperative
d. imprecation is to licentious

10. contretemps is to **embarrass** as
a. carte blanche is to inhibit
b. faux pas is to enthuse
c. quandary is to baffle
d. accolade is to constrain

Word Associations

In each of the following groups, circle the word that is best defined or suggested by the given phrase.

1. "May you never have a moment's peace!"
a. bromide **b. imprecation** c. curmudgeon d. vestige

2. "By the way . . ."
a. bauble b. contumacious **c. apropos** d. unconscionable

3. put his foot in his mouth
a. protocol **b. faux pas** c. fustian d. jeremiad

4. infighting among the company's directors
a. factionalism b. convolution c. contretemps d. probity

5. told a story to teach a moral
a. populous b. unconscionable **c. didactic** d. chauvinist

6. put off by their snootiness
a. populous b. exculpate c. mercurial **d. hauteur**

7. not interested in the opinions of others

a. ascetic   (b. dogmatic)   c. disparate   d. sub rosa

8. their greatest moment

a. acerbity   b. accolade   (c. apogee)   d. imprecation

9. the usual collection of platitudes

(a. bromide)   b. jeremiad   c. apotheosis   d. volition

10. squabble over trifles

a. expound   b. stigmatize   (c. bicker)   d. coalesce

11. as honest as the day is long

a. accoutrements   b. chauvinist   c. vestige   (d. probity)

12. soften the impact

a. coalesce   b. expound   c. truncate   (d. palliate)

Choosing the Right Meaning

Read each sentence carefully. Then circle the item that best completes the statement below the sentence.

See pages T38–T46 for explanations of answers.

"I have seen
A curious child, who dwelt upon a tract   (2)
Of inland ground, applying to his ear
The convolutions of a smooth-lipped shell,   (4)
To which, in silence hushed, his very soul
Listened intensely."   (6)
(William Wordsworth, *The Excursion*)

1. In line 4 the word **convolutions** most nearly means

a. complications   b. sounds   (c. coils)   d. openings

Judging by the cool embrace and the perfunctory kiss, neither party found the accolade particularly agreeable.   (2)

2. In line 2 the word **accolade** most nearly means

a. praise   (b. greeting)   c. cheers   d. acclaim

Purported to be the memoranda of a series of conspirational meetings between Jews and Freemasons, the *Protocols of the Elders of Zion* were in fact forgeries   (2)
concocted by the Russian secret police.

3. The word **Protocols** in line 2 is used to mean

a. regulations   b. agreements   c. codes   (d. minutes)

Doctors were at a loss to account for the malady, which was as remarkable for its virulence as for the suddenness with which it fulminated.   (2)

4. The word **fulminated** in line 2 is used to mean

a. detonated   b. denounced   (c. exploded)   d. railed against

Antonyms

In each of the following groups, circle the word or expression that is most nearly the **opposite** of the word in **boldface** type.

1. truncate
a. unpack
b. elongate (circled)
c. embark
d. shorten

2. sub rosa
a. secretly
b. overtly (circled)
c. repeatedly
d. illegally

3. exculpate
a. acquire
b. bury
c. deactivate
d. convict (circled)

4. acerbity
a. slander
b. asperity
c. mildness (circled)
d. uncertainty

5. immaculate
a. stained (circled)
b. restrained
c. satirical
d. impeccable

6. populous
a. deserted (circled)
b. teeming
c. unknown
d. urban

7. noxious
a. deleterious
b. arrogant
c. wholesome (circled)
d. isolated

8. contumacious
a. refractory
b. hungry
c. ardent
d. docile (circled)

9. burgeon
a. relieve
b. rest
c. atrophy (circled)
d. flourish

10. apropos
a. irrelevant (circled)
b. pertinent
c. common
d. exotic

11. licentious
a. aggressive
b. chaste (circled)
c. humorous
d. legal

12. disingenuous
a. artless (circled)
b. dissembling
c. resilient
d. resourceful

13. ascetic
a. austere
b. fit
c. dissolute (circled)
d. sedentary

14. ineluctable
a. tolerant
b. avoidable (circled)
c. distorted
d. fragile

15. bicker
a. argue
b. select
c. agree (circled)
d. drive

16. inhibit
a. suppress
b. desert
c. promote (circled)
d. dwell

17. disparate
a. divergent
b. employable
c. similar (circled)
d. distant

18. mercurial
a. lovable
b. sluggish (circled)
c. disdainful
d. capricious

19. unimpeachable
a. irrefutable
b. partisan
c. obligatory
d. questionable (circled)

20. factionalism
a. bigotry
b. multiplication
c. discord
d. unanimity (circled)

Completing the Sentence

From the following lists of words, choose the one that best completes each of the following sentences. Write the word in the space provided.

Group A

apogee	coalesce	opportunist	repartee
beguile	fustian	protocol	volition

1. "Now that I'm at the _____**apogee**_____ of my career," the actress said, "I guess I have nowhere to go from here but down."

2. No one told me to go out for the football team; I did it entirely of my own _____**volition**_____.

3. "_____**Protocol**_____ requires that I report to the foreign office as soon as I arrive," the diplomat observed.

4. His speeches are filled with _____ **fustian** _____ and bombast—in sharp contrast to the subdued, constructive comments of his opponent.

5. He is too much of a(n) _____ **opportunist** _____ to be relied upon to stay with us when the other side begins to move ahead.

Group B

adumbrate	bicker	contumacious	inhibit
ascetic	cull	ineluctable	supervene

1. Far from seeking to _____ **inhibit** _____ political debate, a democratic society welcomes and encourages the free exchange of ideas.

2. The students _____ **culled** _____ statistics from various reference works to use in their research project in economics.

3. While he resided in his little cabin beside Walden Pond, Henry Thoreau lived a life as simple and _____ **ascetic** _____ as that of a monk.

4. I think your accounting of the costs is wrong, but it is beneath my dignity to _____ **bicker** _____ with you over a few dollars.

5. In her opening remarks, the prosecutor briefly _____ **adumbrated** _____ the case that the state would bring against the defendant.

Word Families

A. *On the line provided, write the word you have learned in Units 13–15 that is related to each of the following nouns.*
EXAMPLE: supervention—**supervene**

1. license, licentiousness — **licentious**
2. contumacy — **contumacious**
3. disparateness — **disparity**
4. inhibition, inhibitor — **inhibit**
5. population, populace, populousness — **populous**
6. exculpation — **exculpate**
7. palliation, palliator — **palliate**
8. fulmination — **fulminate**
9. mercury, mercurialness — **mercurial**
10. stigma, stigmatization, stigmatic — **stigmatize**
11. didact, didacticism, didactics — **didactic**
12. resplendence, resplendency — **resplendent**
13. beguilement, beguiler — **beguile**
14. ineluctability — **ineluctable**
15. disingenuousness — **disingenuous**

B. *On the line provided, write the word you have learned in Units 13–15 that is related to each of the following verbs.*

EXAMPLE: apotheosize—**apotheosis**

16. impeach   unimpeachable

17. polemicize   polemic

18. dogmatize   dogmatic

19. acerbate   acerbity

20. convolute   convolution

Two-Word Completions

Circle the pair of words that best complete the meaning of each of the following passages.

See pages T38–T46 for explanations of answers.

1. In the 18th century, all art had two _____ purposes: "to point a moral or adorn a tale." Accordingly, no work was judged to be really complete if either the _____ or the decorative element was not in evidence.
a. vestigial . . . dogmatic
b. ineluctable . . . licentious
c. complementary . . . didactic
d. unimpeachable . . . chauvinistic

2. "The man is not a disinterested observer of the passing scene," I said. "He is essentially a(n) _____ who uses his column in the newspaper as a kind of soapbox from which to _____, like some Old Testament prophet, against the iniquities of those around him."
a. curmudgeon . . . exculpate
b. chauvinist . . . palliate
c. opportunist . . . truncate
d. polemicist . . . fulminate

3. During the election of 1860, the Democrats could not present a united front because the party was torn asunder by _____ strife and petty regional _____.
a. factional . . . bickering
b. contumacious . . . attrition
c. dogmatic . . . repartee
d. unconscionable . . . vainglory

4. During the Civil War, Robert E. Lee's freedom of choice was seriously _____ by the fact that the South could never replace the losses it sustained through normal battlefield _____.
a. palliated . . . volition
b. inhibited . . . attrition
c. truncated . . . convolution
d. adumbrated . . . imprecation

*Read the following passage, in which some of the words you have studied in Units 13–15 appear in **boldface** type. Then complete each statement given below the passage by circling the item that is **the same** or **almost the same** in meaning as the highlighted word.*

Vocabulary in Context

Working on a Ledge

(Line)

Birds aren't the only ones who can enjoy a bird's-eye view of things. The intrepid workers who wash the windows of skyscrapers and other

(5) tall buildings share that lofty position.

Working hundreds of feet above the sidewalk is not for everybody, certainly not for anyone who is **inhibited** by a fear of heights. But

(10) heights are just one of the hazards faced by window washers. **Mercurial** weather conditions also put workers at risk. They must learn to deal calmly and cautiously with wind and rain and

(15) snow. They deserve our **accolades** for their courage and the skill with which they do their difficult job.

Tall buildings have various kinds of windows. Some can be cleaned

(20) while the worker stands inside the building. Others can be opened halfway or tilted inward and cleaned by leaning out while remaining inside. Still others cannot be opened

(25) and must be cleaned from the outside. To do this, workers may have to stand on a narrow ledge or on a platform that is suspended by cables from a building's roof.

(30) Workers wear safety harnesses that they secure to the window frames while they use their squeegees to clean the glass. Window washers also need gloves, safety goggles,

(35) and respirator masks to protect them from caustic cleaning substances. Most important of all, they should always check their equipment before beginning work to

(40) make sure that everything is in good condition and fastened securely.

People who become window washers generally do so of their own **volition**. They say that the perks of

(45) the job outweigh the dangers. First of all there is the satisfaction of keeping windows **immaculate**. Then, of course, there are those bird's-eye views. Window washers

(50) can look out over the **resplendent** tops of magnificent tall buildings gleaming in the sunlight and enjoy the panorama of the city.

---

1. The meaning of **inhibited** (line 9) is
a. made dizzy
c. prohibited
(b. held back)
d. unnerved

2. Mercurial (line 11) most nearly means
(a. volatile)
c. stormy
b. flighty
d. predictable

3. Accolades (line 15) is best defined as
a. criticism
c. smiles
b. thanks
(d. praise)

4. The meaning of **volition** (line 44) is
a. compulsion
c. whim
b. preference
(d. choice)

5. Immaculate (line 47) most nearly means
(a. spotless)
c. safe
b. sealed
d. soiled

6. Resplendent (line 50) is best defined as
a. dramatic
(c. dazzling)
b. decorative
d. varied

temp—time

Building with Classical Roots

This Latin root appears in **contretemps** (page 157), which means "an inopportune or embarrassing mishap." Some other words based on the same root are listed below.

contemplative	extempore	temperance	tempest
contemporaneous	temperamentally	temperature	tempestuous

From the list of words above, choose the one that corresponds to each of the brief definitions below. Write the word in the blank space in the illustrative sentence below the definition.

1. the degree of hotness or coldness in a body or an environment; the specific degree of hotness or coldness as measured on a scale

The parents worried when the baby continued to run a high _____**temperature**_____ for three days.

2. stormy; violent; turbulent

Their _____**tempestuous**_____ relationship ended when the stress became just too much to bear.

3. existing or occurring at the same period of time

The lives of writer Christopher Marlowe and Sir Walter Raleigh were _____**contemporaneous**_____ with that of William Shakespeare.

4. a violent storm; a tumult, uproar

The small fishing boat foundered in the raging _____**tempest**_____.

5. inclined to consider intently, thoughtful; meditative; pensive

"The Thinker"—Rodin's famed sculpture—shows a man sitting in a(n) _____**contemplative**_____ pose.

6. in an impromptu, unrehearsed manner; on the spur of the moment

After hearing the mayor's disturbing statement, an irate citizen delivered a rebuttal _____**extempore**_____.

7. by nature, disposition; moodily; impulsively

Although she had always dreamed of being an investigative journalist, she soon realized that she was _____**temperamentally**_____ unsuited for the job.

8. moderation, self-restraint; total abstinence from alcohol

My brother, a cautious person, follows the path of _____**temperance**_____ in all areas of life.

From the list of words on page 177, choose the one that best completes each of the following sentences. Write the word in the blank space provided.

1. After the _____tempestuous_____ events of the French Revolution and Napoleonic Wars, Europe settled down to an era of relative peace and quiet.

2. Shakespeare portrays Richard II as more a poet than a prince, and on that account _____temperamentally_____ unfit to rule England.

3. You may regard the controversy as one of far-reaching importance, but in my opinion it is merely another _____tempest_____ in a teacup.

4. The Restoration Period in England was roughly _____contemporaneous_____ with the start of the reign of Louis XIV in France.

5. Once we learned that we were both competing for the one remaining opening on the roster, the _____temperature_____ of our friendship began to cool noticeably.

6. Her memorial tribute to the departed hero was all the more moving because it was delivered _____extempore_____ rather than from prepared notes.

7. Her hatchet raids on saloons made Carrie Nation one of the most celebrated crusaders of the _____temperance_____ movement.

8. In his "Portrait of a Woman Deep in Thought," the painter has magically captured his subject's _____contemplative_____ mood.

---

*Circle the **boldface** word that more satisfactorily completes each of the following sentences.*

1. At the party, one of the guests gave a hilarious (**extempore,** temperamental) imitation of the rock star whose hit song came on the radio as we were leaving.

2. Some people find it far easier to stick to complete self-denial in certain cases than to observe (**tempest,** **temperance**).

3. Rare books and letters will last longer if they can be kept in an environment whose humidity and (**temperance,** **temperature**) levels are carefully controlled.

4. The photographer's most famous work shows a flashy performer, internationally known for his flamboyant manner, in a rare (**contemplative,** tempestuous) moment.

5. The psychologist concluded that the subject is (**temperamentally,** contemporaneously) unable to accept defeat without flying into a rage.

6. After the fury of the (**extempore,** **tempest**) had passed, the air felt strangely calm and clean.

7. A poet observed that while new romance can be agonizingly (**tempestuous,** contemplative), mature love can remain calm.

8. One of the most famous of the many appearances of Halley's Comet was (**temperature,** **contemporaneous**) with the Battle of Hastings in 1066.

Writer's Challenge

Read the following sentences, paying special attention to the words and phrases underlined. From the words in the box below, find better choices for these underlined words and phrases. Then use these choices to rewrite the sentences.

WORD BANK

accolade	apotheosis	contumacious	inhibit	supervene
accoutrement	apropos	hauteur	mete	truncate
acerbity	burgeon	imprecation	probity	unconscionable
apogee	chronic	ineluctable	protocol	unimpeachable

Wilma Rudolph

1. Of America's many sports heroes, Wilma Rudolph may have left behind the most inspiring and <u>beyond reproach</u> legacy.
unimpeachable

_____

2. The twentieth of twenty-two children, Rudolf entered the world in 1940 as a premature baby weighing just four and one-half pounds. At the age of four, she contracted polio—a crippling disease that <u>checks</u> normal growth and mobility.
inhibits

_____

3. Despite poverty and racial prejudice, Rudolf's family worked tirelessly during her childhood to help her overcome <u>often-recurring</u> illness.
chronic

_____

4. By age eleven, Rudolf was finally strong enough to discard the <u>gear</u> of a cripple and become a promising athlete.
accoutrements

_____

5. Rudolph won three gold medals in track at the 1960 Olympic Games in Rome. Against all odds, she had become the true <u>glorified ideal</u> of the Olympic athlete.
apotheosis

_____

6. Her proudest triumph was breaking old racial <u>codes of conduct</u>; for example, she refused to attend her victory celebration in Clarksville, Tennessee, unless the event was integrated.
protocols

_____

7. Wilma Rudolf went on to win <u>acclaim and approval</u> for her work with inner-city youth and university track teams. She died in 1994 of a malignant brain tumor.
accolades

_____

Analogies

In each of the following, circle the item that best completes the comparison.

See pages T38–T46 for explanations of answers.

1. resplendent is to **shine** as
a. effusive is to gush
b. vestigial is to flow
c. sanguine is to trickle
d. abortive is to cascade

2. patrician is to **hauteur** as
a. lackey is to independence
b. curmudgeon is to amiability
c. sycophant is to servility
d. mountebank is to prescience

3. paean is to **joy** as
a. jeremiad is to sorrow
b. aria is to despair
c. lucubration is to elation
d. polemic is to boredom

4. bromide is to **banal** as
a. non sequitur is to logical
b. philippic is to acerbic
c. elixir is to ineffable
d. vignette is to ribald

5. homily is to **didactic** as
a. corollary is to moot
b. caveat is to cautionary
c. mnemonic is to dogmatic
d. liturgy is to ancillary

6. accolade is to **hero** as
a. melee is to vassal
b. apotheosis is to villain
c. imprecation is to saint
d. obloquy is to poltroon

7. apropos is to **apposite** as
a. ascetic is to hedonistic
b. gargantuan is to dwarfish
c. mercurial is to phlegmatic
d. lugubrious is to lachrymose

8. accoutrements are to **wear** as
a. accessories are to pay
b. utensils are to collect
c. durables are to read
d. comestibles are to eat

9. noxious is to **harm** as
a. portentous is to wealth
b. salubrious is to health
c. bilious is to pleasure
d. traumatic is to ease

10. repartee is to **persiflage** as
a. apogee is to nadir
b. macrocosm is to microcosm
c. probity is to rectitude
d. plethora is to dearth

Choosing the Right Meaning

Read each sentence carefully. Then circle the item that best completes the statement below the sentence.

See pages T38–T46 for explanations of answers.

So that the medicine goes down "in the most delightful way," children's painkillers usually consist of an analgesic suspended in an elixir. (2)

1. The best definition for the word **elixir** in line 2 is

a. panacea   b. tonic   c. sweet liquid   d. potion

"In bosky shade of highland glen
where dappled sunbeams fling and flicker (2)
A bonny brook by sylvan sprites is ken
To tumble, traipse, and bravely bicker."
(A. E. Glug, "Forth to the Firth," IV, 103–106) (4)

2. In line 4 the word **bicker** most nearly means

a. plash   b. wrangle   c. quarrel   d. quiver

Until recent times it was the custom for gentlemen to dress in formal wear—including claque and gloves—when attending the opera. (2)

3. The word **claque** in line 2 most nearly means

a. hangers-on   b. fan club   c. flatterers   (d. hat)

A consequence of the Creek War of 1813–1814 was the deracination of the defeated Creek Indians and their forcible relocation to what is now Oklahoma. (2)

4. In line 1 the word **deracination** is used to mean

a. elimination   (b. uprooting)   c. eradication   d. surrender

Two-Word Completions

Circle the pair of words that best complete the meaning of each of the following sentences.

See pages T38–T46 for explanations of answers.

1. The verve and _____ with which the leading lady played her part did a great deal to make up for the _____ and indifferent performances turned in by the rest of the cast.

a. casuistry . . . prolix
b. empathy . . . fervid

c. bathos . . . inchoate
(d. élan . . . lackluster)

2. I began to understand how profoundly John F. Kennedy's assassination had _____ his wife, Jacqueline, when I noticed that she seemed to perform her part in her husband's _____ as if she were sleepwalking.

a. modulated . . . divination
(b. traumatized . . . obsequies)

c. browbeaten . . . emolument
d. immured . . . homily

3. Since the man has repeatedly shown himself to be a self-seeking _____ who achieves his aims by whatever means are at hand, we have every right to question the _____ of his current dealings.

(a. opportunist . . . probity)
b. chauvinist . . . hauteur

c. curmudgeon . . . acerbity
d. ascetic . . . protocol

4. Though George Frederick Handel envisaged *Solomon* more as a pageant than as a(n) _____, the underlying didactic purpose of the work is revealed in the deep sense of spirituality with which the composer _____ the music.

(a. homily . . . imbued)
b. bromide . . . palliated

c. polemic . . . truncated
d. aberration . . . inhibited

5. The _____ of an unsightly larva into a(n) _____ colored monarch butterfly is surely one of the most awesome wonders of nature.

a. vagary . . . effusively
b. acumen . . . fulsomely

(c. metamorphosis . . . flamboyantly)
d. euphoria . . . zanily

Enriching Your Vocabulary

Read the passage below. Then complete the exercise at the bottom of the page.

The Heritage of Literature

Fine literature ennobles the mind and spirit by enthralling readers with fascinating characters, compelling stories, and absorbing questions to ponder. Literature also contributes to the evolution of language itself. Modern English has borrowed numerous words and phrases from the works of famous and not-so-famous writers. One such word is *quixotic*

(Unit 11), which means "extravagantly idealistic." This word derives from the name of the irrepressible main character in *Don Quixote*, the famous comic novel by Spanish Renaissance writer Miguel de Cervantes.

Literature contributes to the development of language by providing a fertile universe of original phrases written by creative authors. From this resource, other writers and speakers borrow expressions and, by using them, distill the concept or idea into familiar words or phrases. What does it mean to be accused of "sour grapes"? This means that a remark

Statue of Don Quixote and Sancho Panza, Plaza de España, Madrid, Spain

came across as belittling or envious. The phrase comes from Aesop's fable "The Fox and the Grapes." It refers to the fox's decision to stop trying to reach for tasty-looking grapes by concluding that they were probably sour anyway, so not worth it.

In Column A below are 6 more words or phrases borrowed from literature. With or without a dictionary, match each word or phrase with its meaning in Column B.

Column A

___d___ **1.** bite the hand that feeds you

___b___ **2.** ragamuffin

___e___ **3.** salad days

___a___ **4.** Scrooge

___c___ **5.** yahoo

___f___ **6.** yeoman service

Column B

a. a miserly and unpleasant person (Source: Charles Dickens's *A Christmas Carol*)

b. a dirty or unkempt child (Source: *A Vision of Piers Plowman*, attributed to William Langland)

c. a crude, brutish, or unrefined person (Source: Jonathan Swift's *Gulliver's Travels*)

d. to show complete ingratitude (Source: Edmund Burke, referring to the public's attitude toward government)

e. one's inexperienced youth (Source: William Shakespeare's *Antony and Cleopatra*, I, v)

f. effective help or assistance, characterized by hard and steady work (Source: William Shakespeare's *Hamlet*, V, ii)

Selecting Word Meanings

*In each of the following groups, circle the word or expression that is **most nearly the same** in meaning as the word in **boldface** type in the given phrase.*

1. took pleasure in pointing out the **solecisms** in my essay
   a. violations of rules
   b. puns and jokes
   c. changing standards
   d. new ideas

2. players who **complemented** each other's abilities
   a. nullified
   b. reinforced and completed
   c. praised
   d. mocked

3. hit upon an answer after long **lucubration**
   a. delay
   b. silence
   c. experimentation
   d. thought

4. an **inchoate** instrument of government
   a. lacking high ideals
   b. in an early stage of development
   c. corrupt
   d. bureaucratic

5. wounded in the **melee**
   a. trap
   b. fight
   c. arm
   d. crisis

6. the **jeremiads** of the old preacher
   a. brilliant oratory
   b. prolonged lamentations
   c. sincere appeals
   d. anecdotes

7. discovered that mathematics was her **forte**
   a. weakness
   b. consuming interest
   c. strong point
   d. nemesis

8. the **noisome** stereotypes of racial bigotry
   a. foul and offensive
   b. expressed in a loud voice
   c. perpetuated
   d. misleading

9. a **morass** of doubts and misunderstandings
   a. swamp
   b. comedy
   c. scholarly analysis
   d. collection

10. **adumbrated** the problems facing us
    a. overcame
    b. avoided
    c. outlined
    d. pondered

11. a **lugubrious** expression on his face
    a. mournful
    b. optimistic
    c. determined
    d. panic-stricken

12. remaining **immaculate** in all circumstances
    a. calm
    b. indifferent
    c. spotless
    d. sagacious

13. whose forces were diminished by **attrition**
    a. unnecessary expenditures
    b. gradual wearing away
    c. natural disasters
    d. flagrant inefficiency

14. the **depredations** of the invaders
- a. victories
- b. defeats
- c. strategic plans
- (d. plunder and destruction)

15. some leeway for interpretation within the **parameters** of the style
- a. incidental difficulties
- (b. determining elements)
- c. unknown quantities
- d. revolutionary ideas

16. critical of their **supine** attitude
- a. marked by self-interest
- b. superior
- (c. passive and submissive)
- d. aggressively uncooperative

17. showed great **prescience** in formulating policies
- a. courage
- b. determination
- c. human sympathy
- (d. foresight)

18. could not fail to recognize her **mellifluous** voice
- a. rasping
- (b. smooth and sweet)
- c. shrill
- d. obviously affected

19. not particularly amused by his attempts at **persiflage**
- (a. good-natured banter)
- b. impersonation
- c. mime
- d. bitter satire

20. willing to overlook our **peccadilloes**
- (a. minor faults)
- b. lack of faith
- c. blatant dishonesty
- d. poor taste

21. annoyed by their **niggardly** methods
- a. finicky
- (b. stingy)
- c. dishonest
- d. insulting

22. singularly **maladroit** in making the arrangements
- (a. lacking finesse and skill)
- b. accomplished
- c. considerate of others
- d. wasteful

23. a **schism** in the ranks of the political party
- a. infusion of new strength
- b. spread of corruption
- (c. split)
- d. mass confusion

24. in the **lexicon** of youth
- a. set of values
- (b. vocabulary)
- c. time frame
- d. inexperience

25. is constantly being misled by **mirages**
- (a. illusions)
- b. criminal acts
- c. faulty instructions
- d. inadequate preparation

26. a group torn apart by **factionalism**
- a. quarrels over money
- b. lack of communication
- c. wild emotionalism
- (d. partisan differences)

27. a **harbinger** of happier days
- a. guarantee
- (b. herald)
- c. memory
- d. enjoyment

28. a **disingenuous** reply
- (a. lacking in frankness)
- b. exceptionally creative
- c. devoid of human feelings
- d. genial and warmhearted

29. furniture selected purely for **utilitarian** purposes
a. aesthetic
(b. practical)
c. sentimental
d. economical

30. will not accept such **unconscionable** delays
a. severely damaging
b. repeated many times
(c. utterly unjustified)
d. motivated by malice

Words That Describe People

*The words in Column A are used to describe people. In the space before each word, write the **letter** of the item in Column B that identifies it.*

Column A

d	**31.** fastidious
c	**32.** insouciant
g	**33.** philistine
a	**34.** narcissistic
f	**35.** waggish
b	**36.** curmudgeon
h	**37.** mountebank
i	**38.** poltroon
j	**39.** mercurial
e	**40.** ascetic

Column B

a. stuck on oneself

b. a surly and cantankerous person

c. carefree; not disposed to worry about dangers or consequences

d. much concerned with details and niceties

e. practicing strict self-denial

f. given to making jokes

g. scornful of artistic values or the "finer things in life"

h. trickster or phony

i. showing contemptible cowardice

j. showing rapid changes in temperament and attitude

Words Connected with Occupations

*The words in Column A are associated with professions and other occupations. In the space before each word, write the **letter** of the item in Column B that identifies it.*

Column A

c	**41.** lachrymose
d	**42.** therapeutic
i	**43.** divination
j	**44.** bowdlerize
b	**45.** lampoon
e	**46.** persona
h	**47.** adjudicate
f	**48.** virtuoso
g	**49.** homily
a	**50.** protocol

Column B

a. diplomats

b. satirical writers

c. writers of sentimental tragedies

d. doctors and nurses

e. actors and actresses

f. concert violinists

g. members of the clergy

h. mediators between quarreling groups

i. fortune-tellers

j. editors who seek to make classics "more suitable" for young readers

Word Pairs

In the space before each pair of words, write:

S—if the words are synonyms or near-synonyms;
O—if the words are antonyms or near-antonyms;
N—if the words are unrelated in meaning.

S	**51.** cozen—inveigle		O	**59.** disparate—identical
N	**52.** symptomatic—malleable		N	**60.** bibulous—bilious
O	**53.** quixotic—practicable		S	**61.** coalesce—amalgamate
N	**54.** liaison—protégé		N	**62.** pundit—malcontent
O	**55.** minuscule—gargantuan		O	**63.** plebeian—patrician
O	**56.** obloquy—acclaim		S	**64.** hidebound—stodgy
S	**57.** lackluster—drab		S	**65.** wanton—licentious
O	**58.** microcosm—macrocosm			

Foreign Words and Phrases

Some words and phrases commonly used in present-day English that are taken directly from foreign languages are listed below. Write the appropriate word or phrase on the line next to each of the following sentences.

fait accompli	sic	mot juste	carte blanche
non sequitur	volte-face	cul-de-sac	ad hoc
sub rosa	hoi polloi	de facto	quid pro quo

66. When they returned home and found the business completely reorganized and functioning successfully, they simply had to accept the new situation. _____fait accompli_____

67. The committee has been set up to conduct the investigation, and it will pass out of existence as soon as its job is completed. _____ad hoc_____

68. The author added a word to indicate that the misuse of "disinterested" for "uninterested" actually appeared in the book he was quoting. _____sic_____

69. It is foolish of you to conclude that she is an expert in "Asian philosophy" just because she made a two-week tour of the Far East. _____non sequitur_____

70. The truth is that racial segregation still exists in some parts of the United States, even though it is not sanctioned by law. _____de facto_____

71. The treaty negotiations will be successful only if each of the parties makes concessions to the other, so that both can feel they are obtaining fair compensation. _____quid pro quo_____

72. When Mrs. Roth put Larry in charge of the class play, she gave him full authority to select the cast, prepare the sets, and make all other major decisions.

_____carte blanche_____

73. By my lies and deceptions, I had maneuvered myself into an impossible position from which I could neither advance nor retreat.

_____cul-de-sac_____

74. When Fran referred to him as an "intellectual snob," I felt that she had found the perfect epithet on which to skewer his pretentious personality.

_____mot juste_____

75. I was shocked when he abandoned the cause he had backed so long and became an advocate of a diametrically opposed program.

_____volte-face_____

Word Associations

*In each of the following, circle the word or expression that best completes the meaning of the sentence or answers the question, with particular reference to the meaning of the word in **boldface** type.*

76. Your situation might well be described as **precarious** if you were
a. lolling in a hammock
b. hanging from the edge of a cliff
c. playing tennis with a weak opponent
d. attending the Senior Prom

77. To say that a person is **bickering** over the terms of a contract implies
a. praise for being careful
b. disapproval of the contract provisions
c. complete indifference
d. criticism for being petty

78. From a renowned **raconteur** you would expect
a. a superb dinner
b. an entertaining story
c. expert legal advice
d. the perfect crime

79. An **empirical** analysis of a problem is based primarily on
a. the laws of chance
b. preconceived ideas
c. wishful thinking
d. experience

80. If you refer to someone's reactions as **maudlin**, you are
a. expressing sympathy
b. complaining of excessive sentimentality
c. showing utter indifference
d. charging deliberate misrepresentation

81. Deeds of **derring-do** are associated particularly with
a. knights-errant
b. politicians
c. suburban commuters
d. scholars and intellectuals

82. What advice might you give to a person who is guilty of a **tautology**?
a. "See your doctor immediately."
b. "Don't repeat yourself."
c. "Stop that abusive language."
d. "Speak more slowly and distinctly."

83. A person who has just received a **lagniappe** would most likely
a. take some medication
b. say, "Thanks!"
c. seek revenge
d. mend his or her ways

84. Which of the following indicates **kudos**?
a. "Get out of my life!"
b. "Do what I say, not what I do."
c. "What have I done to deserve this?"
d. "You're the greatest!"

85. People who indulge in **casuistry** are most likely
    a. overeating
    b. spreading rumors
    (c. splitting hairs)
    d. feeling sorry for themselves

86. People who are affected by **xenophobia** are
    a. fond of rich food
    b. afraid of heights
    (c. suspicious of foreigners)
    d. unlucky in love

87. Which of the following might properly be described as a **faux pas**?
    a. scoring the winning touchdown
    (b. attending a formal party in blue jeans)
    c. eating a hearty breakfast
    d. learning to water-ski

88. We would expect **aficionados** of the opera to
    a. picket the local opera house
    (b. attend opera performances often)
    c. sing the lead role in *Carmen*
    d. never go to an opera

89. The expression "**vicissitudes** of life" refers to life's
    a. beginning and end   (b. ups and downs)   c. pleasures   d. side issues

90. What is the prevailing mood of a speaker who delivers a **philippic**?
    a. smug self-satisfaction
    b. joyful approbation
    (c. bitter disapproval)
    d. impartiality

91. Which of the following best describes the mood and atmosphere of a **gothic** novel?
    a. bright and cheerful
    (b. dark and gloomy)
    c. zany and slapstick
    d. sophisticated and satirical

92. A person who may properly be described as an **opportunist** is trying hard to
    a. help others
    (b. get ahead at any cost)
    c. maintain law and order
    d. stay young and beautiful

93. Which of the following expresses the attitude of a **dogmatic** person?"
    a. "I may be wrong."
    b. "I'm waiting for more evidence."
    c. "What do you think about it?"
    (d. "I'm right, and that's that!")

94. Which of the following would be most likely to accept a philosophy of **nihilism**?
    a. a deeply religious person
    b. an accomplished physicist
    c. a conservative
    (d. a sweeping critic of the social order)

95. A **flamboyant** personality suggests a
    a. demure little wren   b. bold eagle   c. perky robin   (d. showy peacock)

96. An editorial writer who refers to a strike as **internecine** believes that
    a. the strike will be successful
    (b. all parties involved will suffer greatly)
    c. labor is justified in calling the strike
    d. the strike will end soon

97. Which of the following might you seek to **deracinate**?
    a. fun and games
    b. old friends and good companions
    (c. tree stumps and bad habits)
    d. patience and fortitude

98. Which of the following is typical of **nepotism**?
    (a. giving good jobs to relatives)
    b. donating large sums to charity
    c. advancing the public interest
    d. suffering delusions of persecution

99. What would be the most logical thing to do if you were in a **labyrinth**?
    a. sit down and enjoy the show
    b. deliver a eulogy to the departed
    c. start the motor and drive off
    (d. try to find your way out)

100. You would be likely to regard it as a **contretemps** if you
    a. improved your vocabulary
    b. won first prize in an essay contest
    c. helped your classmates
    (d. did poorly on this final test)

The following tabulation lists all the basic words taught in the various units of this book, as well as those introduced in the *Vocabulary of Vocabulary, Working with Analogies, Building with Classical Roots,* and *Enriching Your Vocabulary* sections. Words taught in the units are printed in **boldface** type. The number following each entry indicates the page on which the word is first introduced. Exercises and review materials in which the word also appears are not cited.

generic, 78
genesis, 78
genocide, 78
genre, 59
gerrymander, 83
gothic, 125
graham crackers, 83
gratis, 36
gung ho, 116

harbinger, 92
hauteur, 166
hedonism, 92
heyday, 99
hidebound, 22
hierarchy, 22
hoi polloi, 52
homily, 59
homogenous, 78
hubris, 149

icon, 36
iconoclastic, 65
iguana, 116
imbue, 85
immaculate, 151
immolate, 118
immure, 59
impasse, 125
impinge, 132
imperceptible, 118
imprecation, 151
inchoate, 85
incubus, 99
indigenous, 29
ineffable, 52
ineluctable, 151
inference clue, 10
infrastructure, 99
inhibit, 166
in medias res, 66
insouciant, 59
internecine, 66
interstice, 36
inveigle, 99

jeremiad, 166

kowtow, 116
kudos, 99

labyrinth, 132
lachrymose, 29
lackey, 118
lackluster, 92
lagniappe, 100
lampoon, 85
leotard, 83
lexicon, 29
liaison, 118
licentious, 158
literal usage, 7
liturgy, 22
lucubration, 52
lugubrious, 125
lynch, 83

macrocosm, 36
maladapted, 111
maladroit, 66
malaise, 111
malcontent, 92
malfeasance, 111
malformation, 111
malfunction, 111
malice, 111
malingerer, 111
malleable, 85
malodorous, 111
mammoth, 116
matrix, 59
maudlin, 66
maverick, 83
melee, 29
mellifluous, 93
mercurial, 151
metaphorical, 7
metamorphosis, 125
mete, 158
microcosm, 29
minuscule, 29
mirage, 22
mnemonic, 53
modulate, 66
monolithic, 118
morass, 22
mot juste, 119
mountebank, 36
mufti, 116
mumbo jumbo, 116
mystique, 125

narcissism, 132
nemesis, 86
nepotism, 93
niggardly, 132
nihilism, 119
noisome, 22
non sequitur, 125
noxious, 158

obfuscate, 29
oblivious, 22
obloquy, 53
obsequies, 59
opportunist, 166
opt, 86

paean, 36
palliate, 151
panache, 59
pander, 93
parameter, 53
parlous, 126
pastiche, 132
paternalism, 30
patrician, 119
peccadillo, 93
persiflage, 36
persona, 60
phenomenon, 149
philippic, 60
philistine, 86
picaresque, 86
pièce de résistance, 93
plethora, 37
polarize, 30
polemic, 159
poltroon, 23
populous, 159
portentous, 66
pragmatic, 37
precarious, 132
prefix, 15
prescience, 66
probity, 159
prolix, 100
propitiate, 119
proselyte, 23
protégé, 100
protocol, 152
prototype, 100

prurient, 60
psychology, 149
punctilio, 126
pundit, 53
purview, 30

quagmire, 126
quasi, 23
queasy, 86
quid pro quo, 67
quisling, 83
quixotic, 126
quizzical, 37

raconteur, 126
ragamuffin, 182
raillery, 23
rapacity, 37
rapport, 132
refractory, 86
remand, 93
repartee, 159
resemblance, 48
resplendent, 152
restatement clue, 9
ribald, 23
risible, 53
root, 11

sacrosanct, 60
salad days, 182
salubrious, 67
sandwich, 83
sanguine, 30
saturnalian, 67
savoir-faire, 86
saxophone, 83
schism, 37
Scrooge, 182
shawl, 116
shrapnel, 83
sic, 119
sideburns, 83
simile, 48
simulacrum, 48
simulation, 48
simulcast, 48
sine qua non, 126
solecism, 30